Y0-AGC-962

R00083 97346

Ruth Jacobs is Adjunct Lecturer in Music, Continuing Education Department, Queens College of the City University of New York. She has performed professionally in concert and on radio.

Learn the E-Z Numbers Way to Play Guitar Whether or Not You Read Music

THE GUITAR EXPERIENCE

Ruth Jacobs

Prentice-Hall, Inc., Englewood Cliffs, N.J. 07632

Library of Congress Cataloging in Publication Data

Jacobs, Ruth T
The guitar experience.

(A Spectrum Book)
Includes index.
1. Guitar-Methods—Self-instruction. I. Title.
MT588.J3 787.6'1'0712 80-18526
ISBN 0-13-371625-2
ISBN 0-13-371617-1 (pbk.)

Despite an exhaustive search, we have been unable to locate the publishers or copyright owners of some of the songs in this book. Therefore, we have proceeded on the assumption that no formal copyright claims have been filed on these works. If we have inadvertently published a previously copyrighted composition without permissions, we advise the copyright owner(s) to contact us so that we may give credit in future editions.

Editorial/production supervision and interior design by Donald Chanfrau
Illustrations used by permission of Marilyn Rey
Page layout by Gail Collis
Cover design by Michael Aron
Manufacturing buyer: Cathie A. Lenard

A SPECTRUM BOOK

10 9 8 7 6 5 4 3 2 1

Printed in the United States of America

Prentice-Hall International, Inc., *London*
Prentice-Hall of Australia Pty. Limited, *Sydney*
Prentice-Hall of Canada, Ltd., *Toronto*
Prentice-Hall of India Private Limited, *New Delhi*
Prentice-Hall of Japan, Inc., *Tokyo*
Prentice-Hall of Southeast Asia Pte. Ltd., *Singapore*
Whitehall Books Limited, *Wellington, New Zealand*

contents

seven

eight

nine

ten

eleven

PLAYING THE NOTES

twelve

thirteen

fourteen

fifteen

sixteen

seventeen

eighteen

nineteen

twenty

twenty-one

preface

We used to be a nation of dropouts. We've turned that around. Now we're a nation of "drop-ins." We're dropping into everything that can make our lives more than just an everyday drudgery of working, eating, and sleeping. Perhaps something inside of us demands to know who we really are or what we could be outside of that routine. We need a very personal kind of fulfillment and we need it as much as we need food and sleep. Without it, something's missing from our lives. Things may be all right but really not satisfying enough. So, we continue to look for something to drop into, something that will provide us with a sense of self-fulfillment.

One of the things that people are dropping into today is playing the guitar. In fact, the instrument seems to be undergoing a sort of renaissance. One large and popular New York music store claims that 70 percent of its sales come from guitars and guitar accessories. It's become the "now" instrument: stylish, personal, and enjoyable.

One reason so many people have become interested in guitar playing is that it's thought of as a "fun," leisurely activity, rather than a serious musical undertaking. In fact, during the years that I've taught, one thing I've learned from my students is that most people who are interested in knowing how to play the guitar don't read music and don't especially want to learn, at least not in the beginning. This discovery was the inspiration for my book. It's great fun to see the thrilled expression on people's faces when they play tunes for the first time without knowing how to read music. And that happens after just a few minutes.

You'll be shown how to play the guitar in a way that's never been done before. You'll be starting with step-by-step descriptions of how to finger a chord, how to play tunes without reading music, and how to change chords. You'll be taught strum patterns and how to fit them in with your singing, how to improve your singing, and, perhaps most importantly, you'll learn to trust yourself, to discover what you can do, and to relax. There's even a section for left-handed people with accompanying instructions and guitar chords. This is a book for people who want to include music in their lives, to play the guitar without having to go through the rigamarole of conventional music-learning structures.

My method is so easy that after a few weeks of playing you'll be able to teach it to other people. That has actually happened several times. There was a student in one of my classes who was a high school teacher. After attending a few of my classes, she received permission from her principal to let her teach guitar to some of her pupils. She was so proud of herself that I couldn't tell her an eight-year-old student of mine did pretty much the same thing using a couple of friends as "students."

You don't have to read music to play the guitar the E-Z Numbers way. In fact, you don't have to know anything at all about music. If you always thought you were "musically handicapped," then you're the one I wrote this book for.

I'm going to take you on a consciousness-raising guitar trip. You'll discover a lot of things about yourself, along the way. You'll find that a lot of the things you're doing in the E-Z Numbers game reflect the way you do things in other areas of your life. Some of your beliefs will change. Some people might even notice a difference in you. You'll probably meet and make new friends along the way. Eventually, you'll begin to feel less of that sense of vague dissatisfaction about yourself and about the way in which you're creating your life style. No more looking for something to drop into, for awhile. This is the beginning of your musical guitar trip.

Let's play.

CREDITS

Those friends long ago, who sat so patiently through my beginning attempts to sing and to play the guitar, surely had a hand in the creation of this book. And my students of course, are the reason for this book's appearance on the musical scene; I owe them my greatest thanks.

But in the actual mechanics of constructing this book, I

would surely have had a much more difficult time if it weren't for Jerry Silverman: he gave me generous advice, strong encouragement, and urged me to finish when I faltered at the crucial beginning stages.

To my friend, Linda Kabo, I owe a debt of gratitude for the many hours she spent reading my manuscript and making valuable suggestions. Her musicianship and skills were very helpful to me. I want to thank Professor David Walker of the Queens College Music Department, who was never too busy to answer any questions I had. I also want to thank Mark Sikelianos who was so helpful in providing me with research information.

Without the support and many reassurances of my family, this book may not have been finished. To Fred Jacobs, who's sympathy and understanding helped me through a difficult time, even when his own problems seemed insurmountable, I can never express the gratitude I feel. To Scott Jacobs, who consented to test some of my musical ideas, and to Gary Jacobs, who generously gave his time, reading my manuscript and making helpful suggestions from halfway across the country, I offer many thanks.

Most of all, my deepest appreciation goes to my husband, Dick Jacobs, who's never-failing, strong support and kind acceptance of topsy-turvy living made this book possible.

1
LEARNING THE GAME

INTRODUCING THE GUITAR

On any day of the week, turn on your radio and you'll hear a guitar being strummed. Flick on your television and, chances are, you'll see someone playing a guitar. Perhaps you've noticed people lugging guitars around town. Where are they going?

Guitars are appearing more and more frequently, and in places they've never been before. My dentist keeps his guitar tucked away in his office closet and practices his strumming between patients; a politician campaigned for governor accompanied by his guitar; and one of our astronauts commented that if he didn't make it back, he would miss learning how to play his guitar better.

Now, more than ever before, people of all ages and backgrounds are interested in learning how to play the guitar: I recently had a seventy-four-year-old pupil in one of my beginner's classes. I've had sisters and brothers, as well as mothers, daughters, husbands, and wives, take the same guitar classes, all students equally eager. Everyone wants to play. No one is ever too old to learn, but some people just keep putting it off for one reason or another. Lots of people of all ages think they just don't have the time. (But you'll never have more time than you have right now; you've always had all the time there is.)

Certainly, the guitar is the most popular instrument in the country today. Although its jump in popularity is comparatively recent, it's by no means a "new" instrument. It's one of the oldest known: ancient forms of the guitar go back over four thousand years.

Why has it become so popular? One very obvious reason is that it's a lot easier to carry around than some other instruments (such as a piano). The guitar only weighs a little over three pounds. But it's more than portable; it's one of the most personal of instruments, like a close friend or companion. You can *hold* a guitar. Maybe that's why the various parts of a guitar came to be called the head, neck, body, face, and mouth.

Perhaps another reason is that the guitar is one of the easiest instruments to learn. Consequently, it can be learned and played very poorly. Give yourself time to grow with your guitar. Please don't fool yourself by expecting to sound like your favorite player unless, of course, you're willing to put in the hours, days, and years that go into making those sounds you love to hear. You choose how far you want to go. (Incidentally, it's not generally known that several famous composers—Schubert, Berlioz, Rossini, and Verdi, to name just a few—played and even composed their music on the guitar. Even our own Ben Franklin played the guitar; he didn't just play with kites.)

Muscles of Your Mind. Your guitar can be a means for unique personal development. It can be a way to enhance what I call "the muscles of your mind." You'll notice some pleasant changes in the way you think and feel about yourself as we go along. It can help you socially, becoming a natural bridge of communication between you and other people. It seems that singing and playing draw people together and give them a chance to express their feelings, sometimes deep feelings, that they can't express in any other way.

Nylon or Steel Strings?

There's an old controversy still going on about which type of guitar to choose: nylon- or steel-string. (We're speaking of acoustic or non-electric guitars, which is what's recommended for beginners.) In my opinion, the easiest guitar for a beginner to play is a nylon-string guitar. Nylon strings are easier for the left-hand fingers to press down, and since the fingerboard (neck) is wider on a nylon-string guitar, it's easier for the fingers to avoid touching adjacent strings when they shouldn't. However, steel string enthusiasts may argue that a narrower neck makes it easier to finger some chord positions, especially for someone with small hands.

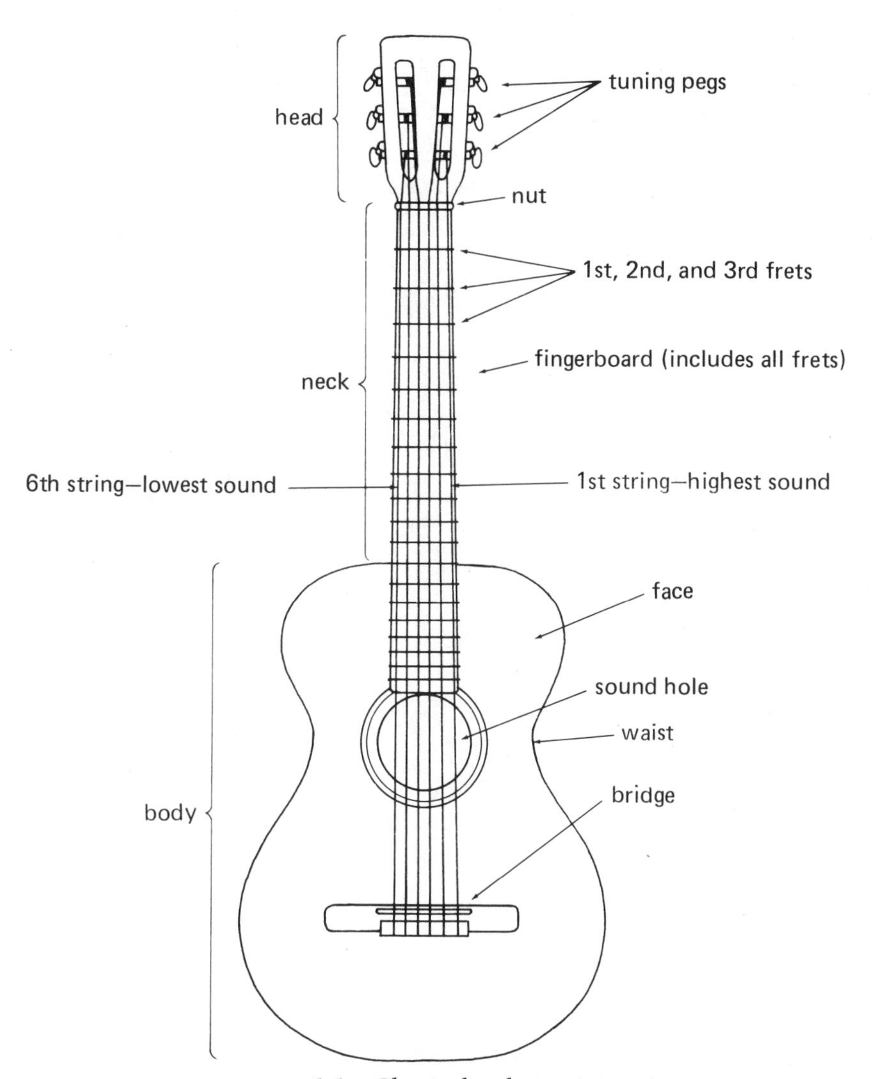

FIGURE 1-1 *Classical nylon-string guitar*

Some Differences. A steel-string guitar has a different inner construction from a nylon-string guitar. For instance, the bracing must be stronger because of the greater tension steel strings exert on the guitar frame. The steel-string guitar has a narrower neck that has fourteen frets[1] up to the point where it meets the body; the nylon-string guitar neck has twelve frets up to the point where it meets the body. Steel-string guitars are often played with a pick, so there's a protective pick guard on the face next to the sound hole. And the nylon-string guitar has an open-slotted head, whereas the steel-string guitar has a closed head, with the tuning gear on top of it.

The sound of a nylon-string guitar is more mellow than a

[1] Frets are the metal strips or crossbars on the guitar fingerboard that run perpendicular to the strings.

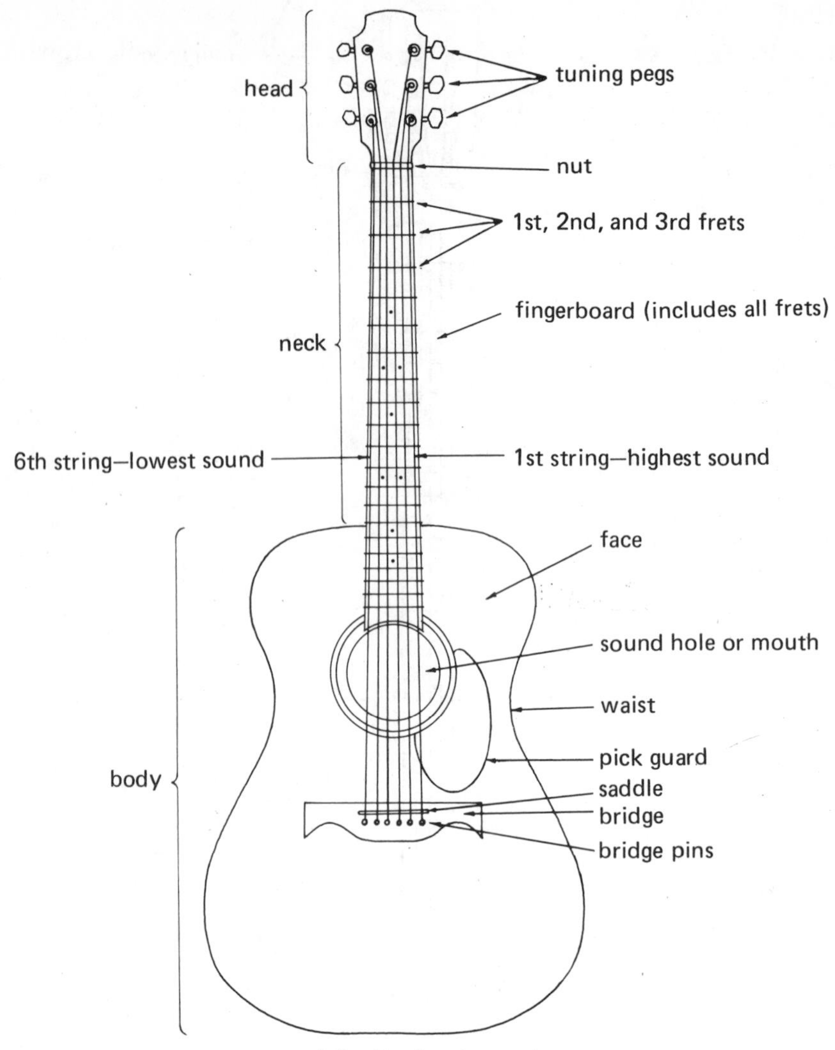

FIGURE 1-2 *Steel-string guitar*

steel-string. However, it's true that the steel-string guitar is more commonly used and has a much greater metallic sound, if that's what you like. If you prefer to be a steel-string player, you should probably start on steel strings. After becoming used to nylon it may be a bit uncomfortable to switch to steel.

How to Select Your Guitar

If you haven't gotten your guitar yet, there are some things you ought to know first. If you've already got one, but notice that a lot of the features I recommend are missing, I suggest you try to exchange it.

Guitars range in price from about forty dollars to well over one thousand dollars. You may find some guitars for less than forty dollars, but inevitably, the cheapest guitars sound the worst. What most people don't realize is that the cheapest guitars are usually the hardest to play. If you have the attitude that playing the guitar is only an experiment, or if you lack confidence, you may wonder why you should buy anything other than the cheapest guitar you can find. The reason is that a badly made guitar can dampen your enthusiasm forever. Why set up barriers for yourself before you even begin? You'll probably set up some barriers after you start.

The following are some of the things you should look for when buying a guitar:

○ Check the body to make sure there are no cracks in the wood.

○ Make sure nothing rattles inside: this could mean that something is loose.

○ Check to see if the guitar is warped (bent in or out) by comparing the neck and the front and back of the body to other guitars. The surface should be straight.

○ Have the guitar tuned up to correct pitch. Press down on the strings all along the fingerboard, one at a time. Be sure that there's no buzzing when you pluck those strings.

○ Check the height of the strings above the frets. This is called the action of the guitar. It should be about one-eighth of an inch above the fingerboard. If the strings are unusually difficult to press down, the action is probably too high. (Keep in mind that it's always a little difficult for a beginner to press down hard on the strings.) If you hear a buzz or rattle when you pluck the strings, they're probably too close to the fingerboard; the action is too low.

○ The frets should not be loose, or stick out so much that it feels uncomfortable to run your finger along the edge of the neck.

If all of this seems like too much responsibility for you to handle, then see if you can take along a friend who knows guitars. If you go alone, the salesperson in a reliable music store should be able to help you choose a good instrument for a price you can afford to pay.

It's not a good idea to buy a guitar without buying a case to keep it in: your guitar needs protection. Cases can range in price from about ten dollars to over one hundred dollars. Obviously, a better guitar deserves a better case for better protection.

How to Care for Your Guitar

Although the guitar is an amazingly sturdy instrument, it is also delicate, and careless handling will certainly damage it. (I've seen great extremes of handling. Some people will go to the trouble of wrapping the guitar in fabric for extra protection, before putting it into its case; others will leave it precariously balanced against a wall or sit it on a table.) It's best to keep your guitar in its case when you're not using it. Remember that temperature extremes can warp your guitar or cause it to crack, so don't rest it against a radiator or a very cold wall. Treat it with consideration, as you would anything or anybody you cared about.

How to Hold the Guitar

The final decision on how to hold the guitar is entirely up to you. After you've tried several possibilities, choose the position that suits you best. It should be most comfortable for *you* because it'll undoubtedly depend on your body build. Even after you've been playing for awhile, don't hesitate to change if you think you can gain more speed or accuracy using some other position. Regardless of which position you choose, make sure you're sitting on a hard surface, like a straight-backed chair, because it'll give you more control over your guitar and allow you to lean back when you feel tired. It may be fun to sit cross-legged on a bed, but it's more difficult to control your guitar playing that way.

Until the time when you're experienced enough and may prefer to stand and strum, the following are some of the playing positions you can choose from:

- Classical guitar players use a small footstand to rest their left foot. It's placed about six inches in front of the player's chair. The guitar waist rests on the left thigh. If you want to use this position but don't have a footstand, a book or a box can be used as a substitute.
- Some people keep their feet flat on the floor and rest the guitar waist on their right thigh.
- Other players cross their right thigh over their left and rest the guitar waist on their right thighs.

Whichever position you choose, make sure that your arm is placed over the body of the guitar, as in Figure 1-3. Your forearm should be angled to rest comfortably on the guitar so that it doesn't move while you're playing. It's the fingers and wrist which do the moving, not the arm.

Left-handedness. There are estimates that approximately 20 percent of the population is left-handed. During the years that I've taught, I've found a number of left-handed people concerned about being able to play a guitar that's commonly

FIGURE 1-3 *How to hold the guitar*

strung for a right-handed person. I used to think that there was absolutely no reason why a left-handed person couldn't play the guitar just as easily as a right-handed person. At the beginning, especially, the left hand does most of the work.

Based on what I thought, I persuaded some left-handed people to try playing the right-handed guitar. Some seemed able to play, with no unusual problems. However, others were quite willing to try, but eventually gave up. I was concerned about this and decided to find out more about left-handedness so that I could understand it in relation to the guitar.

Apparently, it's easier for a left-handed person under the age of fifteen to adapt to a right-handed guitar than for someone over fifteen; the body loses a certain kind of flexibility after that age. Also, family history plays a part in it. People with left-handed parents and grandparents find it easier to play a right-handed guitar than those who are the only lefties in the family. Again, it has to do with flexibility.

If you're left-handed and you can't play a right-handed guitar, you can either order a left-handed guitar from certain manufacturers, or you can buy a right-handed guitar of your choosing and have the strings reversed. Although some guitarists might fear that the guitar will be damaged as a result, that hasn't been my experience.

There's a bit of a problem to consider here. On many of the better guitars, the bridge saddle is slightly slanted. (Usually, this occurs on steel-string guitars.) The slant is made in a certain way to balance the sounds correctly. If the strings are reversed, it will affect the sounds in the higher frets. You could have the bridge changed in a guitar repair or large music shop. They might also want to file the grooves in the nut. The cost would be about thirty or forty dollars. Then, the strings could be reversed.

However, since you won't be playing much above the fifth fret for awhile, you could reverse your strings, get started playing the guitar, and then think about having the repair work done later on. If you decide that playing the guitar is the best thing that ever happened to you, you can always get a better quality, specially-ordered, left-handed guitar. These cost somewhere between fifty and eighty dollars more than an equivalent right-handed model.

If you do decide to reverse the strings, don't remove them all at once because that changes the tension of the guitar too suddenly. Remove the first and sixth strings and reverse them. Then, reverse the second and fifth, and the third and fourth strings in the same way. See the instructions on how to change strings later in this chapter (page 15).

Now, hold the guitar so that the neck is turned toward your right hand rather than toward your left hand. After reversing the strings and placing the guitar in playing position, the thickest string will be closest to your chin and the thinnest string will be closest to your knees. I've included a chart of chords for the left-handed guitar (page 218). Refer to them whenever you're learning new chords and songs.

How to Care for Your Fingers

All you nail biters out there should know that this is one time you won't be disapproved of or frowned upon. The nails of your left hand should not extend beyond the fleshy part of your fingertips. Any amount of nail past that will only prevent you from pressing your fingers down as firmly as you should. The results will be very unmusical to say the least. So keep your nails short by any method you prefer: clipping, cutting, filing, or biting.

EXPLORING THE SOUNDS OF YOUR GUITAR

Now, let's start to get acquainted with your new friend. Put the guitar on your lap, in playing position. Pluck the strings one by one. Listen to the sounds of the guitar. Did you notice that some strings sound lower and some sound higher? Which one sounds the lowest and which one sounds the highest? They're the two outside strings: the highest sounding one is the first string and the lowest sounding one is the sixth string. When you're holding the guitar in playing position, the first string is the one nearest to your knees and the sixth string is the one nearest to your chin.

Use the index finger of your left hand to press down on (finger) the first string anywhere you want to. Use your right hand thumb to pluck the string. Just slide, glide, or brush your thumb across the string. Can you hear that it sounds higher than when you pluck the open string? When a string is plucked open, it's not fingered by your left hand. Try the same thing with some of the other strings. Each time, listen and you'll hear that when you finger any string and pluck it, it sounds higher than when it's plucked open. Experiment with fingering the strings at different places along the fingerboard. Can you hear that the closer you get to the body of the guitar, the higher the sound is? If you can imagine the fingerboard of a guitar being like the keyboard on a piano, then you can see why the higher up you go on the fingerboard of a guitar, towards the body, the higher the sound will be. It's like your fingers moving across the keys of a piano. To get to the higher keys on a piano, your fingers would go from left to right; to get to the higher sounds on the strings of a guitar, you'd finger the strings from left to right also. Each fret on the guitar matches a key on the piano in pitch.[2] For instance, if the first fret on the first string matches the sound of a white key on the piano, then the second fret will match the sound of the black key right after the white one on the piano, and so on.

Naming the Strings—A Way to Remember

This is a good time to learn the names of the strings. You already know that the string nearest to your knees in playing position is the first string. Counting up from that string towards your chin, you'll count six strings. Notice that the first three(treble) strings are not as thick as the last three(bass) strings. The strings have names as well as numbers. Here's a nonsense phrase which should help you to remember the names of the strings. The first letter of each word is the letter name of the string number it's beneath.

[2] Pitch is the high or low quality of a sound.

1 2 3 4 5 6

*E*very *B*aby *G*ets *D*amp *A*fter *E*ating

Or, if you prefer it the other way:

6 5 4 3 2 1

*E*lephants *A*nd *D*onkeys *G*lide *B*ackward *E*asily

If you're inspired to make up your own nonsense phrase, go to it. Of course, this is useful only until you get to know the string names as well as you know your own name.

Tuning the Guitar

One of the most difficult experiences a beginner has to cope with is being able to tune the guitar. In fact, it's easier to learn how to play your guitar than to tune it. There's no way to avoid it. It's best to dig up every bit of patience you've got and go slowly, very slowly, and don't get discouraged. It takes a long time to train your ear to really hear music.

There are several ways to tune the strings. You can decide which way you'd like best.

Do you have a piano? Then you can tune the first string to the E just above middle C; the second string to the B just below middle C; the third string to the G below middle C; the fourth string to the D below middle C; the fifth string to the second A below middle C and the sixth string to the second E below middle C.

If you don't have a piano, there are two tuning devices that can be bought in most music shops: a pitch pipe, which looks like a set of whistles, and a tuning fork. Ask to be instructed in how to use either one by the person who sells it to you.

Although the pitch pipe has six whistles, one for each guitar string, I want you to use the sixth string whistle only. After you tune the low E string to it, you'll be able to tune the rest of the strings to each other. That way, they'll be tuned more accurately. The reason is that pitch pipes don't always have all their whistles in tune.

You tune the guitar by turning the tuning peg counterclockwise, away from you, to raise the pitch of a string. You

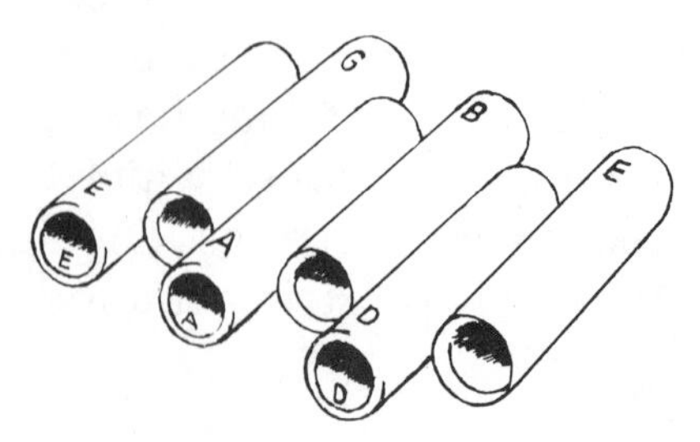

FIGURE 1-4 *Pitch pipe*

turn the tuning peg clockwise, towards you, to lower the pitch of a string.

If you haven't gotten anything to tune your guitar to yet, you can start off by trying to remember, or by guessing the sound of the sixth string when it was in tune.

When you're tuning the strings, if you hum each sound you hear, you'll find that it's easier to recognize whether the sound you hear is lower or higher than you want it to be.

If you're using a pitch pipe, listen carefully to the sound of the sixth string whistle. Hum the sound you hear. Now pluck the open sixth string. Hum the sound you hear from that. Did your voice go up higher or drop down lower when you hummed the sound of the sixth string, as compared to the sound you hummed for the pitch pipe? Which was it? If you're not sure, start again by humming the sound of the sixth string whistle and then the sound of the plucked open sixth string. Listen carefully and don't be afraid of trusting yourself. You can hear the differences more easily if you vary the pitch of your own voice by first saying something

then, higher up.

then, not so low,

low down,

Try it, and remember: trust yourself.

After listening very carefully, if you've decided that your sixth string needs to be tuned, run your finger along the string all the way to the tuning peg it's wound around. That way, you'll be sure you're turning the correct peg when you're tuning. After you've done that, do the following.

1. Press the fifth fret of the sixth string with your left-hand finger. Pluck the sixth string with your right-hand thumb, and then hum the sound you hear. Continue pressing down on the fifth fret of the sixth string while doing the next step.

2. Pluck the open fifth string. Hum the sound you hear. Is it higher or lower than the sound of the sixth string fingered on the fifth fret? Tune it to match the sound of the fingered sixth string, always humming and listening carefully to the sounds you hear. That's the procedure you'll follow to tune the remaining strings.

3. Next, finger the fifth fret of the fifth string. Pluck it. Hum the sound you hear. Now tune the open fourth string to match it.

4. Finger the fifth fret of the fourth string. Pluck it. Hum the sound you hear. Tune the open third string to match it.

5. Next, finger the *fourth fret*(notice the change?) of the third string. Pluck it. Hum the sound you hear. Tune the open second string to match it.

6. Next, finger the fifth fret of the second string. Pluck it. Tune the open first string to match it. All your strings should now be tuned correctly.

Another way to tune is with an A-440 tuning fork. Hold the stem carefully between your thumb and first finger so it doesn't slip out of your fingers when you strike one of the prongs against an object. The action of striking it forces the prongs to vibrate. To hear the musical pitch that this results in, lightly place the end of the stem just inside your ear, or if you'd prefer, just in front of your ear. Another way to hear the pitch is, after striking the tuning fork, place the end of the stem against the body of your guitar. This can be on the bridge, near the sound hole, or anywhere on the face of your guitar. I've even seen a couple of musicians strike the tuning fork against an object and then place the stem lightly against a tooth. Incidentally, don't touch the prongs after striking it or else you'll stop the vibrations. After you've heard the pitch resulting from the vibrations, hum it.

Now, finger the fifth fret of the first string and pluck it. Hum the sound you hear. That sound has to be the same pitch as the vibrating tuning fork. If not, then tune the string to match it. Finger the second string on the fifth fret and hum the sound; that sound must match the sound of the *open* first string. If not, tune the second string to match it.

Next, finger the third string on the *fourth fret*(remember?); it should match the *open* second string. Tune the remaining strings in the same way. You're simply reversing the tuning procedure that you used with the pitch pipe. In fact, you can tune the first string, fingered on the twelfth fret to the high E pitch pipe whistle. Then you can tune the rest of the strings in the same way you did after tuning the first string to the tuning fork. However, I believe it's easier for a beginner to tune from the sixth string pitch pipe whistle.

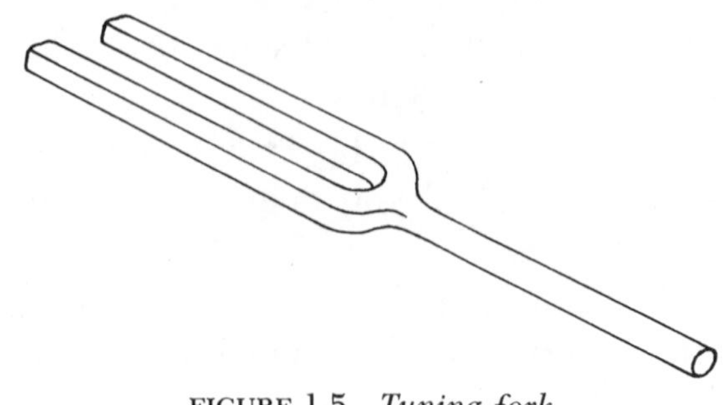

FIGURE 1-5 *Tuning fork*

Don't panic and don't despair if you're not at all sure of what you hear. This is to be expected now. I assure you, if you don't give up, *in time,* you really will begin to recognize sounds. That time may be short for some people and long for others, who like myself, needed more time to learn to really listen and "hear."

Here's another way to tune. It may be easier for some people to recognize the sounds they hear in the following way.

Tune the sixth string to the pitch pipe. Then, starting from the sixth string and going to the fifth string, sing the first four words of "Here Comes the Bride." The sixth string will match the pitch of the first word, "here." The next three words, "comes the bride," should match the pitch of the fifth string. If it doesn't, then tune it to match. Then start all over again with the fifth and fourth strings. The fifth string should match the pitch of 'here' and the fourth string should match the pitch of 'comes the bride.' Do the same with the fourth and third strings.

When you get to the third and second strings, you'll have to change your tune. Either of the first two pitches of the "Blue Danube Waltz," or "Anchors Aweigh," will match the pitches of correctly tuned third and second strings. On the second and first strings, you go back to "Here Comes the Bride."

In addition to "Here Comes the Bride" you can do the same thing with the first couple of pitches of the following tunes: "Old Lang Syne," "Home on the Range," or "Down in the Valley." For the third and second strings, you can also sing the first three pitches of "On Top of Old Smoky." Sing the pitch of 'on top' for the third string and the pitch of the next word, 'of,' for the second string.

You may not think it's necessary to bother with tuning. It's true that you can learn how to play the guitar before you know how to tune it. You can be sure, though, that your guitar playing will sound much, much better on a tuned guitar.

Changing Strings

New strings have a lot of stretching to do and so your guitar will be out of tune much more often at the beginning. Ideally, strings should be changed any time from once a month, for maximum tone, to every three or four months. Realistically, they're changed much less often than that. Don't wait too long though, because the strings will lose their tone and sound dull and lifeless. If a string breaks, you've got no choice but to replace it immediately. It's a good idea to be prepared for that by knowing how to string your guitar. In fact, it's a good idea to always carry around an extra set of strings, just in case that happens.

You might prefer changing your strings one or two at a time, a few days apart, rather than all at the same time. That way, you won't have to suffer with six new, stretching strings, that are out of tune. However, if you can't bear prolonging the tuneless days, then change them all at the same time. Even when you do that, it's best to remove only one or two strings at a time, replace them, and continue changing the rest of the strings the same way. When you remove all the strings at once, the sudden tension change may damage the guitar.

Don't ever substitute steel strings on a nylon-string guitar because steel strings exert about five times the pressure on the body of the guitar that nylon strings do. Steel-string guitars are built with the proper bracing to support that pressure. You can ruin your nylon-string guitar by switching to steel strings.

Figure 1-6a shows how to change a nylon string, starting from the guitar bridge. It's divided into five steps:

1. First you insert the string through the appropriate hole in the bridge.
2. Bring the short end up and under the string in front of the bridge.
3. Guide the shorter end of the string back across the bridge.
4. Loop it through the string in back of the bridge.
5. Pull the string tightly so that it's securely tied into a knot at the back of the bridge. Sometimes, holding it down

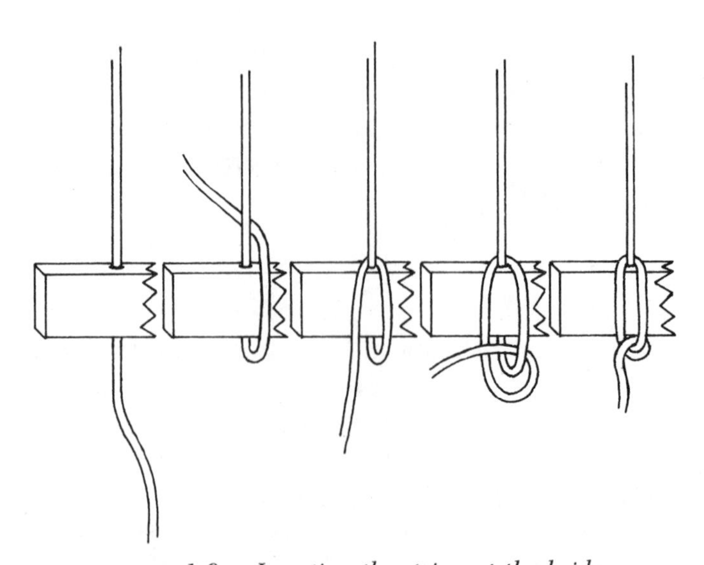

FIGURE 1-6a *Inserting the string at the bridge*

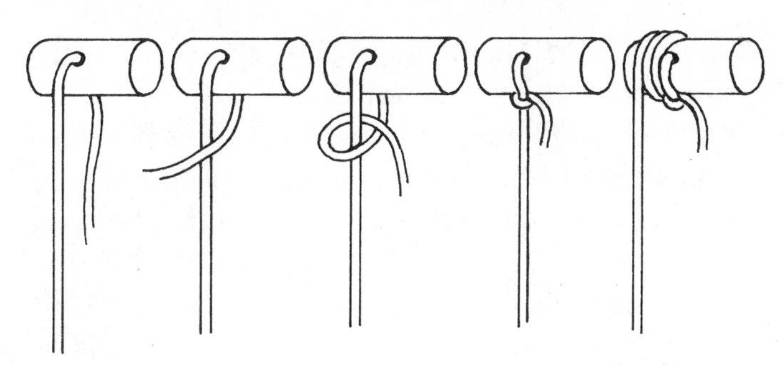

FIGURE 1-6b *Inserting the string at the tuning gear*

with your finger will insure that the knot stays behind the bridge as you pull it tight.

If you have a steel-string guitar, your bridge will probably have bridge pins. If the pin is difficult to pull out, first, you should loosen the string leading to the pin. Then pry the pin loose with a pair of pliers. Be careful that you don't damage the guitar. When you've got the pin out, push the end of the string which has a tiny circular metal piece attached to it down into the hole. Then push the bridge pin back down into the hole, on top of it.

Figure 1-6b shows the other end of the nylon string being inserted into the appropriate hole in the tuning machine head. Then, it's tied and wound around the tuning gear a few times, by turning the peg away from you. (Some guitarists don't bother tying it.) As you turn the peg away from you, counterclockwise, you'll see the string winding around the tuning gear. Don't turn it too fast. You'll either get it so much out of tune that it'll be much harder for you to tune or you may break the string.

Figure 1-6b is also divided into five steps, beginning with inserting the nylon string into the string hole of the tuning gear, and ending by showing the string wound around the tuning gear a few times. If you want to tighten your string and raise the pitch, turn the peg away from you. If you want to loosen your string and lower the pitch, turn the peg towards you. If any one of your strings is doing the opposite of that, then you've strung it incorrectly. You've probably inserted it into the hole going in from the bottom and coming out through the top of the hole. The strings should all be going in the same direction when they're being tightened or loosened. If you've got it wrong, it's best to remove the string and do it correctly.

The other end of a steel string is inserted into the tuning head in the same way as the nylon string, except that the hole for the steel string is on top of the head. When you're tightening the string, hold the bridge pin down to insure that it doesn't jump out of the pin hole.

If the leftover string ends dangling at the tuning head are annoying to you, cut them off. Nylon strings can be cut with a pair of scissors. If the scissors are sturdy enough, they can cut steel strings also; if not, use a wire cutter for the steel strings.

How Long to Practice

Beginners always like to know how long they should practice. That's almost entirely up to the individual. Some people lead extremely active lives, so it's very difficult to fit in more than fifteen or twenty minutes a day. Some can find an hour or even more in their daily schedules for practice. The important thing is not to miss a day's practice, even if there's barely more than a few minutes available. It's just like a sport. If you miss a day's practice, you'll be able to tell the difference when you play the next day, especially if you're just learning the game. To keep up your level of skill in anything you do, you've got to practice. You've got to keep on playing the game to get better at it.

HOW TO READ A CHORD DIAGRAM

Now you're ready to learn how to read a chord diagram. Chord diagrams are always presented to you as though you were looking at the guitar standing on its wider end and facing you, with the sound hole and strings showing. Each diagram is a picture of the guitar fingerboard. Usually, it shows just the first few frets. The six vertical lines represent the guitar strings. The sixth string is the one that's nearest to your chin when the guitar is held in playing position. The short horizontal lines represent the frets. The first fret is the space between the nut and up to, and including, the first metal strip. The second fret is the space between the first metal strip up to, and including, the second metal strip, and so on. So, when we refer to the fret, we're referring to the space *between* the frets as well as to the metal fret strips. However, when any one of your fingers is in a chord position, that finger should be as close as possible to, but not *on,* the fret(metal crossbar strip) that it's supposed to be *in.* For instance, when playing the third fret of the sixth string, your finger should be in the third fret space, closest to the third fret strip (the strip closer to the body of the guitar).

How to Count Your Fingers

Right here and now, I must ask that you memorize the following information. From this day on, you shall know your fingers by this new way of counting them. The pointer shall be called one, or first finger; the middle finger shall be called two, or second finger; the ring finger shall be called three,

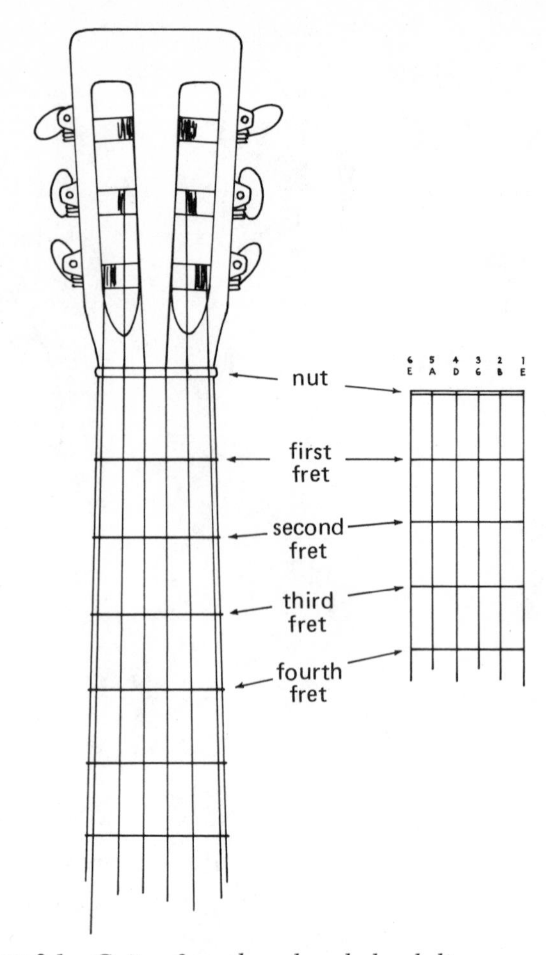

FIGURE 2-1 *Guitar fingerboard and chord diagrams*

or third finger; and the pinky, or little finger, shall be called four, or fourth finger. (However, if you should happen to be looking at a piece of classical music for the guitar, don't be surprised to see that the right hand fingers are called by their Latin names; pollex for thumb, index for pointer, medius for middle finger, and annularis for ring finger. Usually, you'll see those fingers named by their initials: p, i, m, and a.) The fourth finger of the right hand isn't used in plucking the strings. In my method of teaching, the only function of the left hand thumb is to press against the back of the guitar neck for support.

D CHORD; EASY STRUM

Now that you know how to count your fingers and how a chord diagram is pictured, let's look at the diagram for a D chord.

The circles show you where to put your left hand fingers; the numbers tell you which fingers of the left hand to use. There are several expressions, all meaning the same thing,

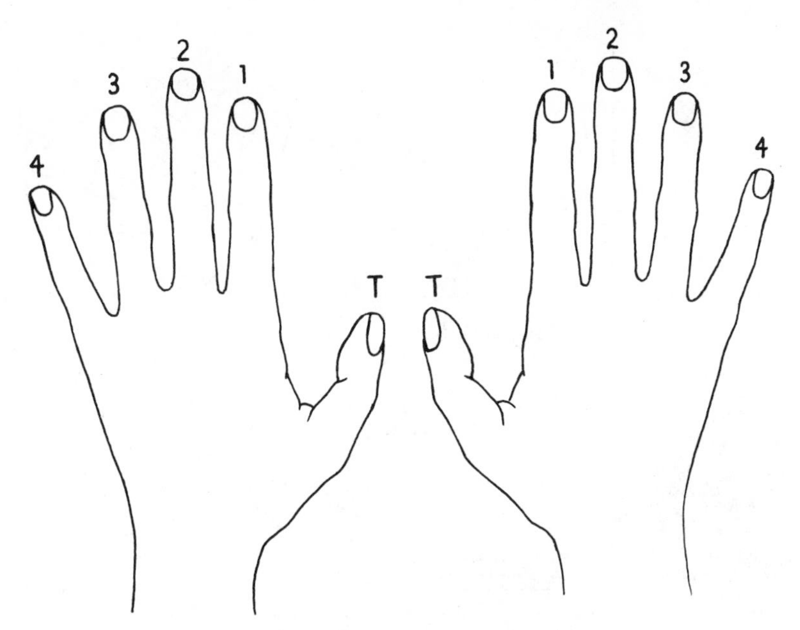

FIGURE 2-2 *How to count your fingers*

to describe playing a chord: pressing down on the string, fingering the string, and fretting the string.

The x above a string means that you don't touch that string when you're strumming with your right hand thumb because it's not part of the chord. The o above a string means that although that string isn't fingered with your left hand, you still can use and include it in your right hand strumming. All the chord diagrams have a tiny black triangle at the bottom, under a string. That shows you which string is the bass string of the chord. We'll cover more information about bass strings a little later.

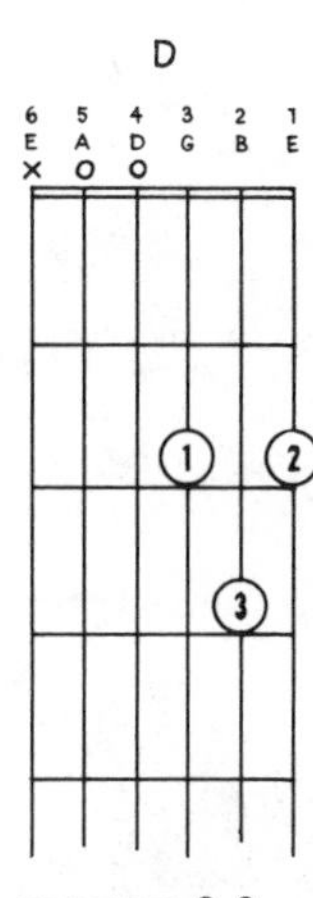

FIGURE 2-3
D chord

Hold the guitar comfortably. Look at the diagram. Figure out, from the diagram, on which strings and which frets to place the fingers of your left hand. Make sure that your fingers take the exact position of the D chord diagram. As you see in the diagram, your first finger should be on the third string, second fret; your second finger should be on the first string, second fret; and your third finger should be on the second string, third fret. Remember, your fingers should be as close as possible to the metal crossbar strip of each fret, (the one closer to the body) without actually being on top of it.

When you've accomplished all that, we'll do the Easy Strum. Starting from the fourth string, strum down over the sound hole by brushing across the strings with the left side of your right hand thumb. The fourth string is the bass of the D chord. Every chord has its bass note or bass string. The bass is the lowest note in a chord. It's the root of the chord and is very important because the chord grows from

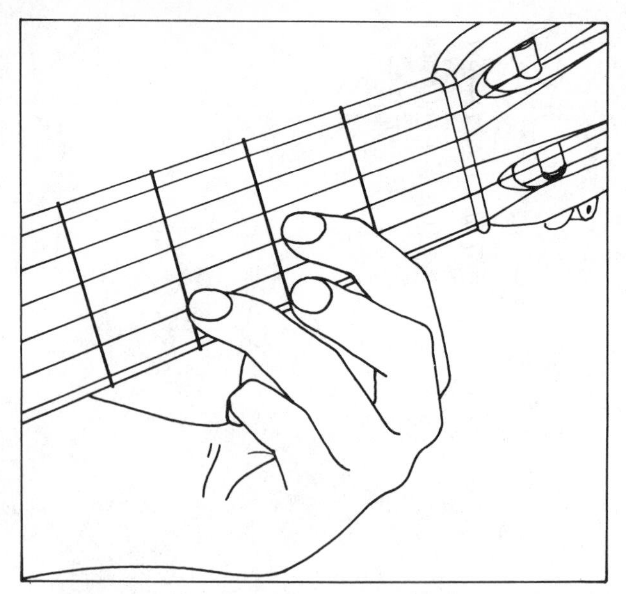

FIGURE 2-4 *D chord finger positions*

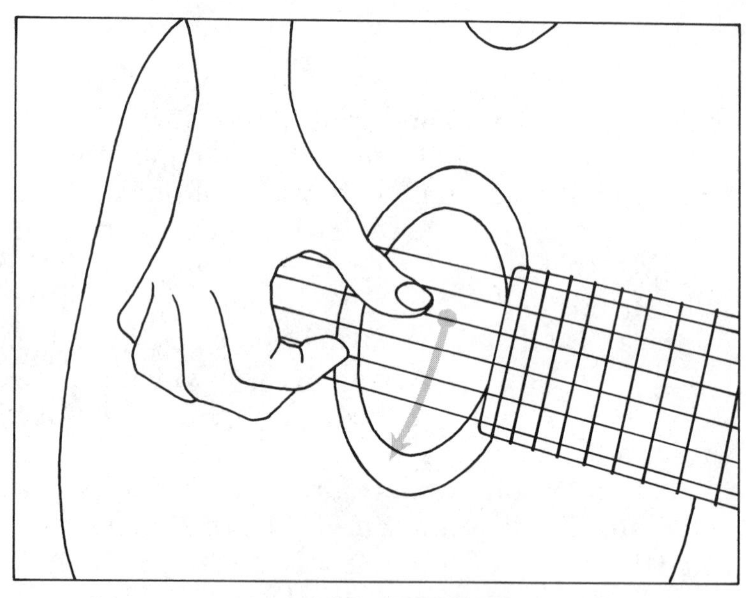

FIGURE 2-5 *Easy Strum*

that root. Be sure that you *always* strum a chord beginning with the bass string; the bass string sound identifies the chord you're strumming.

How to Make It Sound Better

If your chord sounds less than lovely, and it usually does at this time, check these ways to make it sound better:

1. Are your left hand fingers curved as in the illustration, so that only the tips of your fingers are pressing down on the strings, instead of laying flattened out on the strings? Flattened fingers that touch strings they aren't supposed to will result in bad sound.

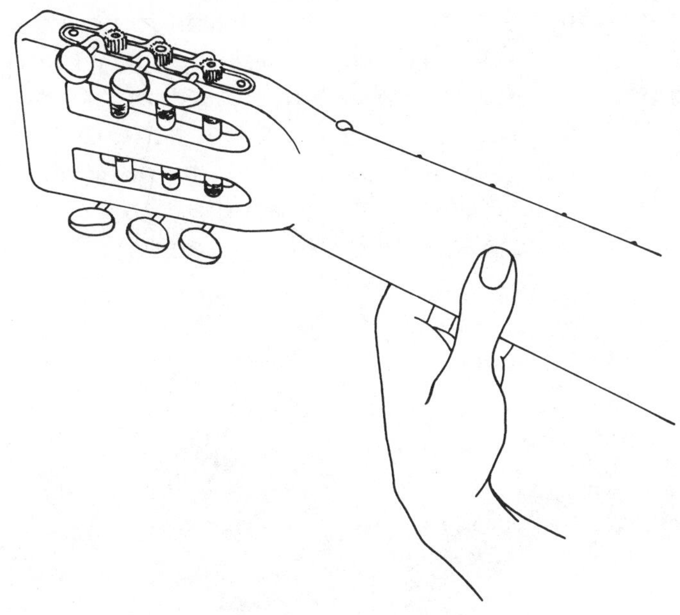

FIGURE 2-6 *Thumb position in back of guitar neck*

2. The palm of your left hand should not touch the guitar. There must be space between the palm of your left hand and the guitar. If not, your fingers won't be free enough to give you a sound that's clear and bright; it will be muffled and dull. Also, your potential for speed will be decreased.

3. Is the thumb of your left hand relaxed in back of the guitar neck and just about opposite to where your first finger is? It shouldn't be up so high that it sticks out from in back of the guitar neck. As the illustration shows you, it should be about half way down on the back of the guitar neck to allow you more leverage and freedom of movement in your fingers.

4. Are your fingers as close to the frets as possible without being on top of them? (Don't forget, that's the metal strip that's closer to the body of the guitar.) The closer your fingers are to the frets, the better the sound will be.

5. Are you pressing as hard as you can with your left hand fingers? You are? Well then, press even harder, even if it hurts. Eventually, those sensitive tips of your fingers will become calloused and toughened so that it won't bother you at all. This won't affect the appearance of your fingertips.

After checking all these points, strum the D chord several times, from the fourth string down. Make sure you're strumming with the left side of your right hand thumb. Don't tense your thumb and then strum down stiffly with the tip of it. Strum casually, as though you're caressing the strings. Beginners tend to strum too loudly. That's not as pleasant as a softer sound. Don't strum too softly either, because nobody will hear it, except you. That may be just what you're hoping, right now, but if you get into that habit, you'll be sorry later on when you want people to hear you. Make the strum sound with one smooth action across the strings, from the fourth string to the first string. If you're satisfied with the sound, how about strumming the D chord while you sing *Three Blind Mice?* You can do the whole song with just that one D chord.

THREE BLIND MICE

D

Three blind mice, three blind mice,
See how they run, see how they run,
They all ran up to the farmer's wife,
She made them dance to the tune on her fife,
Did you ever see such a sight in your life,
As three blind mice?

THE "E-Z NUMBERS GAME"

When I first started teaching, and for some time afterward, when we'd learn the new songs I'd sing them first and then we'd all do it together several times. Repetition was always helpful. It was a way to get acquainted with the tune even if the students had never heard it before. However, from time to time there were some who forgot parts of the tune between sessions. This presented a problem. Of course, one way to solve the problem, would be to learn to read music. The trouble with that solution is that so many people who start guitar playing are doing it more for fun than for a serious study of music. They aren't really interested in learning how to read music, at least not at the beginning. So learning how to read music in order to hear the tune wasn't the answer. Based on this concern, I developed the "E-Z Numbers Game," which begins below.

string	1	1	2
fret	2	0	3

The top numbers tell you which *string* to pluck with your right hand thumb, while you're fingering that *same string* with your left hand.

The bottom numbers tell you which *fret* to finger, on that top number string. The 0 means open string. An open string isn't fingered with your left hand. It's just plucked with your right hand.

Although Figures 2-7a through 2-7c show only the left hand first finger pressing down on (fingering, fretting) the strings, you don't have to limit yourself to one finger. In fact, I prefer that you don't be a one finger player. It's better if you use all four fingers of your left hand when you play the E-Z Numbers Game. I'd like you to use your first finger in the first fret, your second finger in the second fret, your third finger in the third fret, and your first, second, third or fourth finger for any fret above the third fret. It might seem easier to use only the first finger at the beginning but it's more practical and easier to use all the fingers in the long run. Keep your left hand fingers hovering closely over the strings whenever you're not fingering them. If you move them far away from the strings, it'll be harder and take longer to get them back to fret a string.

The first top number is 1 and the first bottom number is 2. This means, press down on the first string in the second fret with your left hand finger, while you pluck that first string with your right hand thumb (see Figure 2-7a).

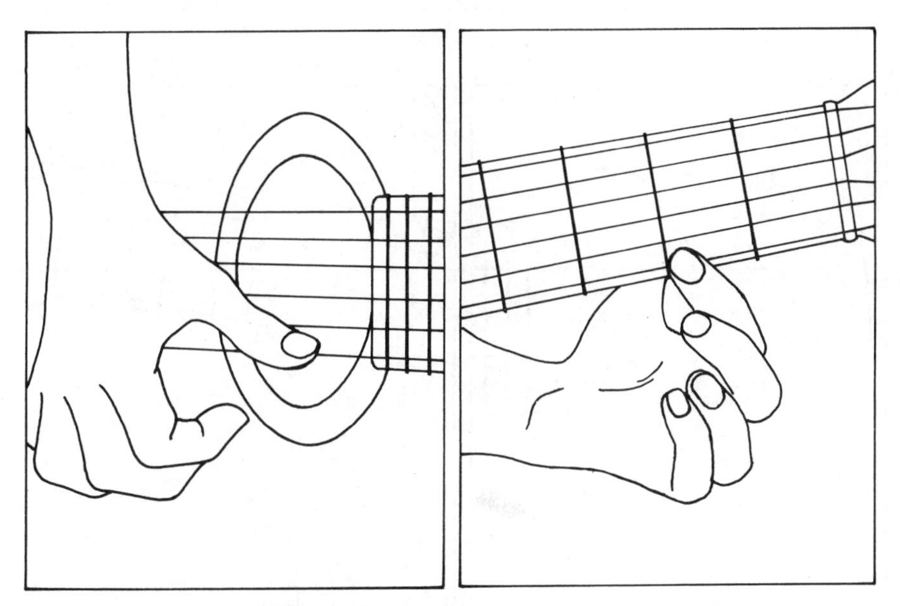

FIGURE 2-7a *"Three Blind Mice": string 1, fret 2*

The next top number is also 1 and the next bottom number is 0. Since 0 means an open string, don't finger the string with your left hand. Just pluck that first string with your right hand (see Figure 2-7b).

The last top number is 2 and the last bottom number is 3. Finger the second string in the third fret with your left hand and pluck that second string with your right hand (see Figure 2-7c).

Make sure your right hand is plucking the correct string according to the numbers and that your left hand is pressing on the correct fret(according to the numbers) of that *same* string.

If you play these numbers a couple of times, it should sound like the beginning of "Three Blind Mice." Why don't you

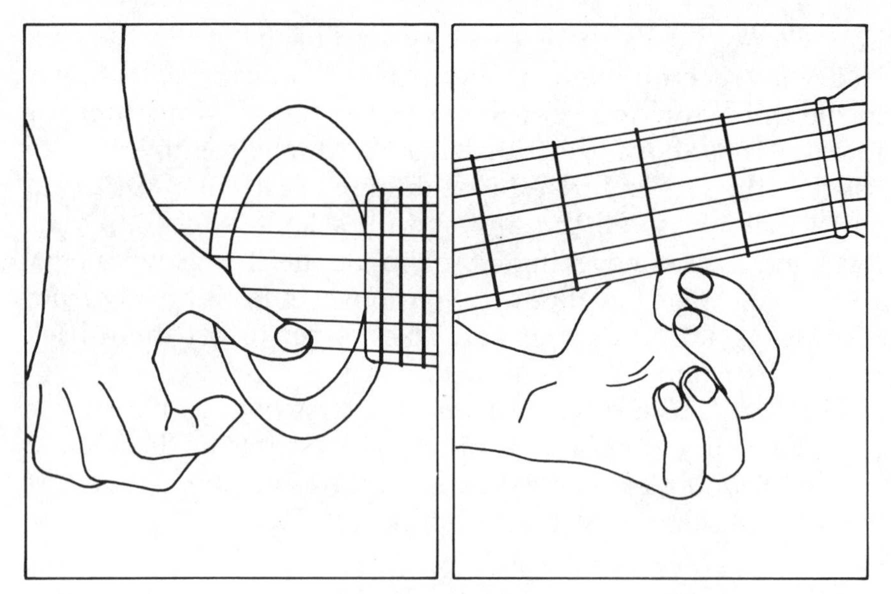

FIGURE 2-7b *"Three Blind Mice": string 1, fret 0*

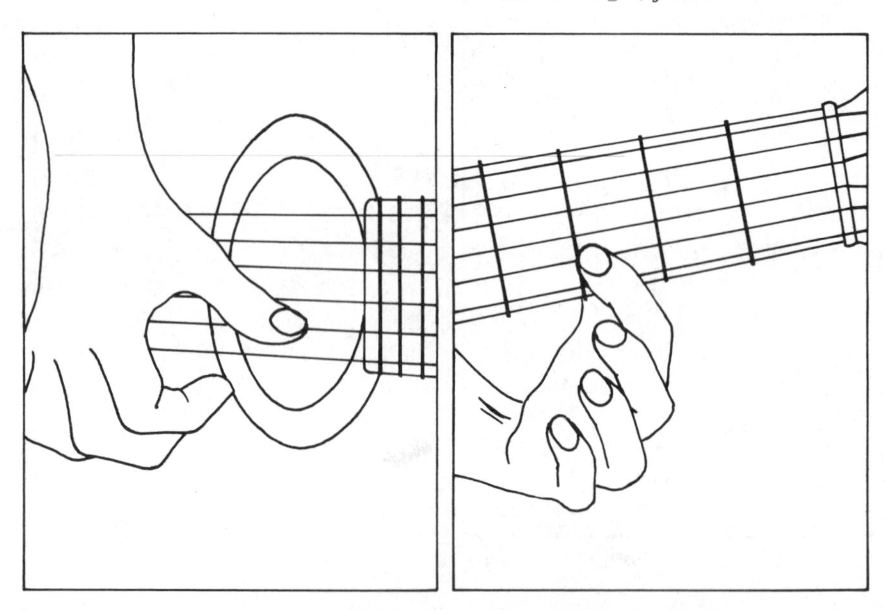

FIGURE 2-7c *"Three Blind Mice": string 2, fret 3*

try this? Play the E-Z Numbers two times. After that introduction, start singing "Three Blind Mice" while accompanying yourself throughout the song with the D chord. If the numbers in the introduction start your voice singing too high for comfort, then start the introduction with the numbers at left instead. It's the same tune, just sounded lower.

string 4 4 4
fret 4 2 0

However, before you start singing, there's one more thing I want you to know. When you sang "Three Blind Mice" earlier, accompanying yourself with the D chord, you probably wondered where and when to strum. If you've forgotten what the D chord looks like, refer to the chord chart at the back of the book.

I've put slanted marks, or slashes, to show you where to strum as you sing. I'll continue to put them on the first verses of songs that you'll be learning. After you've been strumming away for awhile, you won't need to see them anymore. By then, you'll have developed a sense of where to strum. It's something you'll feel within yourself, a pulse or rhythm.

Strum Marks

string 1 1 2
fret 2 0 3

or

string 4 4 4
fret 4 2 0

THREE BLIND MICE

D

Three blind mice, three blind mice,
See how they run, see how they run,
They all ran up to the farmer's wife,
She made them dance to the tune on her fife,
Did you ever see such a sight in your life,
As three blind mice?

Have you guessed it yet? The numbers stand for notes, so believe it or not, you're already playing a tune. Can you "hear" the tune? If it's at all possible to get some kind of recording device, it's very helpful to tape yourself while you're playing the numbers. Then, when you play it back, you can hear the tune you're playing more easily. While you're playing, you're probably concentrating so hard that you're not listening to the tune too well.

Another Song with the E-Z Numbers Game and the D Chord

Now that you know how to play the game, here's the tune for "Frère Jacques." Play the numbers. After you've finished each line of numbers, repeat the whole line again.

string 2 1 1 2
fret 3 0 2 3

Repeat

string 1 1 1
fret 2 3 5

Repeat

string 1 1 1 1 1 2
fret 5 7 5 3 2 3

Repeat

On this third line, you can slide your fourth finger from the fifth fret to the seventh fret and back to the fifth fret again.

string 2 3 2
fret 3 2 3

Repeat

Play the numbers as many times as you need to. It's very important that you feel comfortable with it. That way, you won't be struggling and concentrating so hard on playing the numbers that you forget to listen to the tune. When you're at the point that you feel comfortable with it, play the numbers as an introduction, then sing the song, accompanying yourself with the D chord.

string	2	1	1	2	2	1	1	2
fret	3	0	2	3	3	0	2	3

Fre - re Jacq - ues, Fre - re Jacq - ues,

1	1	1	1	1	1
2	3	5	2	3	5

Dorm - ez vous, dorm - ez vous,

1	1	1	1	1	2	1	1	1	1	1	2
5	7	5	3	2	3	5	7	5	3	2	3

Son - nez les mat - in - es, son - nez les mat - in - es,

2	3	2	2	3	2
3	2	3	3	2	3

Ding, dong, ding; ding, dong, ding.

Are you playing with one finger? Don't forget to use your left hand first finger in the first fret, second finger in the second fret, third finger in the third fret and first, second, third or fourth finger in any fret after that.

Many guitars have fret marker guides. These are little white dots that are either under the strings, or on the side of the neck, starting at the third or fifth fret. Use it to help you find the fret you want.

D

Frere Jacques, Frere Jacques,
Dormez vous, dormez vous,
Sonnez les matines, sonnez matines
Ding, dong, ding; ding, dong, ding.

Are you sleeping, are you sleeping,
Brother John, Brother John,
Morning bells are ringing, morning bells are ringing,
Ding, dong, ding; ding, dong, ding.

Ahkinu Yakov, Ahkinu Yakov,
Altishan, altishan,
Hapahamon mezalzel, hapahamon mezalzel,
Ding, dong, ding; ding, dong, ding.

Brat Eevan, Brat Eevan,
Spesh-lee ti, spesh-lee ti?
Zvoneet kolokolcheek, zvoneet kolokolcheek,
Bim, bam, bim; bim, bam, bim.

Fra Felipe, Fra Felipe,
Duermes tu, duermes tu,
Toca la campana, toca la campana,
Ding, dong, ding; ding, dong, ding.

Now you know verses in French, English, Hebrew, Russian and Spanish, all contributed by students.

Reviewing How to Make It Sound Better

Were you satisfied with how the D chord sounded? If not, check the points from 1 to 5 on page 22 to make it sound better. All this information may be a bit overwhelming at the start, but don't worry. You've got a lot of company.

What Do We Do about That Voice?

For some of you, your singing voice may not be much of a problem. For most of you, it probably is. My experience has been that beginners often are convinced they sound awful and that they absolutely can't "sing a note." You don't have to have a good voice to sing and play the guitar. Would you believe there actually was a time not too long ago that a guitar strummer with a trained voice was rare? All you've got to do is sing in tune and you'll sound fine. Everybody will enjoy listening to that, including yourself.

Singing in Tune. If you've never sung in tune in your entire life, chances are, you never really listened. It's the rare exception to come across a person who's really tone deaf due to physical reasons. The majority of so-called "tone deaf" people are just people with lazy ears, who've never bothered to really listen. The irony is that many years ago, those people were labeled "listeners" when school teachers divided the classes into sopranos, altos, tenors, and baritones.

To help you get started on your way to really listening, here are some things you can do. Get a few containers of some kind; paper cups will do, or anything else that's available. In one, put a handful of raw rice grains. In another, put a handful of grains of sand. In another, you can put some pebbles, paper clips, buttons, or beans. If none of these things are available to you, use any kinds of particles that you can find. As long as it will make some kind of sound, it's useful.

If you've got someone who can help you do this, that's fine, but not necessary. Close your eyes and ask a friend to shake one of the containers. Identify which one it was. For example, were you able to recognize the sound when the rice was being shaken in the container? Or the sand, or the pebbles, or whatever else was being used? Play this game as often as you can. The more you play, the sooner you'll have trained those lazy ears of yours to get into the habit of really listening.

If you don't have anyone to help you, put the containers in back of you. Reach for one carefully, so you don't knock it over. Shake it. Identify it and then check it to see if you heard correctly. When you get really good at recognizing what's in the shaking containers, then do the following. Pluck the guitar strings individually and each time, hum the sound you hear. Be sure to hum the exact sound of the string. If you learn to trust yourself, you'll notice whether your voice went up higher or down lower in pitch than the string sound. If it did go up or down in pitch instead of humming the exact pitch of the string, try it again. When you pluck the string and listen very carefully to the sound, you'll hum exactly what you hear. You won't hum a higher sound and you won't hum a lower sound. You'll hum a sound that's exactly on the same pitch level, right on target. Here's a visual description of what I mean:

guitar string sound ____ voice humming sound ____

not

guitar string sound ____ voice humming sound
____

or

____
guitar string sound ____ voice humming sound

but always

guitar string sound ____ voice humming sound ____

All of these things will actually help you sing in tune. That's because singing in tune is imitating what you've heard, when you're really listening. Once you're singing in tune, you won't think you've got an awful voice any more and that you can't 'sing a note.' You'll feel a lot better about singing.

A parent came to see me one day with her fourteen-year-old son, who was "driving his parents up the wall." He sang constantly and was always out of tune. I asked him to sing *"Three Blind Mice."* If you can imagine a visual picture of the melody, it might look like this, when sung in tune.

Three Three
Blind Blind
Mice Mice

He sang it something like this.

Blind Mice
Three Blind
Mice Three

After having him listen to shaking containers for several months, his "ear" got so good that he became the lead singer of an amateur group.

A nurse who never sang out loud in front of anyone was initially a very shy, timid woman. But after shaking containers for a time, she became less shy and gradually changed into a more comfortable and confident person. She admitted that the discovery that she could sing in tune, something she thought was hopelessly impossible, had encouraged her to think differently about herself.

"E-Z Relaxation" Time

This is a good time to become acquainted with the "E-Z Relaxation" method. In addition to reenforcing your learning experience, it's a wonderful way to get rid of the tensions all of us acquire daily.[1] I want to emphasize that although this works for me and for others as well, it's not *necessary* in order to learn how to play the guitar. But tensions will set up blocks in your memory. When you're relaxed, it does help your mind remember what you learned.

Put your guitar down. Find a comfortable chair in a quiet spot, away from ringing telephones, extremely loud noises, or any possible interruptions. Sit back in a comfortable position and close your eyes. Repeat silently, over and over, E-Z, E-Z, E-Z, over and over, for about fifteen or twenty minutes. You can use your natural breathing pattern as a way to start it. For instance, you can breathe in on E and out on Z or you can breathe in on E-Z and out on E-Z, or you can breathe in on E-Z and breathe out. If you should happen to change your silent repetition from one of these to another, it doesn't matter. It doesn't matter if you repeat it quickly or slowly. It doesn't even matter if your mind is cluttered with other concerns while repeating it. Don't *force* yourself to concentrate on it. Just relax and let it come into your mind casually and easily, like a thought.

If you should notice that your mind has wandered and you've stopped the repetition of E-Z, E-Z, E-Z, that's alright. Just start repeating it again. If you should happen to doze off, when you awaken and see that your fifteen or twenty

[1] I'm not advocating this as a substitute for TM.

minutes is not over, continue repeating E-Z, E-Z, E-Z, until your time is up.

During the fifteen or twenty minutes, if something should distract you, like an itchy nose, an oncoming sneeze, or whatever, don't sit there trying to suppress the sneeze or fight off the urge to scratch your nose. That's not relaxing. Take care of it and continue your E-Z Relaxation. Even if you're unavoidably interrupted by a phone call, answer it, be very brief, and then continue your E-Z Relaxation. You'll become aware, after about five minutes of repeating E-Z, E-Z, E-Z, over and over again, of a pleasant sense of relaxation and a lovely, quiet feeling.

When you're finished repeating E-Z, E-Z, E-Z, continue sitting with your eyes closed for another minute or two. Open your eyes slowly and luxuriate in the wonderful, refreshing feeling of relaxation.

The very least it can do is give you a few minutes of rest, during your day's activities. Although fifteen or twenty minutes is better, if you can't spare more than ten minutes, it's better than nothing. You can get into the habit of doing it every day at the end of your guitar practice, or even before it, if you prefer. You might like to try it.

Trust Yourself. You're the best judge of the pace that's suitable for you. You've got to be the one to decide how long you want to stay with any part of this book and when you're ready to go on. Don't pressure yourself to go faster than you want to, or even slower than you really need to. Don't make the mistake of judging yourself by other people's standards.

THE A7 CHORD

The A7 chord is easier to finger than the D chord. It's strummed from the fifth string. (As you already know, the fifth string is the A string, which is the bass string for the A7 chord.) Strum it casually a few times. Review steps 1 to 5 on page 22 on how to make it sound better. When you've done that, strum the A7 chord a few times more.

Changing Chords

First, practice changing back and forth between the D and the A7 chords, strumming each chord a few times. Make sure you're strumming both chords from their proper bass strings. Then try it again, changing to a slow but steady beat. Strum the D chord four times and then the A7 chord four times. Continue changing back and forth steadily, strumming each chord four times. It doesn't matter how slowly you're changing, as long as you keep it going steadily.

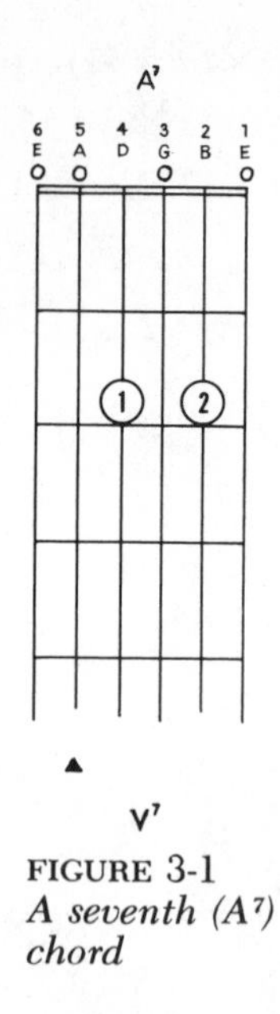

FIGURE 3-1
A seventh (A^7) chord

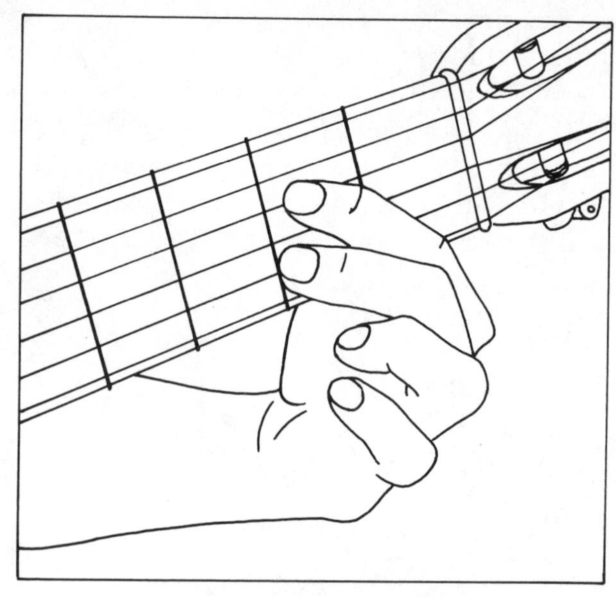

FIGURE 3-2 *A^7 chord finger position*

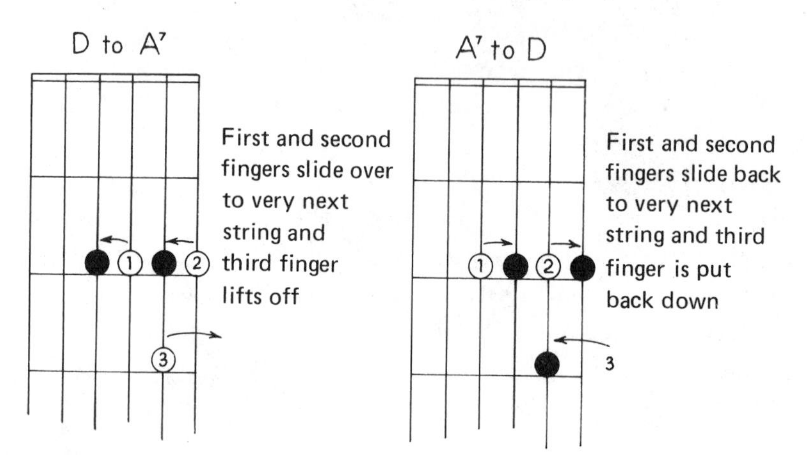

FIGURE 3-3 *Changing from D to A^7 to D*

Tips on Filling in the Empty Spaces. Does it seem like forever before you've changed from one chord to another? Here are some tips for filling in the empty spaces between chord changes.

Notice that on the D chord, if you slide your first and second fingers over to the very next strings in the same second fret, going in the direction of your chin (when your guitar's in playing position), and lift off your third finger, you've got an A^7 chord. When you're on the A^7 chord, if you slide your first and second fingers back to the very next strings (still in the second fret), going in the direction of your knees, and put your third finger back, you're back on a D chord. Now, practice the same chord changes as before, with these tips in mind.

PLAYING THE E-Z NUMBERS GAME WITH SOME SONGS

The next tune you can 'hear' while playing the E-Z Numbers Game is "Skip To My Lou."[1] After you've played the numbers a few times, sing the song, accompanying yourself with the D and A^7 chords. Make sure your guitar is in tune or else you won't hear what you want to hear. Do the Easy Strum with this and follow the strum marks. Get ready to change an instant before you actually have to. This means that as you finish singing the word that's just before a chord change, your fingers should begin the change.

SKIP TO MY LOU

Chorus

1	2	1	1	1	1
2	3	2	2	2	5
Skip,	*skip,*	*skip*	*to*	*my*	*Lou*

1	2	1	1	1	1
0	2	0	0	0	3
Skip,	*skip,*	*skip*	*to*	*my*	*Lou*

1	2	1	1	1	1
2	3	2	2	2	5
Skip,	*skip,*	*skip*	*to*	*my*	*Lou*

1	1	1	1	1	2	2
0	3	3	2	0	3	3
Skip	*to*	*my*	*Lou*	*my*	*dar -*	*ling.*

Chorus

D
Skip, skip, skip to my Lou
A^7
Skip, skip, skip to my Lou
D
Skip, skip, skip to my Lou
A^7 D
Skip to my Lou my darling.

For the purpose of having an entire song to sing, here are three verses sung to the same tune as the chorus of "Skip To My Lou." After each verse, the chorus is repeated. As

[1] Although we've eliminated the words, string and fret next to the top and bottom numbers, here's a reminder. The top numbers are the strings to be plucked by the right hand and at the same time, fingered by the left hand. The bottom numbers refer to the frets these strings are fingered in with the left hand.

you're singing the tune of the verses, you must change chords in the same places as you did for the chorus.

D
Flies in the buttermilk, shoo fly shoo
A⁷
Flies in the buttermilk, shoo fly shoo
D
Flies in the buttermilk, shoo fly shoo
A⁷ **D**
Skip to my Lou my darling.
Chorus

Chords are not indicated after the first verse and chorus (if there is one), for this reason: Even at the beginning, I don't want you to be lulled into always looking to see where you've got to change to the next chord. You should get used to listening and to 'hear' what you're listening to. That's how you'll know when to change chords.

A "Hearing" Test. If you don't think you're capable of playing without chords indicated yet, take this test. Start singing the first verse of the chorus, only this time, instead of changing to an A^7 on the second line, keep on strumming a D chord. On the third line, instead of strumming a D chord, change to an A^7 chord. Can you bear to go on? Sounds pretty awful, doesn't it? So you see, you can 'hear' if you really listen.

Stretch and Squeeze. Keep in mind that although all the verses are sung to the same tune, some verse lines are longer in one verse than those same lines in another verse. That's because, in some verses, there may be more words on a line than that same line in other verses. You've got to fit the verse line to the tune by squeezing the words in as you sing. Similarly, a shorter line will have to be stretched out to fit the tune.

Now, let's continue with "Skip to my Lou." You've done the chorus, first verse, and chorus again. Here are the next two verses, each followed by the chorus:

Lost my partner, what'll I do
Lost my partner, what'll I do
Lost my partner, what'll I do
Skip to my Lou my darling.

Chorus

I'll find another one better than you
I'll find another one better than you
I'll find another one better than you
Skip to my Lou my darling.

Chorus

Please don't get discouraged if, in spite of all the guidelines I've given you, you're still changing chords very slowly and, as a result, the song seems to be never-ending. This is only the beginning. When I first learned how to play the guitar, some friends of mine had a get-together and asked me to bring my guitar along. Of course, I was asked to play and sing. I only knew one song and that's the one I happily obliged with. Believe me when I tell you that only very kind, caring, and patient friends could have sat through the interminable time it took me to make those chord changes. Don't get discouraged.

SHOO FLY

Adapted and arranged with new words by R.T. Jacobs
(Based on a traditional song)

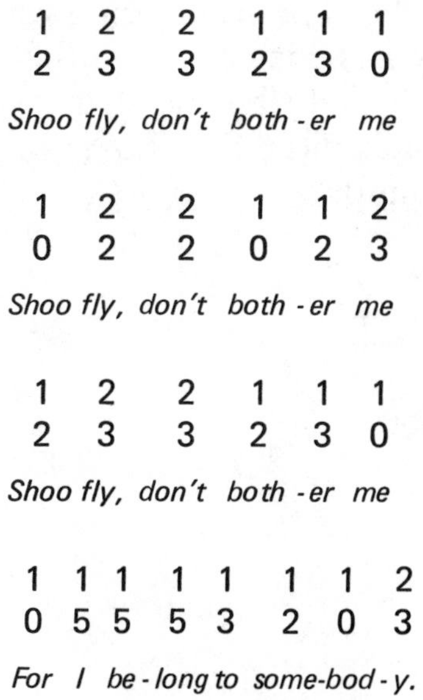

1 2 2 1 1 1
2 3 3 2 3 0

Shoo fly, don't both-er me

1 2 2 1 1 2
0 2 2 0 2 3

Shoo fly, don't both-er me

1 2 2 1 1 1
2 3 3 2 3 0

Shoo fly, don't both-er me

1 1 1 1 1 1 1 2
0 5 5 5 3 2 0 3

For I be-long to some-bod-y.

D A7
Shoo fly, don't bother me
D
Shoo fly, don't bother me
A7
Shoo fly, don't bother me
D
For I belong to somebody.

Did you notice that on three of the verse lines, you strum between words? Sometimes that happens; just keep strumming.

It's some one cute with eyes so blue
It's some one cute with eyes so blue
It's some one cute with eyes so blue
And I don't have to tell you who.

A little bird sang the other day
A little bird sang the other day
A little bird sang the other day
But who it is, she'll never say.

Repeat first verse.

(Have you been using all your left-hand fingers to play the numbers? Have you used the first, second, third and fourth fingers of your left hand to finger the frets?)

THE DOWN–SLAP-DAMP STRUM

In this next song, I'd like you to try a new strum. What you're going to do is called "damping" the strings. Wherever you see a slash for the strum mark, strum down hard with your thumb. Then, still holding the chord position, bring your right hand up quickly and slap the strings hard with the palm of your hand. Don't over do it and slap the strings so hard that you hurt your hand, or your guitar. Slap the strings nearer to the bridge for a larger sound.

LA CUCARACHA

Adapted and arranged with new words by R.T. Jacobs
(Based on Mexican folk song)

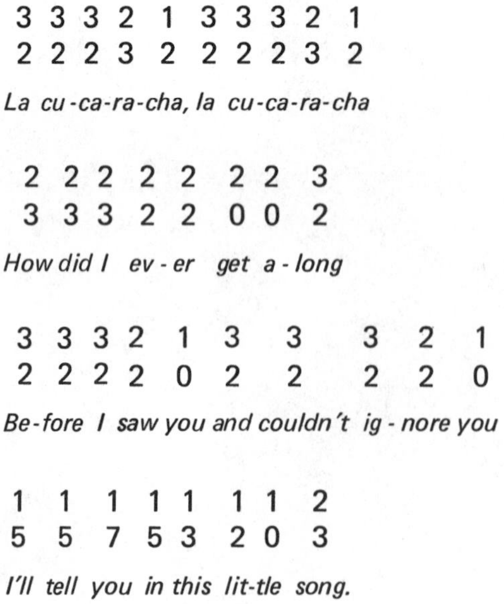

3 3 3 2 1 3 3 3 2 1
2 2 2 3 2 2 2 2 3 2

La cu-ca-ra-cha, la cu-ca-ra-cha

2 2 2 2 2 2 2 3
3 3 3 2 2 0 0 2

How did I ev-er get a-long

3 3 3 2 1 3 3 3 2 1
2 2 2 2 0 2 2 2 2 0

Be-fore I saw you and couldn't ig-nore you

1 1 1 1 1 1 1 2
5 5 7 5 3 2 0 3

I'll tell you in this lit-tle song.

D

Down-slap Down-slap

La cucaracha, la cucaracha

A7

Down - slap Down-slap

How did I ever get along

Down-slap Down-slap

Before I saw you and couldn't ignore you

D

Down - slap Down-slap

I'll tell you in this little song.

2 *La cucaracha, la cucaracha*
Summer, Winter, Spring and Fall
You're always here now, forever near now
I can't get rid of you at all.

3 *La cucaracha, la cucaracha*
Morning, noon and even night
When skies are grey or blue, I'm always chasing you
Because you're never out of sight.

4 *La cucaracha, la cucaracha*
When I see you racing by
I'm sure I'll get you, but never, ever do
Because you have more legs than I.

Have you been stretching and squeezing with "La Cucuracha"?

The "Charley Horse Shake." Muscles that may have never been used before will ache and feel sore when they're first put to use. No doubt, you've discovered this already. You can ease the soreness somewhat by shaking your wrists loosely, as if you're shaking water off your hands. (I call it the "charley horse shake"). If the fingers of your left hand are sore, and they usually are at the beginning, then gently rub them with your right hand thumb. Don't let the string mark indentations on your fingertips scare you. They're not permanent reminders of your beginner's woes; in fact, they'll disappear whenever you're not playing.

four

High and Low, Up and Down. When we talk about the strings, it's easy to get confused with high and low and up and down. High and low refers to the *sounds* of the strings. We're not referring to where they're strung on the guitar. The lowest *sounding* string is the highest one in space away from your knees: that's the sixth string. You can't think of it as the highest string because the highest sounding string is the first string, the string furthest from your chin.

It's true that you strum *down,* but we're talking about space again, not sound. You're strumming down across the space of the strings. You're strumming down from the lower sounding bass strings to the higher sounding treble strings. If you memorize the names and numbers of the strings and always think of them by their names and numbers, you won't get confused.

THE G CHORD

The G chord is quite a stretch. It may seem impossible to do now, but believe me, it won't seem so impossible after your muscles get used to the stretch.

I've given you two sets of fingerings for the G chord and I'll explain why a little later. The bass string for the G chord is the sixth, or E string. This is the string to strum down from. This may change a mistaken belief: Did you think that a bass string is always the very next lower *sounding* string to the chord? Did you think it's always an open string? You

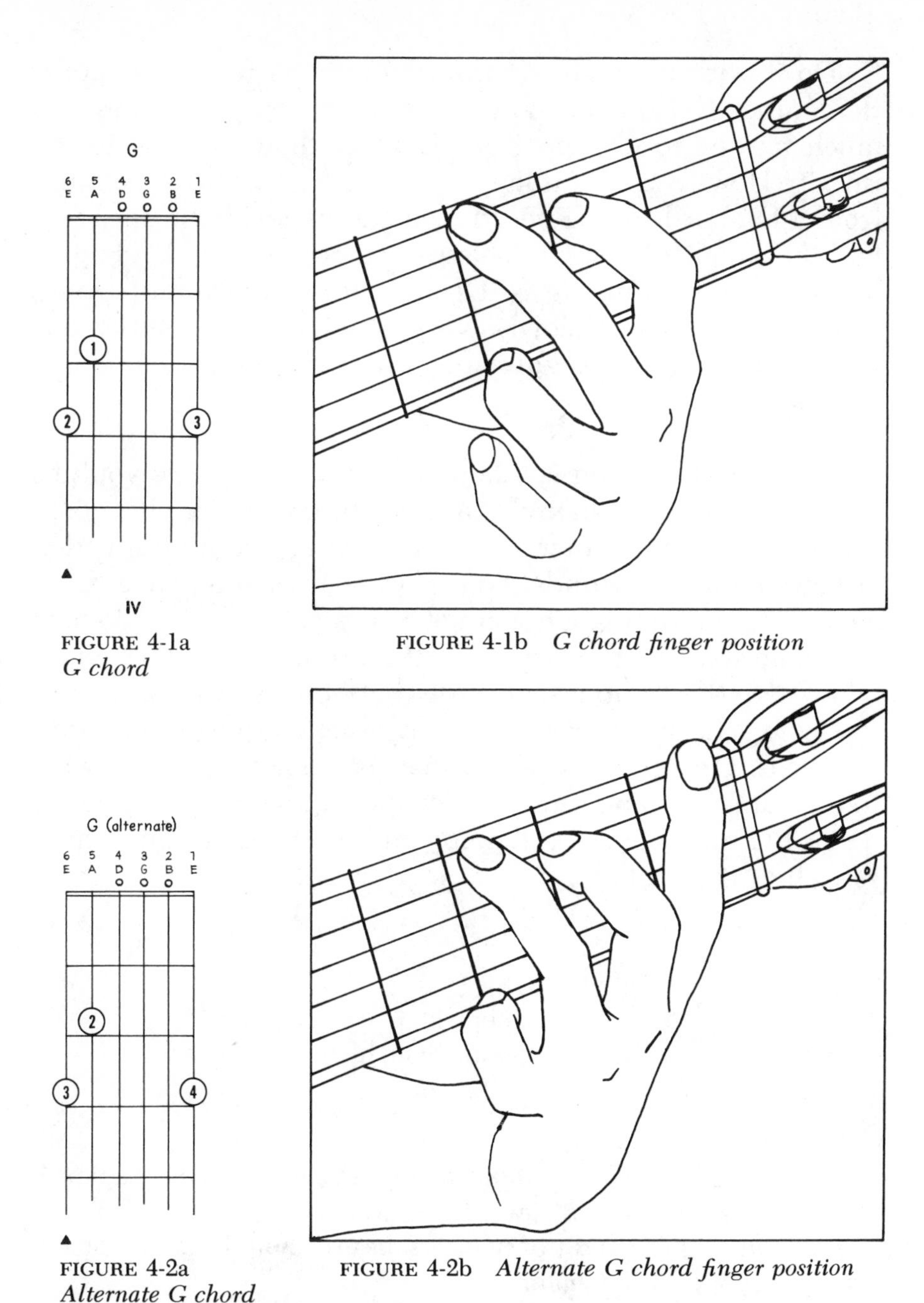

FIGURE 4-1a
G chord

FIGURE 4-1b *G chord finger position*

FIGURE 4-2a
Alternate G chord

FIGURE 4-2b *Alternate G chord finger position*

can see from the figures that the bass string on the G chord happens to be fingered and it's part of the chord position.

The second diagram fingering is easier to use when changing from the G to certain other chords. However, it's more difficult to begin with and fewer beginners can manage it. Although I'm giving you the option of choosing one or the other, the first diagram fingering is the one most people prefer to start with. Even the simpler version of the G chord is a bit of a stretch.

Strum the chord a few times, casually. Review steps 1–5 on page 22 to make it sound better. After you've done that, practice changing from D to A^7, to G, and also, from D to

G. Do it with a steady rhythm, four times for each chord. Remember the tips on how to fill in the empty spaces. It's much harder to change from D to G than from D to A^7, isn't it? However, if you look at your fingers while changing from a D chord to a G chord, you can experiment until you find the smoothest way to change according to which fingering you're using on the G. Do the same experiment, going from G to D. Do it slowly, very slowly at first, until your fingers finally seem to go where you want them to.

RHYTHM AND TIMING MARKS—THE LONG AND SHORT OF IT

Since the next song is a familiar tune to many of you, it's a good time to introduce rhythm and timing marks. It's going to help you to recognize a tune by giving you a better idea of how the music sounds. You know that as you sing a tune, all parts of the tune are not equal. Some notes are held longer and some are sung more quickly. It's important to know when and where this happens, because that helps you to recognize the tune. The markings are not as exact as musical notation timing is. On occasion, there may be more or fewer beats to the bar than some musicians would expect. If you've never heard the tune before, it'll help you get a sense of the timing as well as the melody.

1 count	_	hum
2 counts	L	hum, hum
3 counts	⊔	hum, hum, hum
4 counts	□	hum, hum, hum, hum
quick count	•	
very quick count	:	

This mark _ above a set[1] of numbers means: hold[2] it for the time it takes you to say, or think the word, "Hum."

This mark L above a set of numbers means: hold it for the time it takes you to say, "Hum, hum."

This mark ⊔ above a set of numbers means: hold it for the time it takes you to say, "Hum, hum, hum."

This mark □ above a set of numbers means: hold it for the time it takes you to say, "Hum, hum, hum, hum."

This mark • above a set of numbers means: play it quickly, about twice as fast as the numbers with the single line rhythm mark above them.

This mark : above a set of numbers means: play it very quickly, about twice as fast as the numbers with this mark • above them.

[1] A set of numbers refers to the two vertically aligned numbers that show you which string and fret to play.

[2] When you *hold* a set of numbers, your left hand finger stays down on that string and fret for the amount of hums required, and then goes on to the next set of numbers.

If there's a rhythm mark with no set of numbers beneath it, hold the previous set of numbers for the amount of hums it should get *and* for the amount of hums the mark, without numbers beneath, should get. For example, at right:

—	—	—	•	•	□	□
2	2		2	2	2	
3	3		1	1	0	

The first set of numbers will be held for one hum, or one count. The second set of numbers has a one count hum mark above it also. The one count hum mark after that has no set of numbers below it: hold the second set of numbers for one *plus* one counts: hum, hum. The next two sets of numbers are played twice as fast as the sets of numbers below the one count rhythm marks. The last set of numbers should be held for four counts *plus* four more counts; that's eight counts, or as long as it takes to say eight hums. Now, play those numbers, humming or counting according to the rhythm marks above them.

— — — • •	□	□ ‖
2 2 2 2	2	
3 3 1 1	0	

These are the same numbers and rhythm marks, but now, I've added something called "bar lines." The bar lines between the numbers will make it easier for you to keep track of where you are rhythmically as you're playing. In music, bar lines group beats together. The double bar lines tell you it's the end of the tune.

Occasionally, you'll see the letter "R," after a set of numbers. The R stands for "rest." Do just that. When you see the R, stop and rest for a bit before playing the other numbers.

OLD MACDONALD HAD A FARM

— — — —	— — L	— — — —	⊔ —
1 1 1 2	2 2 2	1 1 1 1	1 2
0 0 0 0	2 2 0	4 4 2 2	0 0

— — — —	— — L	— — — —	⊔ • •
1 1 1 2	2 2 2	1 1 1 1	1 2 2
0 0 0 0	2 2 0	4 4 2 2	0 0 0

— — — • •	— — L	• • — • • —	• • • • — —
1 1 1 2 2	1 1 1	1 1 1 1 1 1	1 1 1 1 1 1
0 0 0 0 0	0 0 0	0 0 0 0 0 0	0 0 0 0 0 0

— — — —	— — L	— — — —	⊔ ‖
1 1 1 2	2 2 2	1 1 1 1	1 R
0 0 0 0	2 2 0	4 4 2 2	0

I'm not going to give you any chords to strum with "Old MacDonald's Farm," but the words to the tune are as follows:

Old MacDonald had a farm, E-I-E-I-O
And on this farm he had some chicks, E-I-E-I-O
With a chick chick here and a chick chick there
Here a chick, there a chick, everywhere a chick chick
Old MacDonald had a farm, E-I-E-I-O.

Now, we'll play a song using the E-Z Numbers Game as an introduction. Then we'll sing the song and accompany it by playing the chords with the Easy Strum.

WHEN THE SAINTS GO MARCHING IN

```
—  —  — |□ |—  —  —   — |□ |—
5  4  4 |4 |   5  4   4 |4 |
0  0  2 |4 |   0  0   2 |4 |
```

Oh when the Saints go march - ing in

```
—  —  — |L  L |L   L |□ |—
5  4  4 |4  4 |4   4 |4 |
0  0  2 |4  0 |0   4 |2 |
```

Oh when the Saints go march - ing in

```
—  —  — |⊔  — |L  —  — |—  ⊔ |—
4  4  4 |4  4 |4  3  3 |3  3 |
2  4  2 |0  0 |4  2  2 |2  0 |
```

Oh Lord I want to be in that num - ber

```
L  — |L  L |L  —  — |□ ||
4  3 |3  4 |4  4  4 |4 ||
4  0 |2  4 |2  4  2 |0 ||
```

When the Saints go mar - chi - ing in.

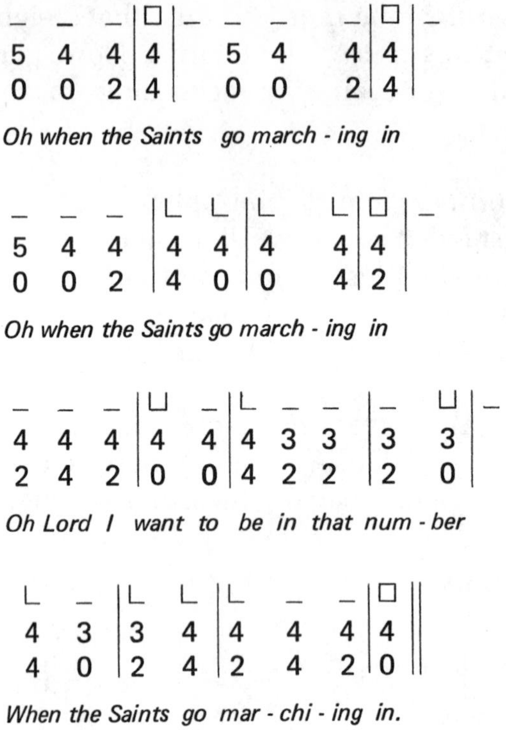

```
                D
Oh when the Saints/go marching in /
                                A7
Oh when the Saints go marching in /
            D                G
Oh Lord I want to be in that number /
            D      A7        D
When the Saints go marching in. /
```

Why don't you try singing the first three words, 'Oh when the,' as you play the first three sets of numbers on the first line, then continue singing the song, accompanying yourself with the Easy Strum? Here are some more verses.

2 *And when the sun begins to shine*
And when the sun begins to shine
Oh Lord I want to be in that number
When the sun begins to shine.

3 *And when the moon drips red with blood, etc.*

4 *And when the Revelation comes, etc.*

Repeat the first verse.

Have you noticed that although you are playing on strings which you haven't used before, it makes no difference? However you played the first three (treble) strings, you can play the same way for the last three (bass) strings.

KEY OF D: THE FAMILY

You have just sung and played in the key of D. Now, I don't want to sneak any theory into a book that's written for people with no musical background. Yet, there are some concepts you should understand. If musical terms scare you, there's another way to think about it. If you could think of a key as though it was a family, with a family name, then the chords are simply members of that family.

In a similar way, D, A⁷, and G belong to the family(key) of D. That's their family name. One does not a family make, but two could begin a family and three can certainly be called a family: there are three main chords in any key. If you know the three main chords in several keys, you can play and sing thousands of songs (if you knew the words and tune, also). If you want to be adventurous, try playing in the key of D with some songs that you already know. If you absolutely

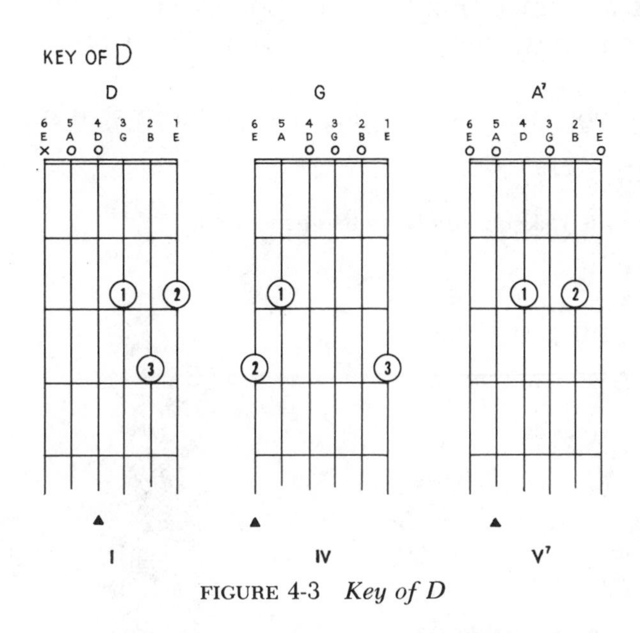

FIGURE 4-3 *Key of D*

can't figure out which chord sounds better in which place, don't get discouraged. It's only a matter of ear training, and that will come to you in time as you continue playing, singing, and really listening to what you're doing.

KEY OF D FAMILY: HOW TO FIND THE THREE MAIN CHORDS

The musical alphabet starts with A and ends with G. Then it starts all over again. The three main chords in any key are always constructed from the first, fourth, and fifth letters of its musical alphabet. The musical alphabet for a key begins with its family name. For example, in the key of D,[3] the musical alphabet would go like this:

D E F *G A* B C, *D* E F *G A* B C, etc.
1 2 3 *4 5* 6 7 *1* 2 3 *4 5* 6 7

In music, chords are indicated by roman numerals, so D would be the I (one) chord, G the IV (four) chord, and A or A^7 the V (five) or V^7 (five seventh) chord. Most often, V^7 chords are used instead of V chords. Both are the same V (five) chord of the musical alphabet. The V^7 chord has an extra note added to it, which gives it a more familiar sound in our music.

You can find the three main chords, the I, IV, and V chords of any key by counting in the same way as you did for the key of D. (Just in case you're wondering why you'd ever have to bother learning these initial concepts, think about this: suppose you were driving a car and knew nothing about the car, except how to drive it, and the car got stuck. Perhaps with some minor adjustments, you could get the car started again and be on your way. Similarly, if you were singing a tune in a key that was uncomfortable for your voice, you'd be stuck, unless you knew the three main chords in other keys.)

In the next song, you can use the down-slap damp strum.

FRANKIE AND JOHNNIE

Adapted and arranged by R.T. Jacobs (Based on traditional song)

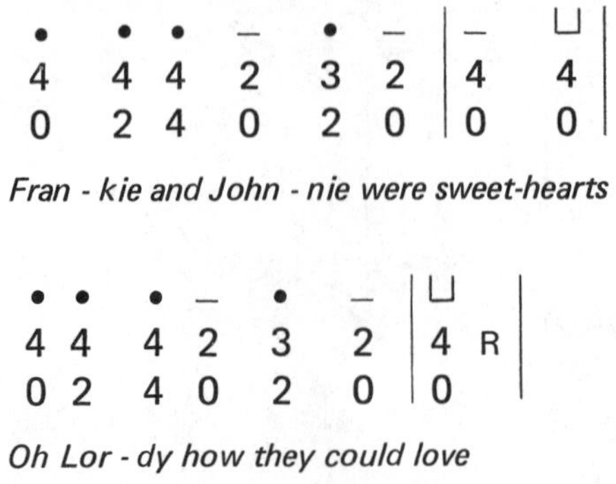

•	•	•	–	•	–	|	–	⊔	|
4	4	4	2	3	2	|	4	4	|
0	2	4	0	2	0	|	0	0	|

Fran - kie and John - nie were sweet-hearts

•	•	•	–	•	–	|	⊔		|
4	4	4	2	3	2	|	4	R	|
0	2	4	0	2	0	|	0		|

Oh Lor - dy how they could love

[3] The key of D has something called a key signature that we won't take up now.

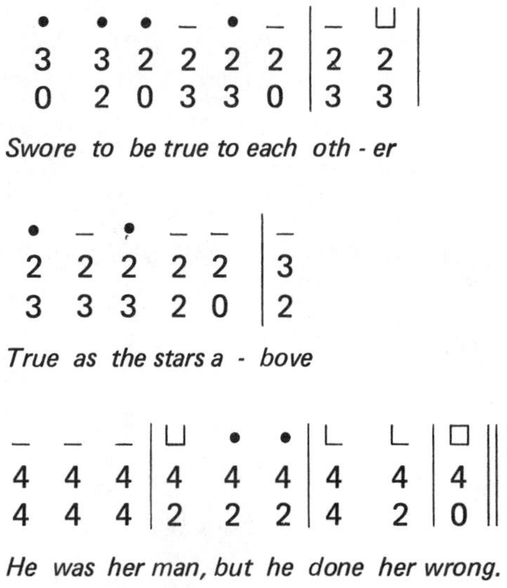

• • • _ • _ | _ ⊔ |
3 3 2 2 2 2 | 2 2 |
0 2 0 3 3 0 | 3 3 |

Swore to be true to each oth - er

• _ • _ _ | _
2 2 2 2 2 | 3
3 3 3 2 0 | 2

True as the stars a - bove

_ _ _ | ⊔ • • | L L | □ ||
4 4 4 | 4 4 4 | 4 4 | 4 ||
4 4 4 | 2 2 2 | 4 2 | 0 ||

He was her man, but he done her wrong.

D
Frankie and Johnnie were sweethearts
Oh Lordy how they could love /
G
Swore to be true to each other
D
True as the stars above
A7 **D**
He was her man, / but he done her wrong. /

2 *Frankie and Johnnie went walking*
Johnnie in his brand new suit
Oh good Lord, said Frankie
Don't my Johnnie look so cute
He was her man but he done her wrong.

3 *Johnnie said I've got to leave you*
But I won't be very long
Don't wait up for me honey
Or worry while I'm gone
He was her man but he done her wrong.

4 *Frankie got off at South Twelfth street*
Looked up in a window so high
And there she saw her Johnnie
Hugging that Nellie Bly
He was her man but he done her wrong.

5 *Frankie stepped back on her right foot*
She took out her little forty four
Root a toot, she shot three time
And dropped him right to the floor
She shot her man 'cause he done her wrong.

6 *The judge he said to the jury*
I know that you'll all agree
This woman shot her lover
It's murder in the second degree
He was her man but he done her wrong.

7 *This story has a good moral*
This story has no good end
It only goes to show you
You'll land right in the pen
You know two wrongs don't ever make a right.

The next song should sound familiar. Play the Easy Strum.

GOOD MORNING TO YOU

Traditional

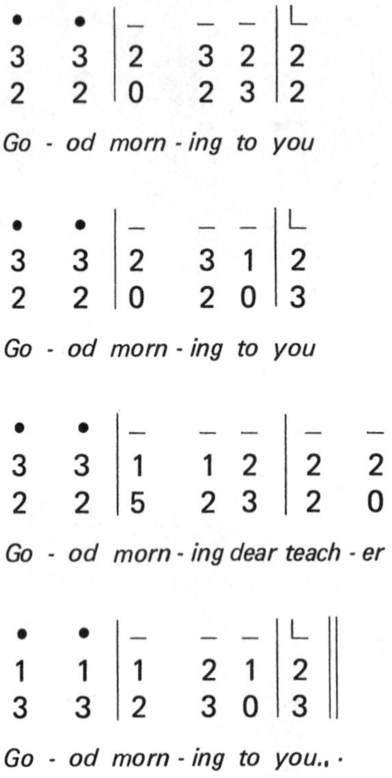

```
•   •  | _   _  _ | L
3   3  | 2   3  2 | 2
2   2  | 0   2  3 | 2
Go - od  morn - ing to  you
```

```
•   •  | _   _  _ | L
3   3  | 2   3  1 | 2
2   2  | 0   2  0 | 3
Go - od  morn - ing to  you
```

```
•   •  | _   _  _ | _   _
3   3  | 1   1  2 | 2   2
2   2  | 5   2  3 | 2   0
Go - od  morn - ing dear teach - er
```

```
•   •  | _   _  _ | L ||
1   1  | 1   2  1 | 2 ||
3   3  | 2   3  0 | 3 ||
Go - od  morn - ing to  you.. .
```

```
        D        A7
Good morning to you /
                 D
Good morning to you /
                    G
Good morning dear teacher
       D       A7 D
Good morning to you.
```

On the last line when you strum the last three chords, sing and strum very slowly.

Have you gotten into the habit of taking the time out for your E-Z Relaxation every day? If not, do so; remember, a relaxed mind learns better (besides that, it feels good, too).

THE D^7 CHORD

Having learned the G chord, let's add the D^7 chord to your repertoire. The combination of G and D^7 gives us the opportunity to play and sing some more songs, using only those two chords. Remember when we were talking about keys being like families? We said that two chords could start a family; that's what G and D^7 will do.

Look at the D^7 chord diagram. Do you notice a resemblance between the D and the D^7 chords? You press down on the same two strings in the second fret as you did on the D chord. However, with the D chord, the second string is played in the third fret; in the D^7 chord, you play the second string in the first fret. The D^7 is something like a mirror image of the D chord. Be careful not to get them confused with one another.

Can you guess which string is the bass string for the D^7 chord? If you guessed the fourth or D string, you're right. It's the same bass string for any kind of D chord (D, D^7, and so on). In the previous chapter we learned that chords are constructed from the musical alphabet. So any D chord is based on the letter D. Therefore, the lowest note of a D chord is the letter D. Since you know the fourth string is the D string, then that's the bass string for any D chord.

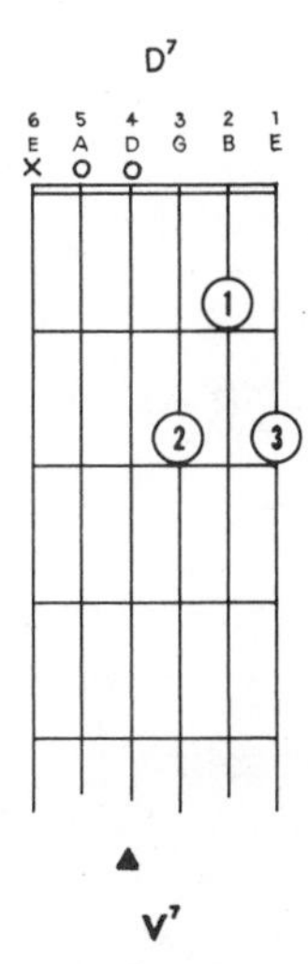

FIGURE 5-1
D seventh
(D^7) chord

Changing between G and D^7, with Tips for Filling in the Empty Spaces

Try playing the D^7 by strumming it down from the fourth string a few times. Review the ways to make it sound better. Now practice changing between the G and D^7 chords. Here's a tip on how to make the change smoother: If you're using the first, second, and third fingers on the G chord, as you change to a D^7, slide your third finger from the third fret on the G chord to the second fret for the D^7 chord. That motion will enable the other fingers to locate their places more easily on the D^7 chord. Then, at the same time that your first finger moves from the fifth string, second fret, to the second string, first fret, your second finger should move from the sixth string, third fret, to the third string, second fret.

To repeat, when changing from G to D^7:

1. Slide your third finger on the first string, from the third fret to the second fret, and
2. Simultaneously, transfer your first finger from the fifth string, second fret, to the second string, first fret, and your second finger from the sixth string, third fret, to the third string, second fret. Practice this change several times until you get used to the way it feels.

In changing back to the G chord from the D^7, slide your third finger from the second fret up to the third fret. That motion will lift up your other fingers and help you locate the rest of the G chord. At about the same time that you're sliding your third finger, move your second finger towards the sixth string. After awhile, your first finger will transfer to the fifth string without you even having to think about it.

If you're using your second, third, and fourth fingers on the G chord, when you change to the D^7, do the following:

1. Put your first finger down on the second string, first fret. This action will allow your other fingers to lift up.
2. Move your second finger from the fifth string, to the third string, second fret; at about the same time, your third finger switches from the sixth string, third fret, to the first string, second fret.

When changing from D^7 back to G, reverse this action. Probably, your fourth finger will be the last to cooperate. Whenever you play a chord with a fingered bass string, try to get your bass string finger down first. We'll see later how that helps to fill in the empty spaces.

THE B-DOWN STRUM

Up to now, you've been doing the Easy Strum, or the down–slap-damp strum, with your songs. Now, let's go one step further and learn the B-down strum.[1] You remember that on the Easy Strum, you brushed across all the strings with the left side of your right hand thumb, starting from the bass string. On the B-down strum, you divide that movement into two steps:

1. Using the left side of your right-hand thumb, brush firmly across the bass string, coming to rest for a moment on the very next string. (On the G chord, that would be the fifth string; on the D^7 chord, it's the third string).

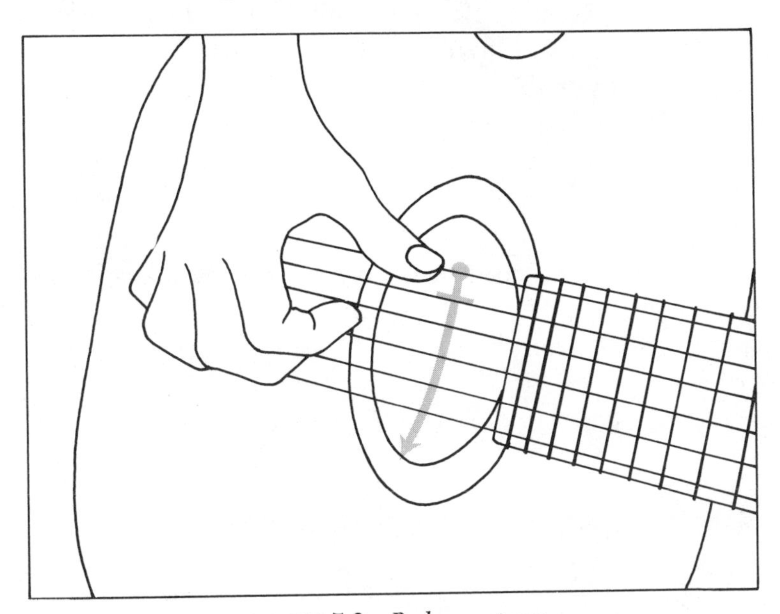

FIGURE 5-2 *B–down strum*

2. Now continue, brushing the thumb down across the rest of the strings. Since the B-down strum is a two-step strum, think of it as ONE-two, ONE-two, ONE-two. Emphasize the bass by playing it a little louder: ONE-two, ONE-two, ONE-two.

Practice the B-down strum with the G and D^7 chords. It's going to make your accompaniment sound more interesting. If you'd like, try this new strum with some of the old songs.

MORE TIPS FOR FILLING IN EMPTY SPACES

Get ready to change an instant before the actual chord change takes place. Here's a way to fill in the empty spaces when going from G to D^7. In that instant when you're getting ready to change, brush the open fourth string with your

[1] If you haven't guessed yet, B stands for bass string.

thumb and come to rest on the third string, while your fingers find their way to the D^7 chord. Since you've already "done" the bass of the D^7 chord, just continue the down strum of the B-down pattern. (A pattern is the form or design of a particular strum, such as, the Easy Strum, the down-slap damp strum, the B-down strum.) On the B-down strum the pattern begins with the bass and ends with the down motion.

When you're getting ready to change from D^7 to G, put down whichever finger you use on the G chord bass string. Brush the sixth string with your right hand thumb, coming to rest on the fifth string, while your fingers locate the rest of the chord. (Remember, always try to get the bass string finger down first.) When you're brushing the bass string, you're filling in the empty space of silence with sound.

The more you go over these changes, the faster your fingers will find their places. Keep that in mind when playing your old songs with the D and A^7 chords. For either chord, in that instant when you're getting ready to change, brush the bass string of the chord you're going to while your fingers locate their places. The sound of the bass string always helps to fill in the empty spaces.

The next three songs can be accompanied with the B-down strum pattern.

HEY LOLLY

Adapted and arranged by R.T. Jacobs (Based on a calypso folk song)

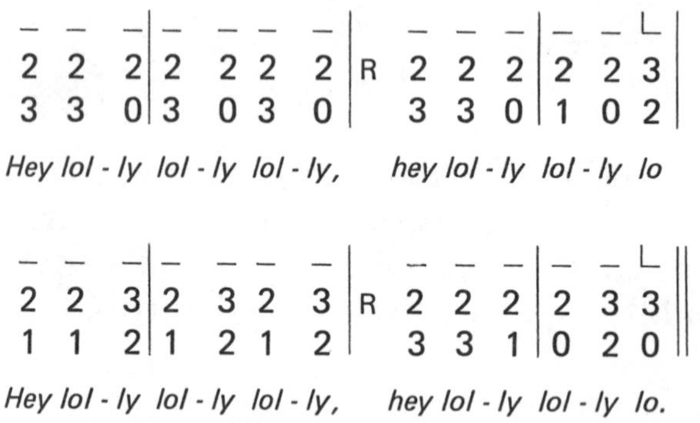

```
—  —  —|—  —  —  —|   —  —  —|—  —  L|
2  2  2|2  2  2  2|R  2  2  2|2  2  3|
3  3  0|3  0  3  0|   3  3  0|1  0  2|
Hey lol-ly lol-ly lol-ly,  hey lol-ly lol-ly lo
```

```
—  —  —|—  —  —  —|   —  —  —|—  —  L||
2  2  3|2  3  2  3|R  2  2  2|2  3  3||
1  1  2|1  2  1  2|   3  3  1|0  2  0||
Hey lol-ly lol-ly lol-ly,  hey lol-ly lol-ly lo.
```

G $\qquad\qquad\qquad\qquad$ D^7

/ Hey lølly, lølly, lølly,/Hey lølly, lølly lø

G

/ Hey lølly, lølly, lølly,/hey lølly, lølly lø.

That's the chorus and it's sung at the beginning of the song and then after each verse.

1	2	3	4	5	6	7	8
B-down	B-down	B-down	B-down	B-down	B-down	B-down	B-down
/Hey	*løl - ly*	*løl - ly*	*løl - ly,*	*/Hey*	*løl - ly*	*løl - ly*	*lø.*

What you see is a visual lining out of how you do the strum with this song. Notice that there are eight patterns of beats on a line. They fall in exactly the same places on both lines (this is the same for all the verses). You count the pattern by beginning with the bass. Wherever there is a "B," that's where you brush across the bass for the B-down strum. I've separated each pattern of the strum so you can see exactly where you start with the 'B' and finish the pattern with the "down." Each word is lined out on the strum pattern.

Since "Hey Lolly" is an adaptation of a calypso tune, and calypso rhythms are a bit different from ours, I've put the strum marks on all the verses. The tune is the same for the verse as it is for the chorus; you change chords in the same places. Start the song with the E-Z Numbers introduction (see page 52) and then accompany yourself with the B-down strum. Maybe, if you tap your foot when you brush the bass, it'll make it easier for you to keep time.

G **D7**

2 *Everybødy sing the chørus,/hey lølly, lølly lø*
Either you're against us ør you're før us,/hey lølly, lølly lø.

Chorus

3 *I have a bøy, he's ten feet tall,/hey lølly, lølly lø*
Sleeps in the kitchen with his feet in the hall,/hey lølly lølly lø.

Chorus

4 *My sister plays in a marching band,/hey lølly lølly lø*
Blows nøtes so high they never land,/hey lølly, lølly lø.

Chorus

5 *My old man, he's six feet twø,/hey lølly lølly lø*
Takes all day to tie his shoe,/hey lølly lølly lø.

Chorus

6 *The purpose øf this little søng,/hey lølly lølly lø*
Is to make up verses as you gø aløng,/hey lølly lølly lø.

Chorus

How are you doing at filling in the empty spaces? No matter what strum you use, it's important to keep the music going. But don't rush; after all, slow music is better than no music.

HE'S GOT THE WHOLE WORLD IN HIS HAND

Adapted and arranged by R.T. Jacobs

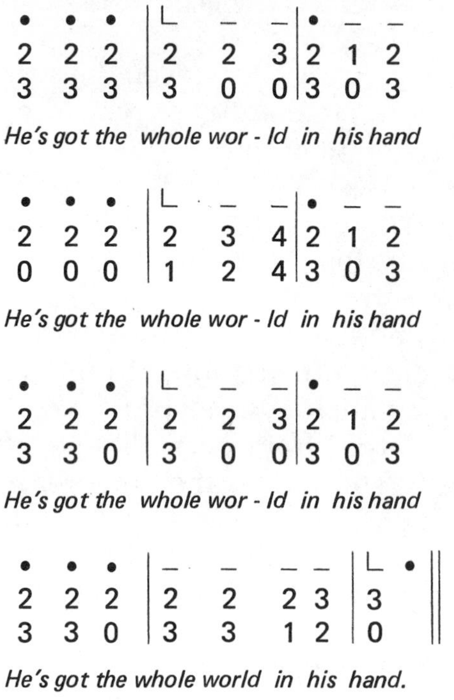

```
•  •  •  | L   _   _ | •  _  _
2  2  2  | 2   2   3 | 2  1  2
3  3  3  | 3   0   0 | 3  0  3
```

He's got the whole wor - ld in his hand

```
•  •  •  | L   _   _ | •  _  _
2  2  2  | 2   3   4 | 2  1  2
0  0  0  | 1   2   4 | 3  0  3
```

He's got the whole wor - ld in his hand

```
•  •  •  | L   _   _ | •  _  _
2  2  2  | 2   2   3 | 2  1  2
3  3  0  | 3   0   0 | 3  0  3
```

He's got the whole wor - ld in his hand

```
•  •  •  | _   _   _  _ | L  •  ||
2  2  2  | 2   2   2  3 | 3     ||
3  3  0  | 3   3   1  2 | 0     ||
```

He's got the whole world in his hand.

```
G
/He's got the whøle wørld i̸n his ha̸nd
                 D7
He's got the whøle wørld i̸n his ha̸nd
                 G
He's got the whøle wørld i̸n his ha̸nd
                             D7    G
He's got the whøle world i̸n his ha̸nd./
```

He's got the river and the mountains in his hand
He's got the river and the mountains in his hand
He's got the river and the mountains in his hand
He's got the whole world in his hand.

2 *He's got you and me brother in his hand, etc.*

3 *He's got you and me sister in his hand, etc.*

4 *He's got the itty bitty baby in his hand, etc.*

5 *He's got the rich and the poor, in his hand, etc.*

Remember, you stretch or squeeze according to shorter or longer lines on all songs.

BILLY BOY

Adapted and arranged by R.T. Jacobs (Based on a traditional folk song)

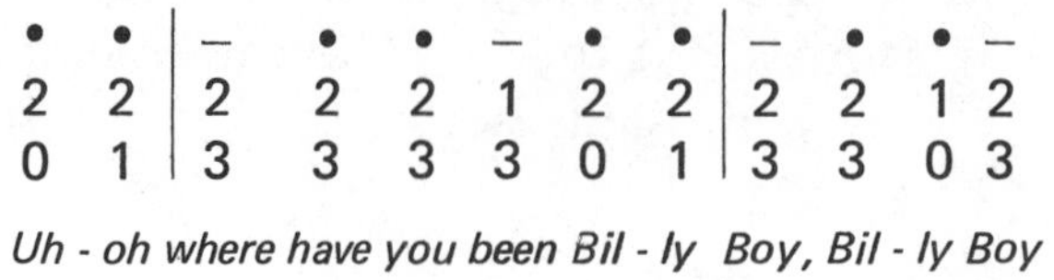

```
•  •  | _   •   •   _   •   •  | _   •   •  _
2  2  | 2   2   2   1   2   2  | 2   2   1  2
0  1  | 3   3   3   3   0   1  | 3   3   0  3
```

Uh - oh where have you been Bil - ly Boy, Bil - ly Boy

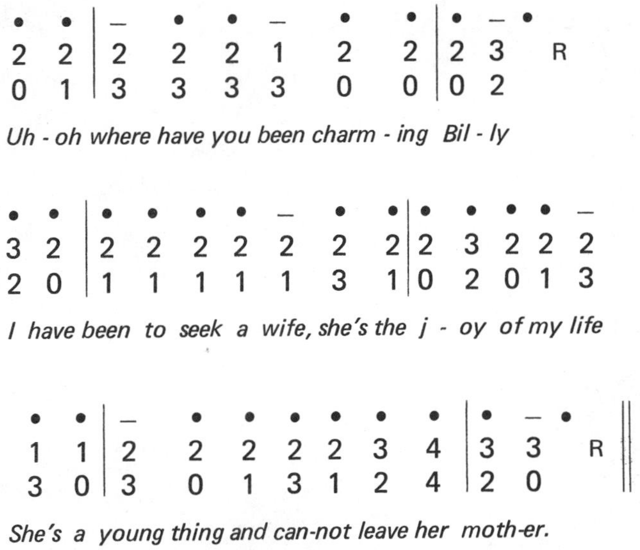

```
•  •  |  —  •  •  —  •  •  |  •  —  •
2  2  |  2  2  2  1  2  2  |  2  3     R
0  1  |  3  3  3  3  0  0  |  0  2
```

Uh - oh where have you been charm - ing Bil - ly

```
•  •  |  •  •  •  •  —  •  •  |  •  •  •  •  —
3  2  |  2  2  2  2  2  2  2  |  2  3  2  2  2
2  0  |  1  1  1  1  1  3  1  |  0  2  0  1  3
```

I have been to seek a wife, she's the j - oy of my life

```
•  •  |  —  •  •  •  •  •  •  |  •  —  •
1  1  |  2  2  2  2  2  3  4  |  3  3     R  ||
3  0  |  3  0  1  3  1  2  4  |  2  0
```

She's a young thing and can-not leave her moth-er.

G

Uh-oh where have you been Billy Boy, Billy Boy

D7

Uh-oh where have you been charming Billy /

G

I have been to seek a wife, she's the joy of my life

D7 G

She's a young thing and cannot leave her mother. /

2 *Did she tell you to come in Billy Boy, Billy Boy*
Did she tell you to come in charming Billy
Yes, she told me to come in and to kiss her on the chin
She's a young thing and cannot leave her mother.

3 *Did she take your fancy cap Billy Boy, Billy Boy*
Did she take your fancy cap charming Billy
Yes, she took my fancy cap and she threw it at the cat
She's a young thing and cannot leave her mother.

4 *Did she seat you on a chair Billy Boy, Billy Boy*
Did she seat you on a chair charming Billy
Yes, she sat me on a chair, but the bottom wasn't there
She's a young thing and cannot leave her mother.

5 *Can she sing a pretty song, Billy Boy, Billy Boy*
Can she sing a pretty song charming Billy
She can sing a pretty song, but she often sings it wrong
She's a young thing and cannot leave her mother.

Maybe some of you were sure that you were musically handicapped and kept "proving" it to yourself all the time. You know, what we believe, we make happen. Since you've come this far and you've accomplished something you once thought impossible, have any of your beliefs changed?

THE A CHORD

Up to now, we've been going from chord to chord in a fairly orderly progression. In this way, you've learned the three main chords in the key of D. So it might seem that the next step should be to complete the key family we started with the G and D^7 chords. You remember that two chords can start a key family. But we're not going to do that; I believe you'll find the learning progression easier if we change the order.

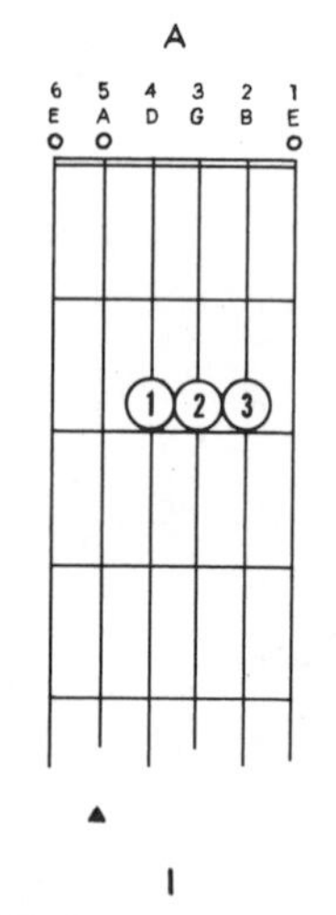

FIGURE 6-1 *A chord*

In a way, the A chord is very easy to play. All the fingers are in the same fret. Yet, it's a bit of a squeeze to get those three fingers in the same fret. Your fingers should be as close as possible to the metal cross bar of the fret, the strip that's closer to the body of the guitar. Obviously, on the A chord, the third finger will be the only one to get that close. By reasons of human anatomy, the first finger will probably find itself closer to the first fret than the second fret. The second finger will be somewhere in between.

Do you notice anything familiar looking about this chord? If you lift off your second finger, the remaining fingers form the A^7 chord. Although you learned to use your first and second fingers on the A^7 chord, if you ever have any fast changing to do between A and A^7, it's easier to just lift that middle finger from the A. Don't confuse the two chords because of their resemblance to one another. If you're supposed to be playing an A chord, an A^7 in its' place won't sound too good.

Do you know which string is the bass string for the A chord? As we've discussed, chords are constructed from the musical alphabet. So, any kind of A chord comes from the A in that musical alphabet. If the bass string is the lowest note in the chord, the note the chord grows from, then you can be sure that the bass is going to be the A, or fifth string.

Look at the A chord diagram. Then strum the chord on your guitar a few times, first with the Easy Strum, then with the B-down strum. *Make sure* all three fingers are in the second fret and that they don't spill over into the adjacent frets.

Playing the Numbers on the A a Fancy Way, from Home Base

Up to now, you've been playing the E-Z Numbers Game moving all your fingers around as needed, from string to string and from fret to fret. However, it's possible to play the numbers using certain chords as home bases. You just lift off, or return your finger back, to the home base of the A chord position as needed. The advantage in playing this way is that from time to time, you can strum down on the chord between numbers. Then, you're playing a combination of melody(the numbers) and harmony(the chords). For example, here are the E-Z Numbers for "Alouette." Take the A chord position and play the numbers from that position, lifting off and returning your fingers to the home base chord where necessary. The entire song can be accompanied by an A chord alone. Do the down–slap-damp strum. (The "S" next to a number means to strum the chord.)

ALOUETTE

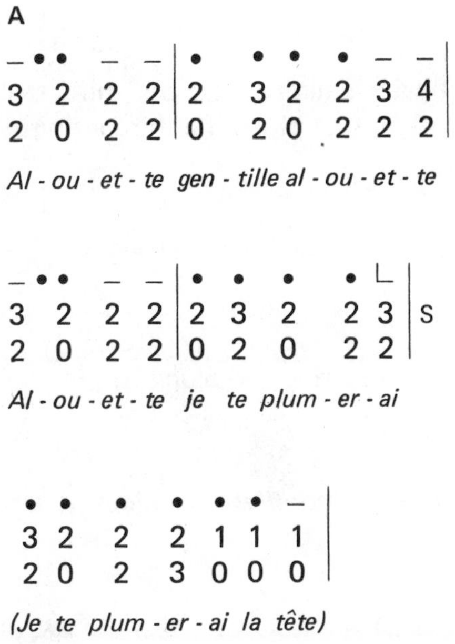

A

```
_••  _ _ | •   • • • _ _ |
3 2 2 2  | 2   3 2 2 3 4 |
2 0 2 2  | 0   2 0 2 2 2 |
```

Al - ou - et - te gen - tille al - ou - et - te

```
_••  _ _ | • • •   • L |
3 2 2 2  | 2 3 2   2 3 | S
2 0 2 2  | 0 2 0   2 2 |
```

Al - ou - et - te je te plum - er - ai

```
• •  •  • • • _ |
3 2  2  2 1 1 1 |
2 0  2  3 0 0 0 |
```

(Je te plum - er - ai la tête)

```
•  •   •     •  •  •  _  |
1  1   1     2  2 2  3   |
0  2   0     3  2 0  2   |
```

Je te plum - er - ai la tête

```
• • _   • • _  | •   •   _   •   •   _ | L   L ||
1 1 1   4 4 4  | 1   1   1   4   4   4 | 1   4 || S
0 0 0   2 2 2  | 0   0   0   2   2   2 | 0   2 ||
```

(Et la tête,) et la tête, (Al - ou - ette,) Al - ou - ette, uh - oh

Start at the beginning again.

A

Alouette, gentille Alouette
Alouette, je te plumerai
(Je te plumerai la tête
Je te plumerai la tête
(Et la tête,) et la tête, (Alouette,) Alouette, uh-oh

Start at the beginning again, substituting the following words for la tête—le bec, les yeux, le nez, les pattes, les ailes, le cou, le dos, les jambes, les pieds, la bazoombaza—repeating all previously used ones in reverse order. If you're singing this with a group, you sing the phrases in brackets, and both you and the group sing the rest of the song together.

Were you able to play the numbers using the A chord as a home base? I'll break it down for you step-by-step. Starting with the first set of numbers on the first line, here's how you do it.

```
_   • •  _  _  | •   •   •   •   _   _ |
3   2 2  2  2  | 2   3   2   2   3   4 |
2   0 2  2  2  | 0   2   0   2   2   2 |
```

```
_
3  Since your left hand second finger is already on the third string,
2  second fret, in the A chord position, just pluck the third string with
   your right hand.

•
2  Lift off your third finger and pluck the open second string.
0

_
2  Return your third finger to the second string and pluck it.
2

_
2  Your third finger is already on the second string. Pluck it again.
2

•
2  Lift your third finger off the second string and pluck the open sec-
0  ond string.
```

•
3 Your second finger is already there. Pluck the third string.
2

•
2 If you haven't returned your third finger to the second string, just
0 pluck the second string. If you've returned it already to its home base, lift it and pluck the open second string.

•
2 Return your third finger to the second string and pluck it.
2

–
3 Since your second finger is already on the third string on the A chord
2 position, pluck the third string.

–
4 Your first finger is on the fourth string in the A chord position.
2 Pluck the fourth string.

That's the end of the first line of numbers. The second line of numbers plays exactly the same, except there's one fewer set of numbers at the end of the line. On the third line of numbers, keeping the A chord home base position, you should know what to do until you get to the fourth set of numbers.

•
2 Just add your fourth finger to the second string, third fret, and pluck
3 the second string. Then, lift it off again.

• • –
1 1 1 On the last three sets of numbers on the third line, keeping the
0 0 0 home base position, pluck the open first string three times. Then, pluck it once more for the first set of numbers on the fourth line.

•
1 For the second set of numbers on the fourth line, keep the home
2 base position and put your fourth finger on the first string, second fret. Pluck the first string and then lift your finger off. You should be able to play the rest of the numbers for "Alouette" without further instruction.

Let's do the same thing with "Row, Row, Row Your Boat." It, too, can be played solely with the A chord. Do it with the Easy Strum. In the first line of numbers, using the A chord for a home base, do just as you did for "Alouette." When you come to the second line of numbers, slide your fingers into the A chord position, up to about the fourth or fifth fret so that you can finger the $\frac{1}{5}$ with your fourth finger. Then, slide back to the second fret and return your fingers to home base when necessary. Remember that S stands for strum.

ROW, ROW, ROW YOUR BOAT

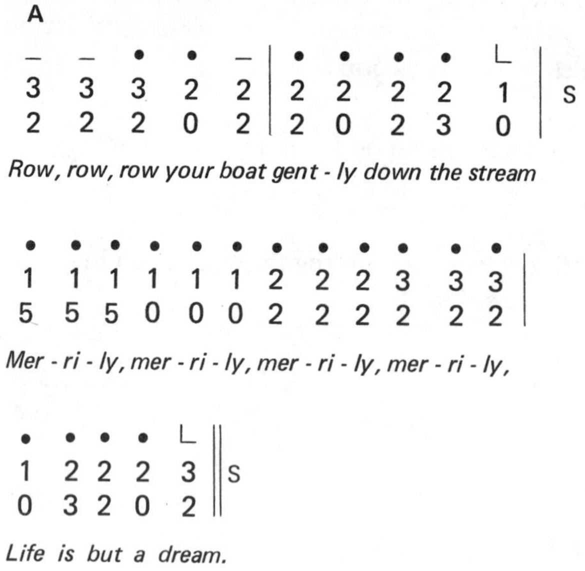

A

—	—	•	•	—	|	•	•	•	•	L	|	
3	3	3	2	2	|	2	2	2	2	1	|	S
2	2	2	0	2	|	2	0	2	3	0	|	

Row, row, row your boat gent - ly down the stream

•	•	•	•	•	•	•	•	•	•	•	•	|
1	1	1	1	1	1	2	2	2	3	3	3	|
5	5	5	0	0	0	2	2	2	2	2	2	|

Mer - ri - ly, mer - ri - ly, mer - ri - ly, mer - ri - ly,

•	•	•	•	L	||	
1	2	2	2	3	||	S
0	3	2	0	2	||	

Life is but a dream.

A

Row, row, row your boat gently down the stream /
Merrily, merrily, merrily, merrily
Life is but a dream. /

The Power of Your Mind. Now, some of you might not believe in the power of your mind and convince yourself that it's absolutely impossible to use the A chord position as home base and to play the numbers that way. Would you believe that a legenday guitarist, Django Reinhardt, became a master in spite of the fact that he had lost the use of two left-hand fingers? Believe me: You absolutely can play "Alouette" and "Row, Row, Row Your Boat" with A as your home base.

As we go on, some songs quite probably will be too difficult for you to play like that, but do so when you can.

THE E^7 CHORD

You can see that the E^7 chord is very easy to finger. The bass string for the E^7 is the sixth or low E string. Practice changing back and forth between the A and E^7 chords. Notice how your fingers move; concentrate closely on the moves that give you the smoothest changes. Practice it with the B-down strum and always pluck the open bass string of the chord you're going to *immediately* after strumming down on the chord you're on.

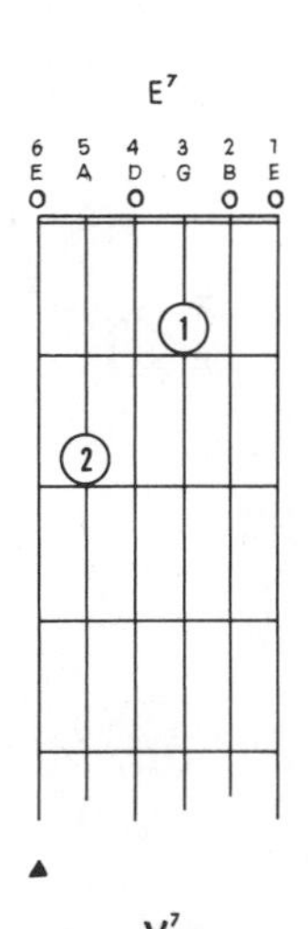

FIGURE 7-1
E seventh (E^7) chord

Changing Chords. Is it better, when you go from A to E^7, to put your second finger down on the fifth string and then locate the third string, first fret, with your first finger? What about the changes from E^7 to A? Is it better to put your first finger down on the fourth string, second fret, and then to let your other fingers just line up after it? Try out several different ways of changing. That's the way you discover and choose what creates the smoothest sounding changes with the least amount of empty spaces. Go slowly. Eventually, you'll begin to feel the strings with your fingers, instead of having to look. Always watching your fingers form the chords is one action that will only slow you down. You may think it's impossible to play the guitar without looking at your fingers, but even blind people can learn to play the guitar well: Jose Feliciano, for instance, is a famous and great guitarist.

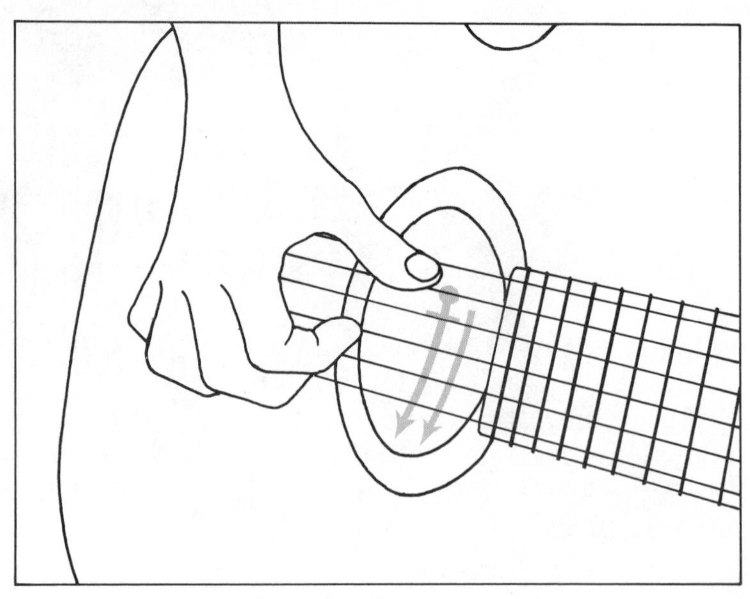

FIGURE 7-2 *Waltz strum: B–down*

WALTZ STRUM: B-DOWN-DOWN

The waltz, or bass-down-down, strum starts out the same as the bass-down strum. However, the B-down strum is a two-step strum and the B-down-down is a three-step strum. On the count of ONE, your thumb brushes firmly across the bass string and comes to rest on the very next string. On the A chord, that's the fourth string; on the E^7 chord, it's the fifth string. On the count of TWO, it continues to brush down across the rest of the strings. On the count of THREE, brush across the strings again, but don't be concerned about which strings to brush. You don't have to go back to the bass string. Whatever strings happen to come under your thumb as you brush are all right.

Emphasize the bass. For example, BASS-down-down, BASS-down-down, BASS-down-down; the first beat is stronger than the other two in the waltz strum pattern. Don't forget to brush with the left side of your right hand thumb.

A Couple of Songs to Waltz with

In "Alouette" and "Row, Row, Row Your Boat," if you played the numbers from an A chord position, here's some fancy playing to add to what you've already done.

DOWN IN THE VALLEY

```
A                              E7
—  —  — | ⊔ | L     — | —  —  — | ⊔ | ⊔ |
4  3  2 | 2 | 3 s 2 | 2  2  3 | 2 | s |
2  2  0 | 2 | 2     2 | 2  0  2 | 0 |   |
```

Down in the val - ley, the val - ley so low

A

—	—	—	⊔	⊔		—	—	—	⊔	
4	3	2	2	2	S	3 3	2		3	S
2	1	0	3	0		1 2	0		2	

Hang your head o - ver, hear the wind blow.

Take an A chord position; lift up and return your fingers to home base as needed for the first line, until just before the last set of numbers. Change to E^7 and play the last set of numbers. Don't forget to strum when you see the 'S'.

Now, you're on the second line. Keep the E^7 position as your home base. For the first set of numbers, put your third finger on the fourth string, second fret. After playing that, lift your third finger off—you should know what to do until you get to the fourth set of numbers—there, put your fourth finger down on the second string, third fret, play the numbers, and lift your fourth finger off. Keep the E^7 position for home base until just before the last set of numbers. Change back to an A chord, play the last set of numbers and then strum down. Now, play the B-down-down pattern twice and start to sing and play with the waltz strum.

Let's Have a Fitting. Here's how you'd fit the singing to the waltz strum. Bass-down-down is the full pattern of the strum. You count a pattern by starting with the bass. You'll see that there are exactly the same number of patterns of strums on each line. Therefore, you've got to squeeze or stretch the words of a line, wherever necessary, to fit the singing to the strum patterns. (B-d-d means Bass-down-down. The numbers stand for the number of patterns on each line.)

B - d - d B-d-d B-d-d B - d - d B-d-d B-d-d
Down in the val - ley, the val - ley so low
1 2 3 4 5 6
B - d - d B-d-d B-d-d B - d - d B-d-d B-d-d
Hang your head o - ver, hear the wind blow.

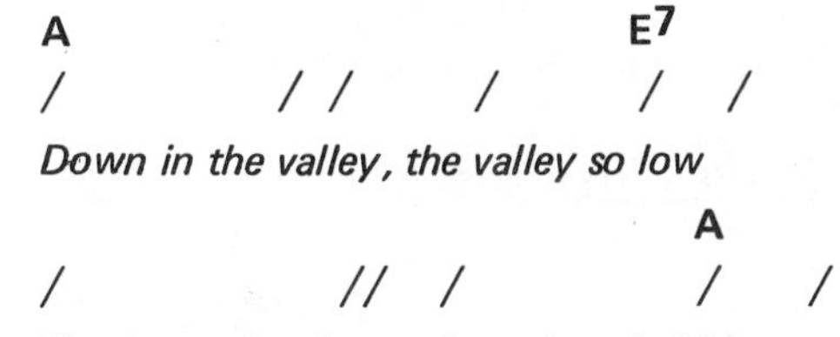

Hang your head over, hear the wind blow.

2 *Hear the wind blow love, hear the wind blow*
Hand your head over, hear the wind blow.

3 *Send me a letter, send it by mail*
Send it in care of Birmingham jail.

4 *Birmingham jail love, Birmingham jail*
Send it in care of Birmingham jail.

5 *Build me a castle forty feet high*
So I can see you as you go by.

6 *As you go by love, as you go by*
So I can see you as you go by.

7 *If you don't love me, love whom you please*
But throw your arms 'round me, give my heart ease.

Repeat first verse

Did you choose to do some fancy playing in the introduction, using the chords as home bases? How does it sound and feel?

The next song, "Clementine," has more chord changes than "Down In The Valley." How about trying it this way? After you've heard the tune by playing the Numbers Game, why don't you play it again, but this time whenever you change chords, just strum the chord. Don't play the numbers beneath the chord. You can even start off by strumming down on the A chord and then going to the second set of numbers. When you've strummed the last chord, the A, play two waltz strum patterns, then start singing and strumming. The verses and the chorus all have the same tune. Stretch and squeeze wherever necessary in order to fit the words to the tune.

CLEMENTINE

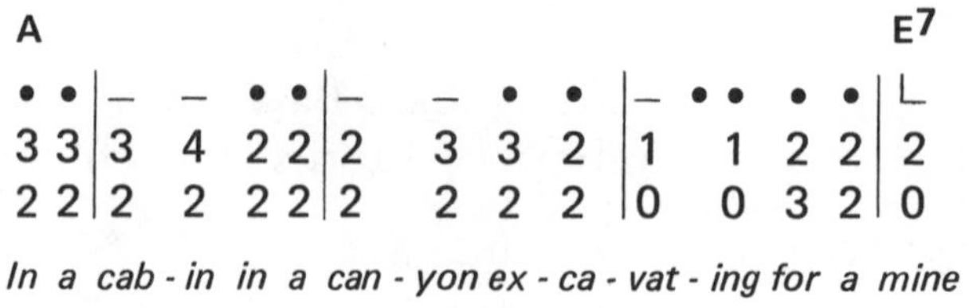

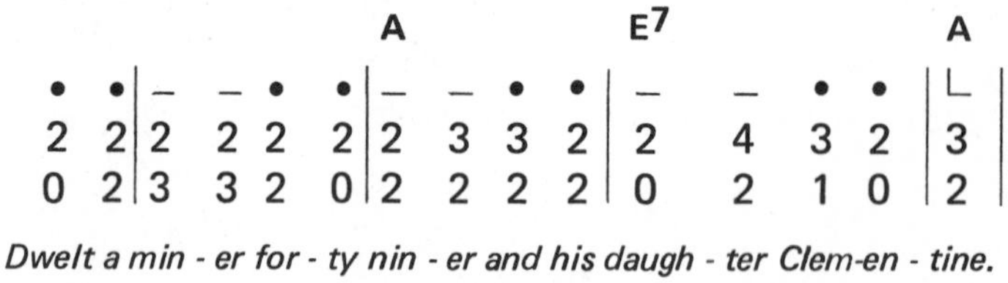

```
A                                         E7
• • | —   —  • • | —    —  •  • | — • •  • • | L
3 3 | 3   4  2 2 | 2    3  3  2 | 1   1  2 2 | 2
2 2 | 2   2  2 2 | 2    2  2  2 | 0   0  3 2 | 0
```
In a cab - in in a can - yon ex - ca - vat - ing for a mine

```
                      A              E7             A
•  • | —  —  •  • | —  —  •  • | —    —  •  • | L  ||
2  2 | 2  2  2  2 | 2  3  3  2 | 2    4  3  2 | 3  ||
0  2 | 3  3  2  0 | 2  2  2  2 | 0    2  1  0 | 2  ||
```
Dwelt a min - er for - ty nin - er and his daugh - ter Clem-en - tine.

Here's the way "Clementine" fits with the waltz strum.

```
         1          2            3           4
B-d-d    B- d- d    B- d-   d    B- d-  d    B-d-
```
In a cabin in a canyon exca-vating for a mine

```
         1          2            3              4
d        B-d-  d    B-d-  d      B-    d-  d    B-d-
```
Dwelt a miner forty niner and his daughter Clementine.

A   E7
In a cabin, in a canyon, excavating for a mine
*   A   E7   A*
Dwelt a miner, forty niner and his daughter Clementine.

You can see that there are the exact same number of waltz strum patterns on each line. You begin the first two words on the down strum for the third step of the pattern. On the last word of the first line, strum the bass-down for the first two steps of the pattern. Can you see that the down strum for the third step of the pattern comes on the first two words of the second line? All the lines of the chorus and verses begin and end the same way. Strum the bass-down at the end of a line and finish the pattern with a down strum at the beginning of the next line. There are two places in the rest of the song where it might be a little tricky for you to know where to strum, so I've inserted strum marks in those places. After you sing the first verse, sing the chorus, and then sing it again after each verse.

Chorus

A   E7
Oh my darling, oh my darling, oh my darling Clementine
*   A   E7   A*
You are lost and gone forever, dreadful sorry, Clementine.

2 *Light she was and like a fairy and her shoes were number nine*
Herring boxes without topses, sandals were for Clementine.

Chorus

3 *Drove she ducklings to the water every morning just at nine*
Hit her foot against a splinter, fell into the foaming brine.

Chorus

4 *Ruby lips above the water, blowing bubbles soft and fine*
Alas for me, I was no swimmer, so I lost my Clementine.

Chorus

5 *Then the miner, forty niner soon began to peak and pine*
Thought he oughter jine his daughter, now he's with his Clementine.

Chorus

6 *How I missed her, how I misser her, how I missed my Clementine*
Till I kissed her little sister, and forgot my Clementine.

Chorus

How are you doing with the waltz strum? You must concentrate on it more than on the other strums you've had so far, but it can be mastered.

In the last few songs, you've been playing melody and chord accompaniment, using chord positions as home bases. It takes time, patience, and good coordination to accomplish this. You probably got confused about which finger to lift off and which finger to return to home base. Sometimes, it probably felt like your fingers belonged to some one else's hand, because the finger you expected to go up or down didn't while others did.

You'll remember that I said you wouldn't be able to play from the base position on some songs because they're too difficult for you now. In the following song, you'll start off playing the numbers from home base chord positions, but you'll have to leave the position at points. In the chorus, when you come to the fifth set of numbers on both lines, you'll see that it would be impossible for you to reach that fourth fret while still holding on to the A chord position. Just leave the position here. Then, return on the very next set of numbers.

In "Clementine," you played the Numbers Game by strumming down whenever you changed chords, ignoring the numbers under the chord change. You can do the same thing on this song. Stretch and squeeze where necessary.

DOWN-UP–SLAP-DAMP STRUM

We're going to use the following variation of the Down–slap-damp strum to accompany a song. In the first step of the original down–slap-damp strum you played the 'down' with your thumb. In this variation, play down-up in the same space of time it took you to do the 'down.' Brush down across the strings with the left side of your thumb and then scrape up across the strings with the flat side of your thumb nail. The second part of the strum is the same as the original down–slap-damp strum:

1. Down with thumb and up with flat side of thumb nail
2. Slap-damp with palm of hand

GO TELL IT ON THE MOUNTAIN

Adapted and arranged with new words by R.T. Jacobs (Based on a spiritual)

Chorus

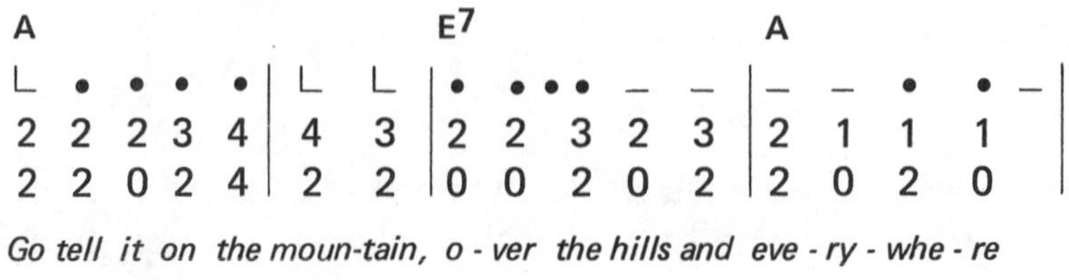

```
A                    E7                  A
L  •  • •  • | L  L | •  • • •  —  — | —  —  •  •  — |
2  2  2 3  4 | 4  3 | 2  2  3 2  3   | 2  1  1  1     |
2  2  0 2  4 | 2  2 | 0  0  2 0  2   | 2  0  2  0     |
```

Go tell it on the moun-tain, o - ver the hills and eve - ry - whe - re

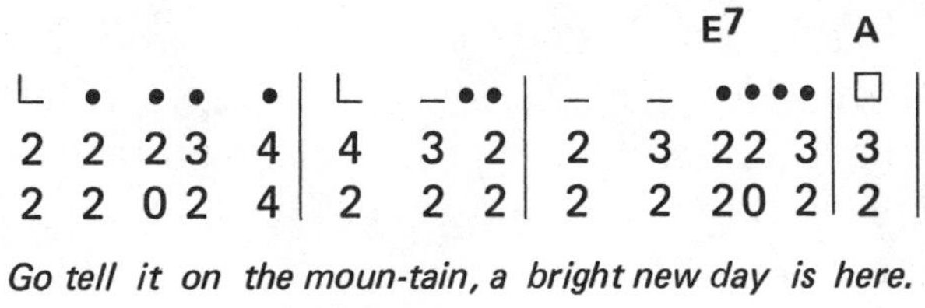

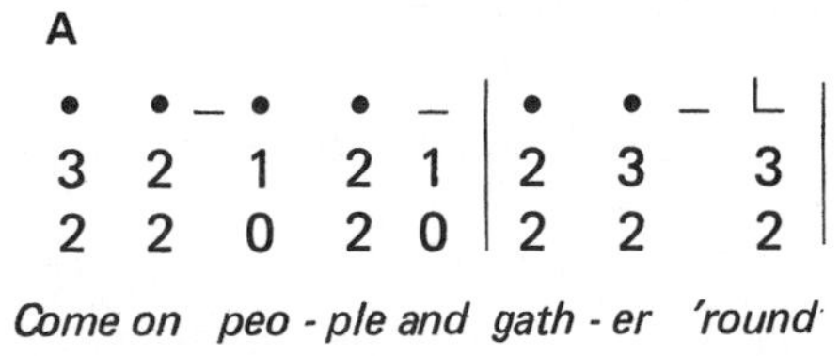

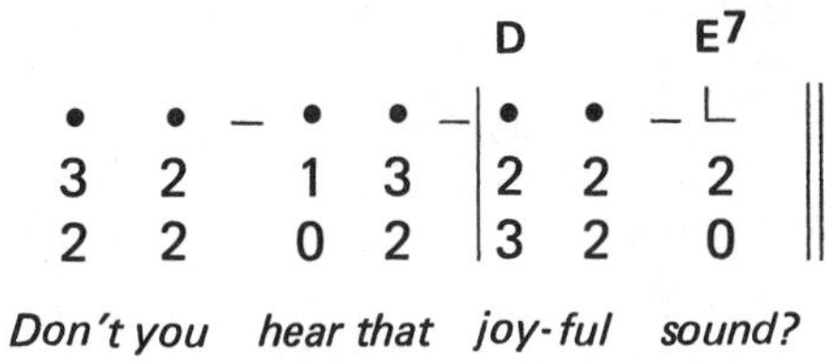

```
                                      E7      A
L  •  ••  •  • | L   _••  | _   _  ••••| □ |
2  2  2 3    4 | 4   3 2  | 2   3  22 3| 3 |
2  2  0 2    4 | 2   2 2  | 2   2  20 2| 2 |
```

Go tell it on the moun-tain, a bright new day is here.

```
A
•   •_ •   •  _ |  •   •  _ L  |
3   2  1   2  1 |  2   3    3  |
2   2  0   2  0 |  2   2    2  |
```

Come on peo - ple and gath - er 'round

```
                       D      E7
•   •  _  •   • _|  •   •  _ L    ||
3   2     1   3  |  2   2    2    ||
2   2     0   2  |  3   2    0    ||
```

Don't you hear that joy-ful sound?

Chorus

A E7 A

Go tell it on the mountain, over the hills and everywhere

E7 A

Go tell it on the mountain, a bright new day is here. /

A

Come on people and gather 'round

D E7

Don't you hear that joyful sound?

Chorus

2 *Don't you cry and don't you moan*
You never have to be alone.

Chorus

3 *Let's join hands with others too*
You know together we'll all come through.

Chorus

4 *Come on people and don't ask how*
Here's the way, get ready now to.

Chorus

THE KEY OF A FAMILY—SAME NAME, DIFFERENT FAMILIES

The very first chord you learned was the D chord. The first key family you learned about was the key of D. You know that in the key of D, the D chord is the I chord. The key of A shows the D chord as the IV chord. Are you wondering how the D chord could be the I chord in the key of D when it's the IV chord in the key of A?

Do you remember how to find the I, IV, and V chords in any key? If not, review it again in chapter 4. In the key of D, the D chord is the I chord in the musical alphabet. In

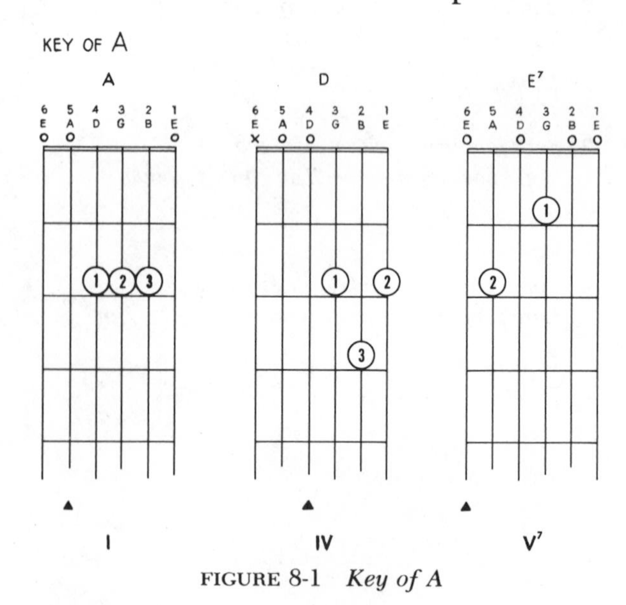

FIGURE 8-1 *Key of A*

the key of A, since you start the counting from A, then A is the I chord. It's as though you know a person who is the head of a family. You could think of that person as the I chord there. At the same time, this person must be somebody's son or daughter, a IV chord in his or her parents' family. It's the same person who assumes different positions in different families. The position depends upon which family-(key) the person(chord) happens to be part of.

Changing between A and D

You've already made the change between A and E^7 in the last few songs in chapter 7. Now, practice changing between A and D. When you want to go from A to D, slide your first and second fingers over to the third and first strings in the same second fret. While your other fingers are doing their sliding, lift your third finger very slightly from the second string, second fret; immediately, put it down on the second string, third fret. Even though your third finger's already on the second string in the second fret, it may not slide easily to the second string, third fret, while your other fingers are changing.

It's no more complicated going from the D chord to the A chord. When you're first learning to change chords, watch what your fingers are doing, very carefully. After you've found the smoothest way to change, start on your eventual goal of not looking, but of mostly feeling the strings, when you're playing.

Again, I want to remind you to avoid empty spaces when you practice changing chords. Immediately after strumming down on the chord, sound the bass of the chord you're going to.

Changing between D and E^7

When changing from D to E^7, slide your first finger from the second fret, third string, to the first fret, third string. Lift your second finger off the first string in the second fret and put it down on the fifth string, in the second fret. While you are doing this, lift your third finger.

We're going to do three songs in the key of A. In the first song, "Oh Susanna," after you play the numbers and 'hear' the tune, play it from home base chord positions. Whenever you've got to change chords, strum down on the chord. Don't play the numbers beneath the chord. Go on to the next set of numbers and continue playing the numbers and strumming down on chord changes. However, on the second and fourth lines of the verses, you have to change chords in the middle of a measure. Therefore, it's easier to do the Easy Strum for the last three strum marks of those lines. Do the

Easy Strum for the last line of the chorus also. The strum for "Oh Susanna" is the B-down strum. The last two lines of every verse have the same tune as the first two lines.

OH, SUSANNA

Words and Music by Stephen Foster

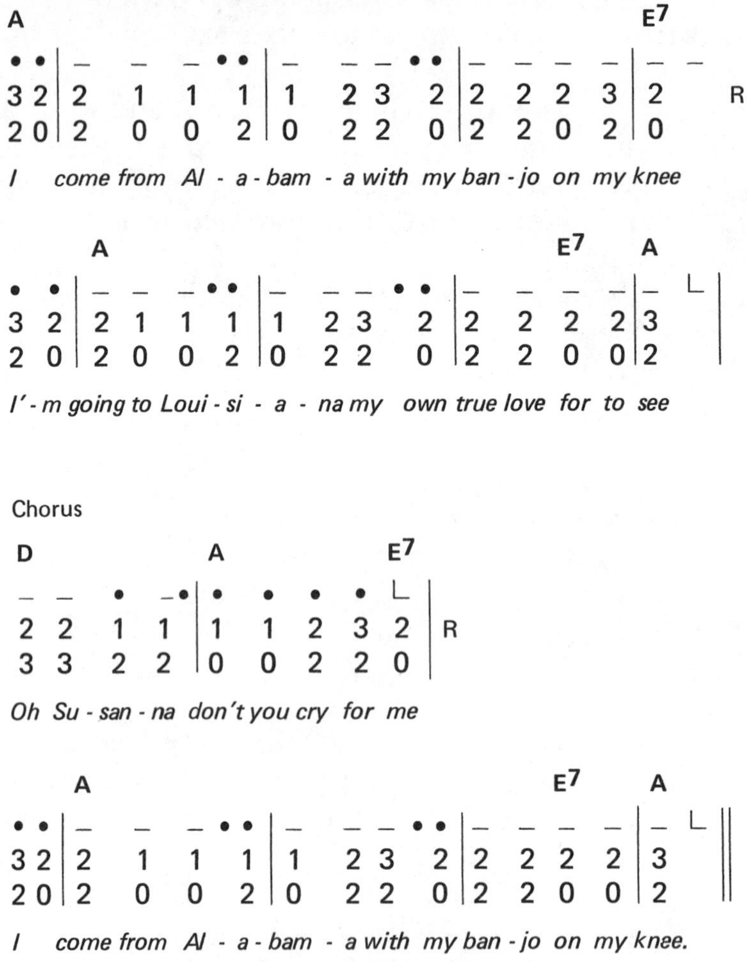

```
A                                                     E7
• • | _    _    _ • • | _    _ _ • • | _   _   _   _ | _  _
3 2 | 2    1    1   1 | 1    2 3   2 | 2   2   2   3 | 2      R
2 0 | 2    0    0   2 | 0    2 2   0 | 2   2   0   2 | 0
I    come from Al - a - bam - a with my ban - jo on my knee
```

```
        A                                    E7      A
•  • | _  _   _ • • | _    _ _ • • | _   _   _   _ | _  L |
3  2 | 2  1   1   1 | 1    2 3   2 | 2   2   2   2 | 3    |
2  0 | 2  0   0   2 | 0    2 2   0 | 2   2   0   0 | 2    |
I'-m going to Loui - si - a - na my  own true love for to see
```

Chorus

```
D                A               E7
_  _    •   _•| •    •    •   •  L |
2  2    1   1 | 1    1    2   3  2 | R
3  3    2   2 | 0    0    2   2  0 |
Oh Su - san - na  don't you cry  for me
```

```
      A                                           E7      A
• • | _    _    _ • • | _    _ _ • • | _   _   _   _ | _  L ||
3 2 | 2    1    1   1 | 1    2 3   2 | 2   2   2   2 | 3    ||
2 0 | 2    0    0   2 | 0    2 2   0 | 2   2   0   0 | 2    ||
I    come from Al - a - bam - a with my ban - jo on my knee.
```

```
A                                        E7
I come from Alabama with my banjo on my knee
     A                                E7    A
I'm going to Louisiana, my own true love for to see
                                                  E7
It rained all night the day I left, the weather is was dry
     A                              E7          A
The sun so hot, I froze to death, Susanna don't you cry.
```

Chorus

```
D                 A                E7
Oh Susanna, don't you cry for me
  A                                  E7        A
I come from Alabama with my banjo on my knee.
```

2 *I had a dream the other night when everything was still*
I thought I saw Susanna a-coming down the hill
The buckwheat cake was in her mouth, the tear was in her eye
Says I, I'm coming from the South, Susanna don't you cry.

Chorus

3 *I'll soon be down in New Orleans, and then I'll look around*
And if I see Susanna, I will faint right on the ground
But if I do not find her, then I will surely die
And when I'm dead and buried, Susanna, don't you cry.

Chorus

There are some quick chord changes in "Oh Susanna," but if you go very slowly at first, you'll soon surprise yourself with your smooth chord changes.

B–FINGERS-DOWN STRUM

With this next song, let's learn another version of the B-down strum. Like the B-down strum, it's also in two steps. I call it the B–fingers-down strum. The first step is exactly the same as the B–down strum. Brush firmly across the bass string with the left side of your right hand thumb, coming to rest on the very next string. The second step is done in one continuing motion. However, I'm going to break it down, so you'll understand it more easily.

Right after your thumb has come to rest on the very next string, turn your wrist a little, so that your hand and fingers turn upward. At the same time, curve your fingers toward the palm of your hand in a partially-clenched fist position. Without stopping, start opening your fingers, and at the same time, quickly strike the strings with the flat part of your fin-

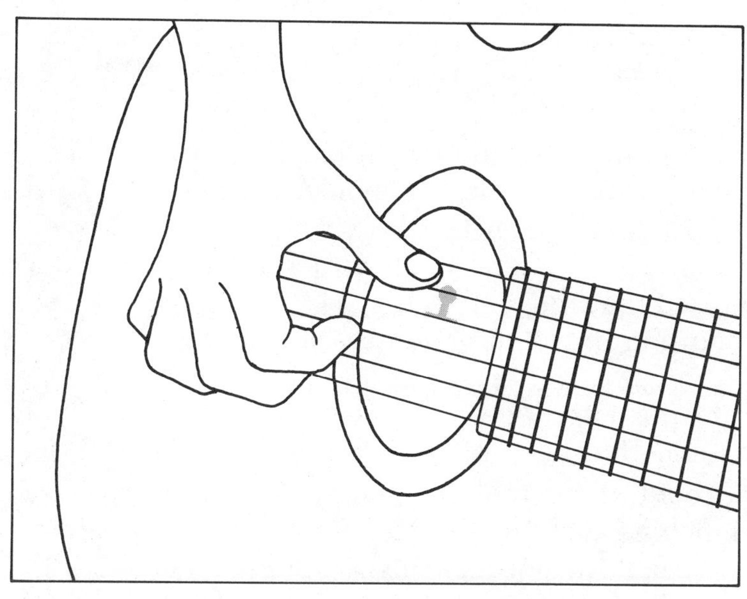

FIGURE 8-2a *Bass–fingers-down strum: Banjo Brush*

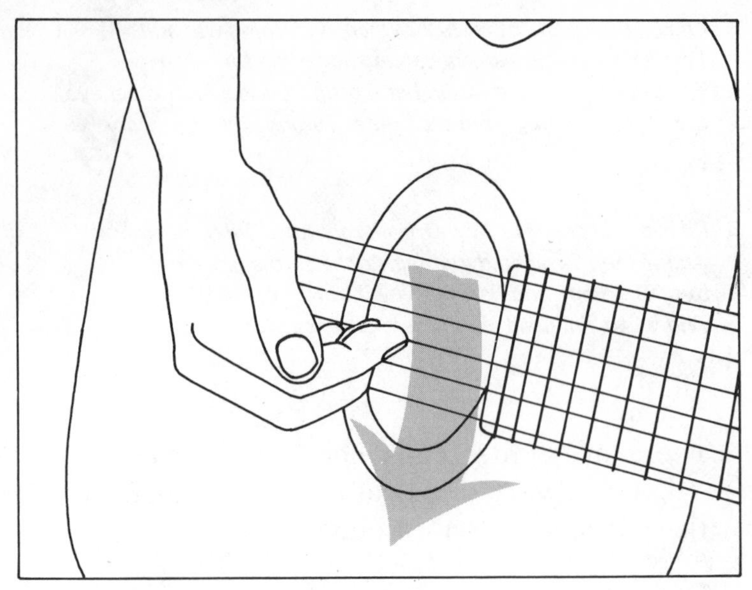

FIGURE 8-2b *Bass–fingers-down strum: Banjo Brush*

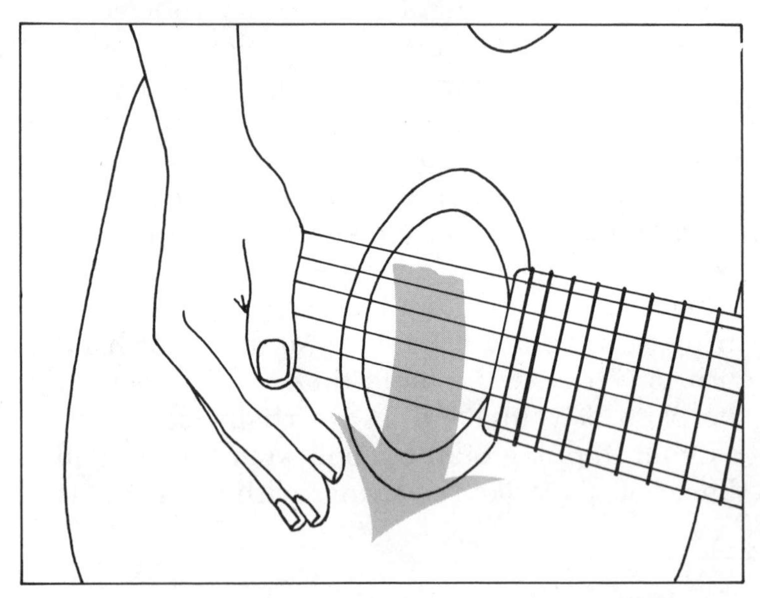

FIGURE 8-2c *Bass–fingers-down strum: Banjo Brush*

gernails. Continuing the motion, your fingernails should scrape the strings and your fingers should turn in an outward and downward direction. After the strings are struck with your fingernails, the momentum of the action will carry your fingers along, so that they'll end the action unclenched, and generally pointing in the direction of the floor.

1. Brush firmly across the bass string with the left side of your right hand thumb, coming to rest on the next string.
2. In one continuing motion, swing your hand upward, partially clenching and then unclenching your fingers and striking the strings with your nails, ending the action with your fingers pointing downward.

Don't be concerned with whether or not all four fingernails strike the strings or with how many strings are struck with your fingernails. Whichever fingers and strings get into the action is all right.

In "Slow Me Down Lord," you're going to play double dot rhythm marks, which are for really fast numbers, for the first time. You should remember that the dot is played twice as fast as the single line. The double dot is played twice as fast as the single dot. In fact, it's so fast that if four double dots stood for the four syllables in the word "huckleberry" (huck-le-ber-ry), you'd have to say the word in the same space of time it previously took you to say "hum"; if two single dots stood for the two syllables of the word "berry" (ber-ry), it would also have to be said as quickly as saying "hum." Since we're comparing timing and counts to fruits, let's substitute the word "grape" for the word, "hum." If you saw a visual picture of huckleberry, it would look like this —, the word berry would look like this ——, and the word grape would look like this ———. These dashes are for *timing*, not spelling.

On the first and fourth lines of the verses and chorus, a single dot rhythm mark is followed by a double dot, another double dot, and then a single line. The visual picture would look like this —— — — ——— You'd sing the word "slow" over the space of the first two lines, the word "me" on the space of the third line, and the word "down" on the space of the fourth line. It doesn't matter how quickly or how slowly *you* play and sing, as long as the rhythm marks bear the proper relationship to each other.

Incidentally, on the third line of the Numbers Game, you'll find it's too tricky to do from home base chord positions.

The tune for the verses and the chorus are exactly the same.

On the first and fourth lines of the Numbers Game, you'll notice an S over the numbers. Strum down on the chord there, as well as when you change chords. Don't play the numbers beneath the chord when you strum down.

I'm going to let you choose one of two possibilities here for the accompaniment. You can do the whole song with the B–fingers-down strum or you can do the B-fingers down strum on the verses only, and the down-up–slap-damp strum on the chorus. They're both two-step strums. On the down-up-slap-damp strum, don't damp the strings with your palm too quickly after you've played the down-up step. If you do, it won't sound like a two-step strum. I'm going to line out a couple of lines of the strum patterns for the chorus, using "D-u" for the down-up action and s-d for the slap-damp action.

```
A                                    E7
D-u-  s-d  D-u-  s-d    D-u-  s-d  D-u-s-d D-u-
Every day every night every day L - o-r  d
                        A
s-d D-     u-s-d     D-u-s-d D-u-etc.
I  know it don't p - a - y
```

You can see that the s-d of the pattern at the end of the second line would come on the first word of the third line. That's how the patterns of the strum are played on the chorus.

SLOW ME DOWN LORD

Words and Music by R.T. Jacobs

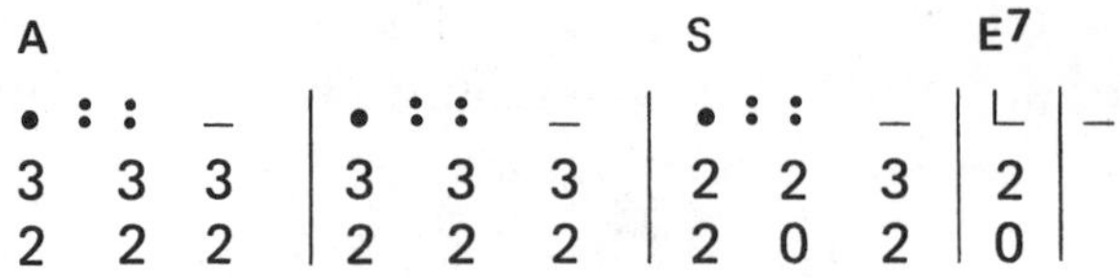

```
A                                  S          E7
• : :  _  | • : :  _  | • : :  _ | L |_
3  3  3   | 3  3  3   | 2  2  3  | 2 |
2  2  2   | 2  2  2   | 2  0  2  | 0 |
Slow  me down,  slow  me down,  slow  me down Lord

              A
_ | •   •   _ | L |_
1 | 1   1   1 | 2 |
0 | 2   0   2 | 2 |
I'm travel-ling too fast

           D                                 E7
_ | _  _ | •    _ • | L |  _   _ | _  _ | L |_
1 | 1  1 | 1    1   | 1 |  1   1 | 1  2 | 2 |
0 | 2  0 | 5    2   | 5 |  5   5 | 2  3 | 0 |
Won't see my broth - er   Lord,    when  he goes past

    A                                  S          E7
_ | • : :  _  | • : :  _  | • : :  _ | L |_
2 | 2  2  3   | 2  2  3   | 2  2  3  | 2 |
0 | 2  0  2   | 2  0  2   | 2  0  2  | 0 |
So slow  me down,  slow  me down,  slow  me down Lord

              A
_ | •   •   _ | L | L |_ ||
2 | 2   2   3 | 3 |   | R ||
0 | 2   0   2 | 2 |   |   ||
I'm travel-ling too fast.
```

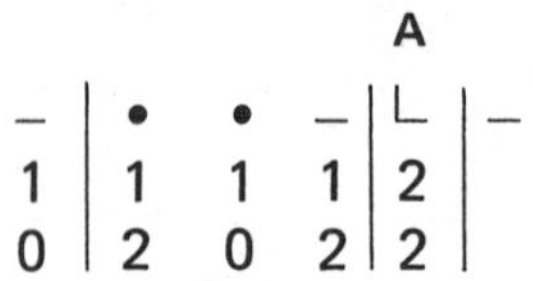

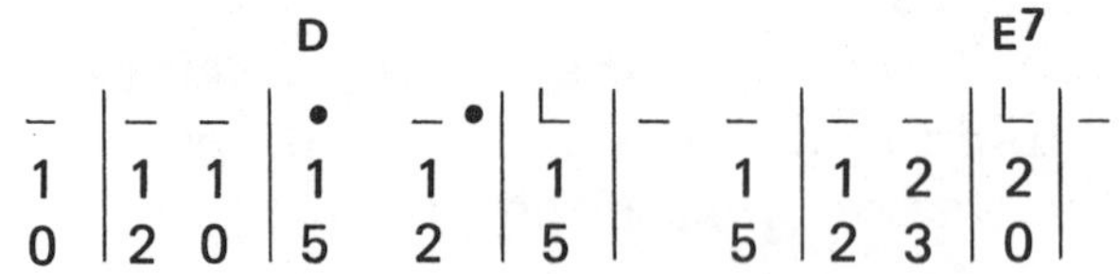

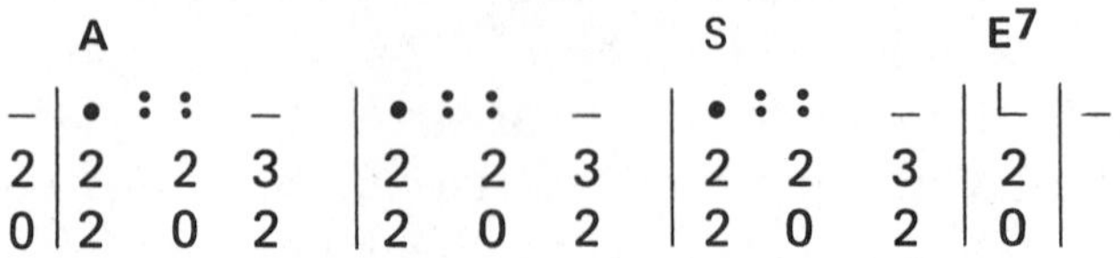

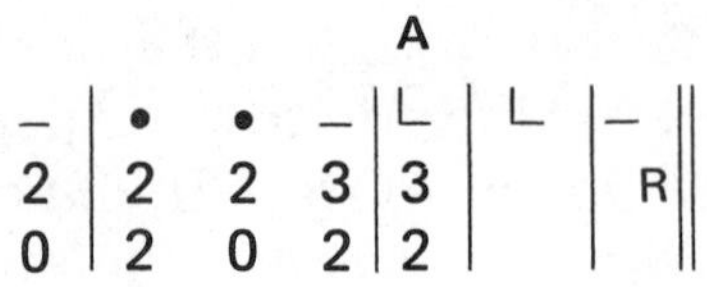

A E7
Slow me down, slow me down, slow me down Lord
A
I'm travelling too fast
D E7
Won't see my brother Lord, when he goes past
A E7
So slow me down, slow me down, slow me down Lord
A
I'm travelling too fast.

Chorus

A E7
Every day, every night, every day Lord
A
I know it don't pay
D E7
I'm in a hurry Lord, and I'll lose my way
A E7
So slow me down, slow me down, slow me down Lord
A
I'm travelling too fast.

2 *Slow me down, slow me down, slow me down Lord*
I'm travelling too fast
Won't see my sister Lord, when she goes past
So slow me down, slow me down, slow me down Lord
I'm travelling too fast.

Chorus

3 *Slow me down, slow me down, slow me down Lord*
I'm travelling too fast
Won't know a blessing Lord, when it comes past
So slow me down, slow me down, slow me down Lord
I'm travelling too fast.

Chorus

Ending after last chorus

A E7
So slow me down, slow me down, slow me down Lord
A-D-A
I'm travelling too fast.

Hymn Ending: I, IV, I. While you're singing the last word "fast," strum down with the Easy Strum on the A chord, then the D chord, then the A chord again. It'll sound like the harmony you hear on a church organ; in fact, it's called a "hymn ending." It's a nice way to end some songs. You might like to try it with some others. Keep singing the last word of the song while you play a I chord, a IV chord, and then a I chord again. Of course, it's got to be the I, IV, and I chords of the key you're singing and playing the song in.

Here and Now. Taking the cue from the song, don't be in a hurry. Take your own time, not somebody else's idea of what your time should be. Slow down. Relax and enjoy what you're doing right now, while you're doing it. Enjoy the time you're using to learn. You don't have to be finished with something before you enjoy it. Enjoy it here and now.

Three Home Bases

In the next song, I'd like you to use all three chords as home base positions. Probably, the only place you'll have to get off the base is on the second line, the next to the last set of numbers. Most of you will find it too tricky to reach that fourth fret on the fourth string, so leave the home base position and then return on the rest of the numbers. Use the B-fingers-down strum here.

GOIN' DOWN THE ROAD FEELIN' BAD

```
    A
• | •  –  •  –  •  • | L •
1 | 1  1  1  1  1  3 | 2
0 | 0  0  0  2  0  2 | 2
```

I'm goin' down the road feel - in' bad

```
    D                  A
• | •  –  •  –  •  • | L •
2 | 3  3  3  2  3  4 | 3
0 | 2  2  2  0  2  4 | 2
```

I'm goin' down the road feel - in' bad

```
    D                  A
• | •  –  •  –  •  • | –  –  •  •
3 | 3  3  3  2  3  2 | 2  1  1  1
2 | 2  2  2  0  2  0 | 2  0  2  0
```

I'm goin' down the road feel - in' bad, Oh Lord

```
        E7                         A
•  • | •  •  •  •  •  •  •  •  | L • ||
1  1 | 1  2  2  2  2  2  2  2  | 3   ||
0  0 | 0  0  0  0  0  3  2  0  | 2   ||
```

And I ain't gon - na be treat - ed this - a way.

```
     A
I'm goin' down the road feelin' bad /
     D                         A
I'm goin' down the road feelin' bad /
     D                         A
I'm goin' down the road feelin' bad, Oh Lord
       E7                         A
And I ain't gonna be treated this-a way. /
```

2 I'm goin' where the chilly winds don't blow
I'm goin' where the chilly winds don't blow
I'm goin' where the chilly winds don't blow, Oh Lord
And I ain't gonna be treated this-a way.

3 I'm goin' where the climate suits my clothes
I'm goin' where the climate suits my clothes
I'm goin' where the climate suits my clothes, Oh Lord
And I ain't gonna be treated this-a way.

4 I'm goin' where a dollar buys something fine
I'm goin' where a dollar buys something fine
I'm goin' where a dollar buys something fine, Oh Lord
And I ain't gonna be treated this-a way.

5 I'm goin' where the water tastes like wine
I'm goin' where the water tastes like wine
I'm goin' where the water tastes like wine, Oh Lord
And I ain't gonna be treated this-a way.

Did you play the numbers using all three chords as home bases? Did you play the numbers using a combination of home-base-chord positions with some and play the others the way you first learned the game? Or, did you choose to play the game with no home bases on any of the numbers? Remember to keep your own pace and to relax in between practice and learning sessions.

nine

Do you remember that we left the key of G temporarily to work on the key of A because the learning progression was more beneficial that way? Now, we'll complete the three main chords in the key of G. We're going to add the C chord, which is the IV chord in the key of G. (If you've forgotten how to find the three main chords in any key family, the I, IV, and V chords, see chapter 4.)

THE C CHORD

The bass string for the C chord is the fifth or A string. Have you wondered why, in every chord you've learned so far, only the G and C chords don't have the same-name bass strings? You already know the fingerboard of the guitar is like the keyboard of a piano. On the G chord, when you finger the bass string(sixth) on the third fret, you're fingering a G note. That makes the string a G bass string during the time it's fingered. On the C chord, when you finger the bass string(fifth) on the third fret, you're fingering a C note. So you're still strumming those two chords from the lowest note, or bass note of the chord.

The C chord is a bit of a stretch but your fingers will get used to it, like they did for the G chord. (Have they, yet?) Practice the C chord with the Easy Strum first and then with the waltz strum.

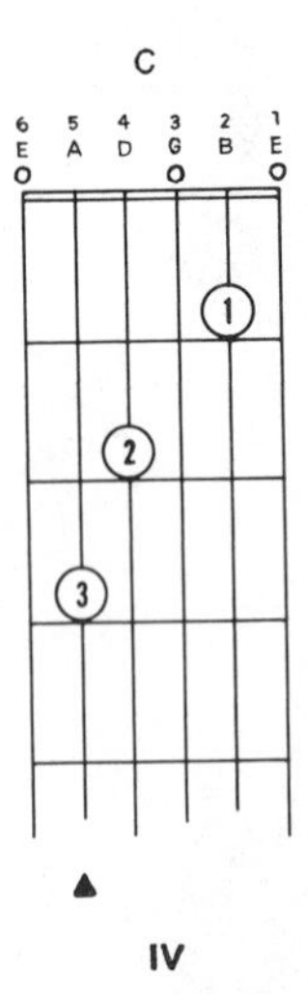

FIGURE 9-1
C chord

Changing between the G and C Chords

After you've practiced strumming on the C chord for awhile, try changing between the G and C chords. Now you know why I changed the progression of chords earlier; it's a bit difficult, isn't it?

Earlier (page 41), I gave you two different fingerings on the G chord to choose from. Those of you who chose the more difficult fingering, using the second, third, and fourth fingers, will find it easier now to change to the C chord. In changing from G to C, the third finger moves over one string to the fifth string in the third fret; the second finger moves over one string to the fourth string in the second fret; and, the first finger goes on the second string, first fret. Your fourth finger lifts off, meanwhile.

In changing back to G again, move your third finger, and then your second finger; as your fourth finger goes on the first string, third fret, your first finger lifts off. Don't forget, although you're practicing the changes this way now, your eventual goal is to move all the fingers at the same time, as you change. When you don't have to think about how your fingers are moving, that's when they'll all move together. Keep in mind that another goal is to avoid looking at your fingers, to *feel* the strings in the changes and when you're playing.

For those of you who chose the easier fingering, using the first, second, and third fingers (and that's probably most of you), you'll have a little more difficulty changing chords. Nevertheless, I suspect you've discovered that you can do anything you choose to do.

In changing from G to C, the third finger moves over to the fifth string, in the third fret, and the second finger goes over to the fourth string in the second fret. As you're moving your second finger into position, your first finger will naturally lift off the fifth string. The first finger then goes over to the second string, in the first fret.

Try changing back to G, starting with the first finger switch. Do this for awhile, back and forth, silently, just moving the fingers into position without strumming. Then, when your fingers seem to go where you want them to, practice changing between the G and C chords with the Easy Strum and then the waltz strum.

In the next couple of keys, don't attempt to play the numbers from home bases. It's too complicated for you to do it in these keys, right now. Later on, when you've done a lot more playing on your guitar, you'll be ready to come back to it.

The song that follows, "On Top Of Old Smoky," should be accompanied by the waltz strum. You learned how to fit the words and singing to the waltz strum with "Down In The Valley" and "Clementine." Remember, wherever you see a strum mark, that's exactly where you begin the pattern of B-down-down.

ON TOP OF OLD SMOKY

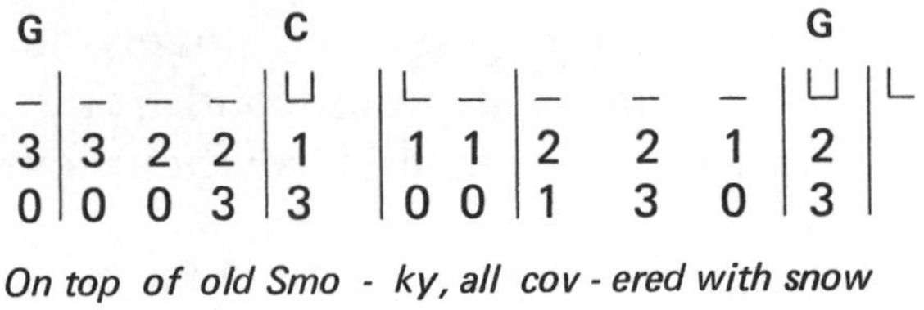

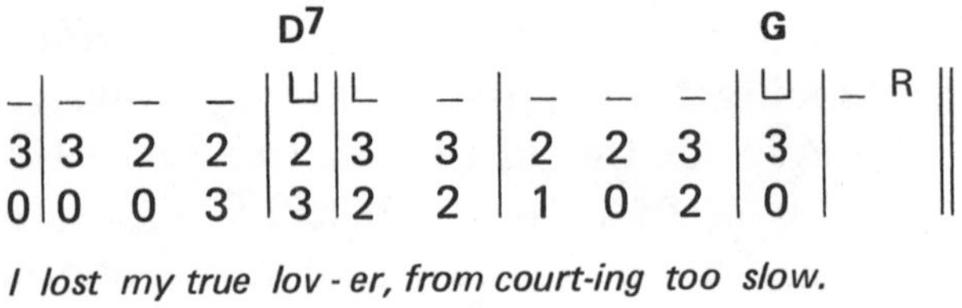

```
G           C                         G
_ |_ _ _ |⊔  |∟ _ |_   _   _ |⊔ |∟
3 |3 2 2 |1  |1 1 |2   2   1 |2 |
0 |0 0 3 |3  |0 0 |1   3   0 |3 |
```

On top of old Smo - ky, all cov - ered with snow

```
            D7                        G
_ |_ _ _ |⊔ |∟  _ |_   _   _ |⊔ |_ R ||
3 |3 2 2 |2 |3  3 |2   2   3 |3 |    ||
0 |0 0 3 |3 |2  2 |1   0   2 |0 |    ||
```

I lost my true lov - er, from court-ing too slow.

G C G
On top of old Smoky, all covered with snow /
D7 G
I lost my true lover, from courting too slow. /

C G
2 *For courting's a pleasure and parting is grief /*
D7 G
And a false hearted lover, is worse than a thief. /

3 *A thief he will rob you and take what you have*
But a false hearted lover will lead you to the grave.

4 *The grave will decay you and turn you to dust*
Not one boy in a hundred, a poor girl can trust.

5 *They'll hug you and kiss you and tell you more lies*
Than the cross ties on the railroads or the stars in the skies.

6 *They'll tell you they love you to give your heart ease*
And the minute your back's turned, they'll court whom they please.

Repeat first two lines of first verse

Did you stretch and squeeze wherever you had to? The next song, "The Sucker's Lament," is sung to the tune of "On Top Of Old Smoky." I've doubled up on the verses, but the tune for the first two lines is identical to that for the last two lines of each verse. Try it out with the waltz strum. Then, we'll do a variation of the waltz strum with it.

THE SUCKER'S LAMENT

Tune of OLD SMOKY, Words by R.T. Jacobs

G C G
If it's a phony, I still wouldn't know how /
D7 G
To say I don't want it, at least not for now /
C G
They tell me it's marvelous, and one of a kind /
D7 G
But after I buy it, what do I find? /

2 *I find that it's yellow and it's big and it's round*
And no matter how hard I try, it won't make a sound
I poke it and squeeze it and push it around
Which isn't so easy, 'cause it weighs fifteen pounds.

3 *I get tired of trying and go for a walk*
Still wondering how I can make that thing talk
And while I'm out walking, what do I see
A lot of my neighbors, no smarter than me.

4 *I couldn't believe it, what I saw that night*
Such poking and squeezing, an incredible sight
My priceless possession, my 'one of a kind'
Had dozens just like it and all of one mind.

5 *Yes, they're big and their yellow, they're heavy and round*
And know what you're waiting for, but won't make a sound.

DOUBLE-BASS–DOWN STRUM

Do this variation of the waltz strum very slowly at first, until you get so used to it that you don't have to think about it. This is a three-step strum. ONE, two, three; ONE, two, three.

1. Brush across the bass string with your thumb, coming to rest on the very next string. (For the G chord, that would be the fifth string, for the C chord, the fourth string, and for the D^7 chord, it would be the third string.)

2. Brush across that very next string also, coming to rest on it's very *next* string. (For the G chord, it would be the fourth string, for the C chord, the third string, for the D^7 chord, the second string. On the D^7 chord, the double bass strings are really not bass strings. They're treble strings. That's because the D chords are shorter(in space) on the guitar, than the others.)

3. Brush down across the rest of the strings.

The pattern for this strum is, B-B-down. Each strum mark starts the pattern with the first bass and ends the pattern with the 'down.' On any songs where you previously waltz strum, you can interchange this strum. You can even try doing the double bass-down strum on some verses and the bass-down-down on others.

KEY OF G FAMILY

Did you notice that the G chord belongs to the key of D *and* to the key of G? Remember, in the beginning of chapter 8 when we compared an imaginary person's different family positions to those of the D chord? The G chord works the same way. The G chord is the IV chord in the key of D and it's the I chord in the key of G. (If you think you've forgotten how to find the three main chords in any key, review chapter 4. As we progress, you'll find more chords that belong to more than one key family.

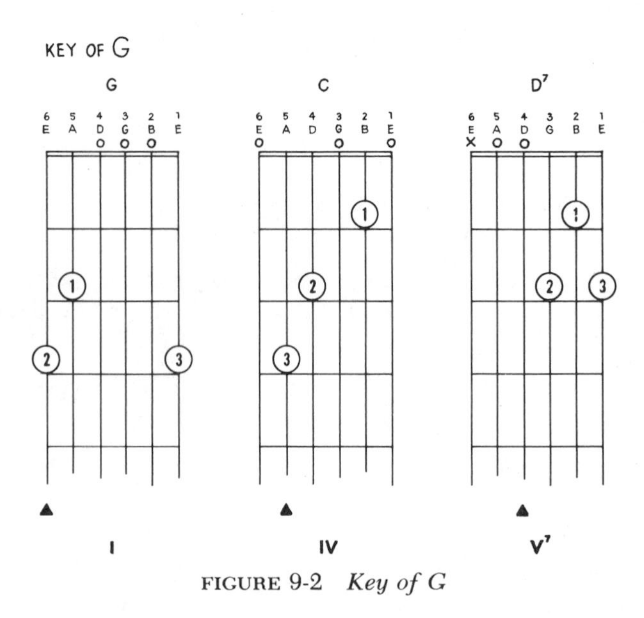

FIGURE 9-2 *Key of G*

Changing from D^7 to C

On the next song, "Hangman," you'll use an easy chord change. When going from the D^7 chord to the C chord, the first finger doesn't move; it stays on the second string, first fret for both the D^7 and the C chords. The second finger moves from the third string, second fret, to the fourth string, second fret. The third finger transfers from the first string, second fret, to the fifth string, third fret. Practice this easy change with any of your two-step strums. Then we'll try a new strum for the "Hangman" song.

"HANGING LOOSE" DOWN-UP STRUM

This strum "hangs loose" because there's no bass string to brush. It's a two-step strum that's almost as easy as the Easy Strum.

1. Brush down with your thumb across the strings just as you did in the Easy Strum.

2. Brush up with your first finger and don't worry about which strings your first finger brushes.

Do the strum in a loose, casual, almost circular motion, so that your first finger is brushing up on the strings closer to the bridge. (This will give a larger, more metallic sound, and also, will be an interesting variation.) This is how the strum looks: "T" means thumb and 1 means first finger.

```
Down-up, Down-up, Down-up, etc.
T    1 T    1 T    1
```

It's easy, isn't it? I remember when I first learned this strum, I made very exaggerated circular motions, thinking I looked very professional strumming that way.

THE HANGMAN

Adapted and arranged by R.T. Jacobs

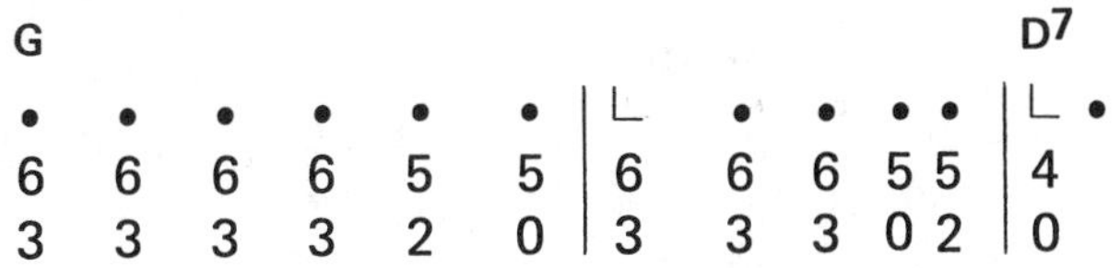

```
G                                         D7
•   •   •   •   •   •  | L   •   •  • •  | L •
6   6   6   6   5   5  | 6   6   6  5 5  | 4
3   3   3   3   2   0  | 3   3   3  0 2  | 0
```

Hang-man hang-man slack your rope, slack it for a - while

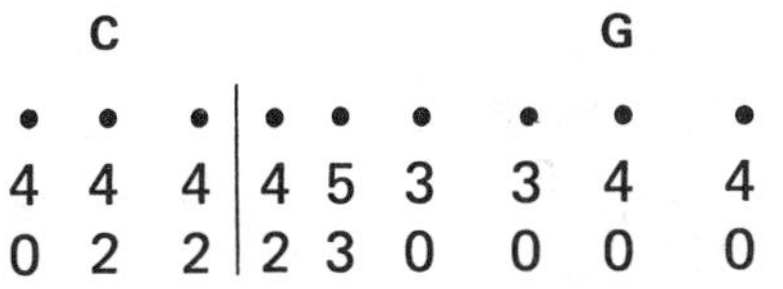

```
  C                      G
•  •  • | •  •  •   •  •   •
4  4  4 | 4  5  3   3  4   4
0  2  2 | 2  3  0   0  0   0
```

I think I see my fa - ther com - ing

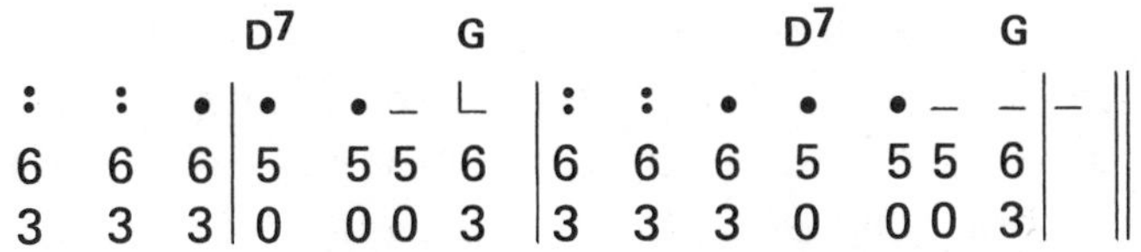

```
            D7      G                  D7      G
:   :   • | •   • _ L | :  :  •  •   • _ _ | _ ||
6   6   6 | 5   5 5 6 | 6  6  6  5   5 5 6 |   ||
3   3   3 | 0   0 0 3 | 3  3  3  0   0 0 3 |   ||
```

Rid - ing for man - y a mile, rid - ing for man - y a mile.

G **D7**

Hangman hangman slack your rope, slack it for awhile

C **G**

I think I see my father coming

D7 **G** **D7** **G**

Riding for many a mile, riding for many a mile.

2 *Father dear, what brought you here, did you bring me gold*
To save me from the cold clay ground and
My neck from the gallows pole, alone on the gallows pole.

3 *No oh no I brought no gold, no gold to set you free*
For I have come to see you hang
All alone on the gallows tree, alone on the gallows tree.

4 *Mother dear, what brought you here, did you bring me gold*
To save me from the cold clay ground and
My neck from the gallows pole, alone on the gallows pole.

5 *No oh no I brought no gold, no gold to set you free*
For I have come to see you hang
All alone on the gallows tree, alone on the gallows tree.

6 *Lover dear, what brought you here, did you bring me gold*
To save me from the cold clay ground and
My neck from the gallows pole, alone on the gallows pole.

7 *Yes oh yes, I brought you gold, gold for all to see*
I have not come to see you hang but
To take you back home with me, yes to take you back home with me.

ALTERNATING BASSES

Up to now, we've been careful to use the "proper" bass string for all our chords. Those 'proper' bass strings are called the "primary" basses. The primary bass is the lowest note of the chord. It's the note that the chord is constructed from, the first note or root of the chord. However, there are also secondary basses. In fact, you already used them when you did the double-bass-down strum. These could be the third or even the fifth note of the chord. On this next song, we're going to alternate between the primary bass and the secondary bass strings of the chords.

For the G chord, alternate between the sixth string and the fifth string basses. Practice it by changing back and forth, with the bass-fingers down strum, which we'll be using on the next song, "John B. Sails." On the D^7 chord, alternate between the fourth string bass and the fifth string bass. On the C chord, we'll alternate basses between the fifth string and the fourth string. After you've spent enough time, to your own satisfaction, alternating basses on all three chords, try it out with "John B. Sails." It makes the accompaniment more interesting. Don't forget that whenever there's a strum mark, that's where you play one of the alternating basses. You do the "fingers down" between the strum marks. The tune is the same for the chorus and the verses.

JOHN B. SAILS

Adapted with new words by R.T. Jacobs (Based on a calypso folk song)

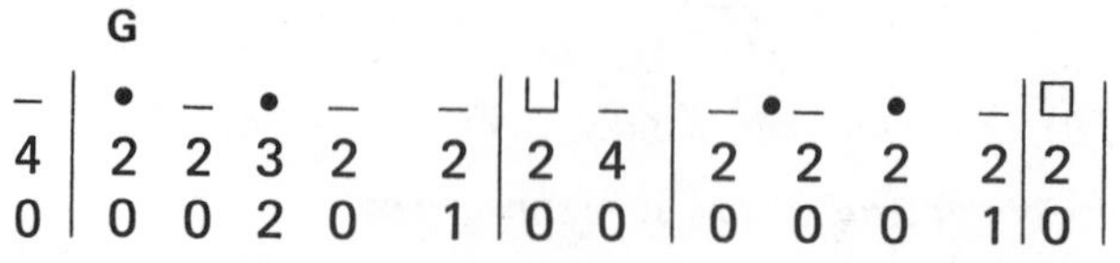

```
    G
—  | •  —  •  —     —  | ⊔  —  | — • —  •     — | □ |
4  | 2  2  3  2     2  | 2  4  | 2   2  2     2 | 2 |
0  | 0  0  2  0     1  | 0  0  | 0   0  0     1 | 0 |
```

We came on the ship John B. my grand-fa - ther and me

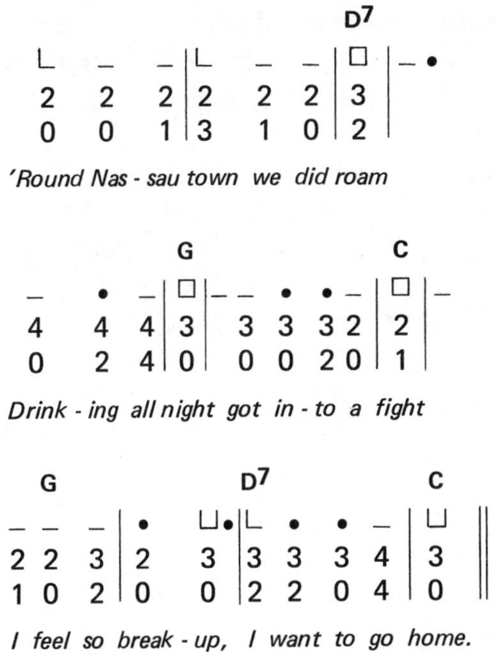

D7

L _ _ | L _ _ | □ | _ •
2 2 2 | 2 2 2 | 3 |
0 0 1 | 3 1 0 | 2 |

'Round Nas - sau town we did roam

G C

_ • _ | □ | _ _ • • _ | □ | _
4 4 4 | 3 | 3 3 3 2 | 2 |
0 2 4 | 0 | 0 0 2 0 | 1 |

Drink - ing all night got in - to a fight

G D7 C

_ _ _ | • ⊔• | L • • _ | ⊔ ||
2 2 3 | 2 3 | 3 3 3 4 | 3 ||
1 0 2 | 0 0 | 2 2 0 4 | 0 ||

I feel so break - up, I want to go home.

G
We came on the ship John B./my grandfather and me /
D7
'Round Nassau town we did roam /
G C
Drinking all night,/got into a fight /
G D7 G
I feel so break up,/I want to go home.

Chorus

G
So hoist up the John B. Sails, see how the mains'l sets
D7
Send for the captain ashore, let me go home /
G C
Oh let me ho home,/I want to go home /
G D7 G
I feel so break up,/I want to go home.

2 *The first mate he got drunk, he broke up the people's trunk*
Constable had to come and take him away
Oh Sheriff John Stone, please leave me alone
I feel so break up, I want to go home

Chorus

3 *The third mate, he got stewed, broke dishes and threw around food*
Constable had to come and take him away
Oh Dr. Freud, we're all getting schizoid
I feel so break up, I want to go home.

Chorus

Where's your left hand thumb? Is it halfway down the back of the guitar neck, just about opposite to your first finger, or is it peeping up over the top of the sixth string? Make sure it doesn't do the latter.

You've learned several things in this chapter: a new chord, new strums, and a new key. If you tried playing the numbers from their home-base chord positions, that was an additional challenge. It might be a good idea to spend some extra time practicing at this point. Choose your own pace.

ten

We're going to switch tracks on the progression of chords again for good reasons. You'll see why, later on.

THE E CHORD

Do you see anything familiar about this new chord? It's an E^7 chord with the third finger added right behind the second finger, making it an E chord. The bass string of the E chord is the same as it is for the E^7 chord: the low E or sixth string. (Had you guessed that already?) Strum the E chord a few times. It's such a lovely chord that it's used as an extra means of checking whether or not the guitar is in tune; the E chord has the *do, mi, sol, do* in it that singers tune their voices to, and some guitarists also like tuning their guitars to it. Once you're familiar with the sound of the E chord (from a tuned guitar, of course), do this. Brush your thumb across each string from the sixth string bass all the way down to the first string. You'll recognize any out-of-tune or sour-sounding strings. After brushing or gliding across each string with your thumb, come to rest for a moment on the very next string before going on. That way you'll be able to hear each string individually, and therefore, more clearly.

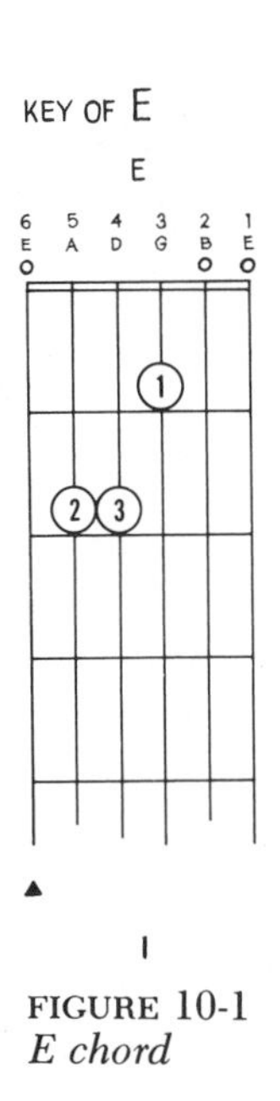

FIGURE 10-1
E chord

The next song, "Swing Low, Sweet Chariot," can be accompanied by an E chord alone. Later on, when you know how, you can add the other main chords in the key of E, but for now, just the E will do. We'll be alternating basses with the bass-fingers down strum in the following way: sixth string bass-fingers down, fourth string bass-fingers down, sixth string bass-fingers down, fourth string bass-fingers down, and so on. Change back and forth steadily between the sixth and fourth strings. After each bass, you'll do the 'fingers down' to complete the pattern of the B-fingers down strum. At the very end of the song, strum down once using the Easy Strum. It's a little trickier to skip a string when you're alternating basses, but it's a very interesting sound; try it.

Make sure you don't confuse yourself by forgetting that the E chord is not an E⁷ chord. An E⁷ chord won't give you the musical sound you want here.

SWING LOW, SWEET CHARIOT

Adapted and arranged by R.T. Jacobs

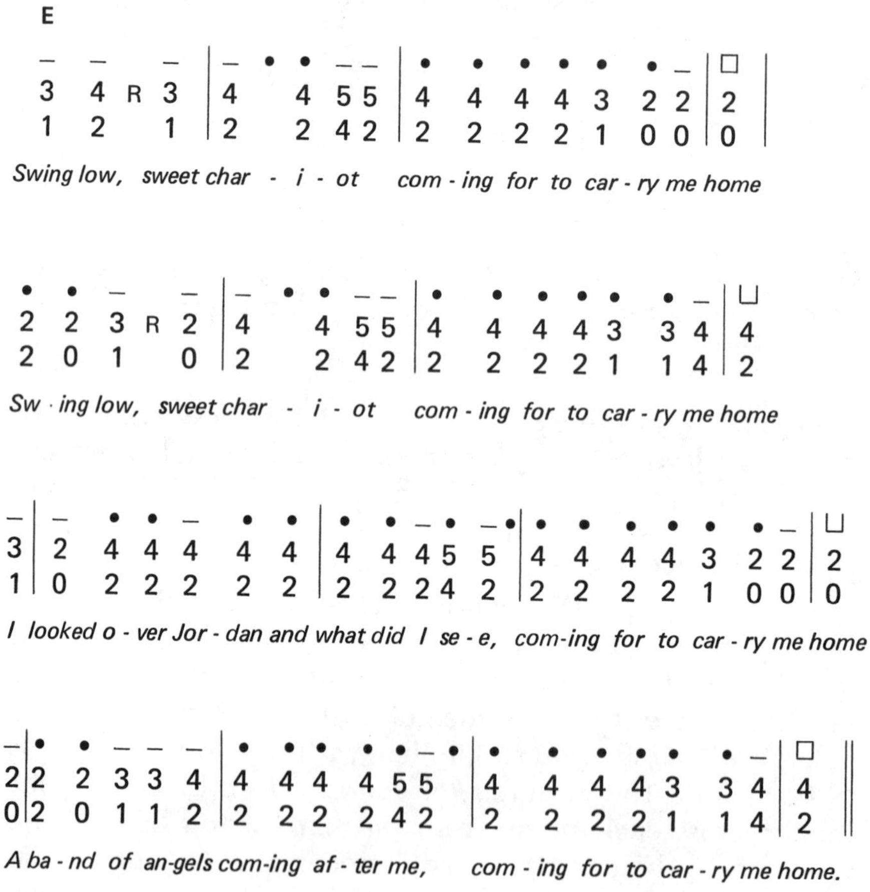

E

```
— — — | — • • — — | • • • • • • — | □ |
3 4 R 3 | 4 4 5 5 | 4 4 4 4 3 2 2 | 2 |
1 2 1 | 2 2 4 2 | 2 2 2 2 1 0 0 | 0 |
```

Swing low, sweet char - i - ot com - ing for to car - ry me home

```
• • — — | — • • — — | • • • • • • — | ⊔
2 2 3 R 2 | 4 4 5 5 | 4 4 4 4 3 3 4 | 4
2 0 1 0 | 2 2 4 2 | 2 2 2 2 1 1 4 | 2
```

Sw · ing low, sweet char - i - ot com - ing for to car - ry me home

```
— | — • • — • • | • • — • — • | • • • • • • — | ⊔
3 | 2 4 4 4 4 4 | 4 4 4 5 5 | 4 4 4 4 3 2 2 | 2
1 | 0 2 2 2 2 2 | 2 2 2 4 2 | 2 2 2 2 1 0 0 | 0
```

I looked o - ver Jor - dan and what did I se - e, com-ing for to car - ry me home

```
— | • • — — — | • • • • • — • | • • • • • • — | □ ||
2 | 2 2 3 3 4 | 4 4 4 4 5 5 | 4 4 4 4 3 3 4 | 4 ||
0 | 2 0 1 1 2 | 2 2 2 2 4 2 | 2 2 2 2 1 1 4 | 2 ||
```

A ba - nd of an-gels com-ing af - ter me, com - ing for to car - ry me home.

E

Swing low,/sweet chariot, coming for to carry me home
Swing low,/sweet chariot, coming for to carry me home
I looked over Jordan and what did I see, coming for to carry me home
A band of angels coming after me, coming for to carry me home.

2 *Swing low, sweet chariot, coming for to carry me home*
Swing low, sweet chariot, coming for to carry me home
If you get there before I do, coming for to carry me home
Please tell my friends I'm coming too, coming for to carry me home.

THE B^7 CHORD

Don't be intimidated by this chord. It looks more complicated than it really is.

Look at the diagram very carefully and notice that your first finger goes on the fourth string, first fret. That's the only finger playing in the first fret. Next, see that in the second fret, you've got a finger on every other string. It's true that this is the first time many of you have put your fourth finger to work on a chord. But if you've been using it to play the numbers, it shouldn't feel so strange. It fits in very easily on the first string, second fret.

The B^7 chord is strummed from the fifth or A string, its bass string. If you think that's because you're fingering a B note on the fifth string, you're right. Strum the B^7 chord several times with all your two-step strums. We'll do the bass–fingers-down strum with alternating basses for the next song, "I'm Gonna Sing." Make sure you don't accidentally touch the sixth string. That's the low E string and there's no E in a B^7 chord, so it won't sound right if it's included.

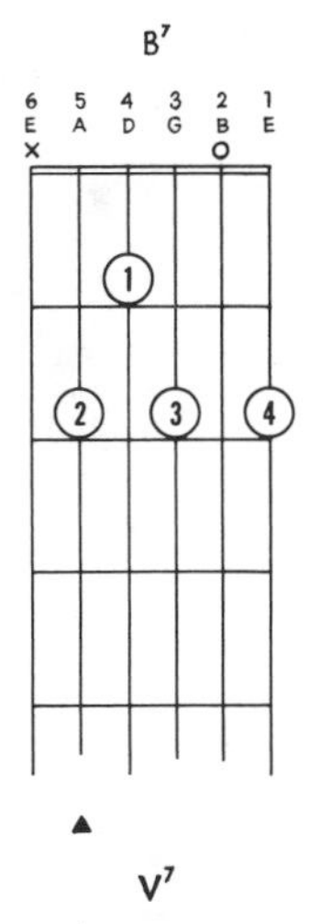

FIGURE 10-2 *B seventh (B^7) chord*

Changing from E to B^7 to E

Take an E chord position. In changing from E to B^7, your *second finger doesn't move* from the fifth string, second fret. Keep that idea in your mind, or else you'll find that the second finger will lift off every time you try to change. That extra action is an unnecessary complication that you don't need. Your third finger moves over one string while your fourth finger transfers to the first string. All this takes place in the second fret. In the first fret, your first finger moves over one string, from the third string to the fourth.

When changing from B^7 to E, reverse these moves. Again, the second finger *doesn't move.* The third finger moves over one string and is then right behind the second finger, in the second fret. Lift the fourth finger off the first string. In the first fret, the first finger moves over one string, from the fourth string to the third string. Keep the following thought in the back of your mind: Eventually, all your fingers

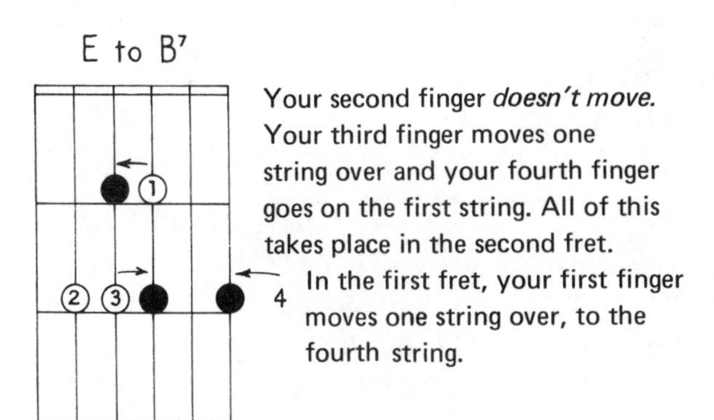

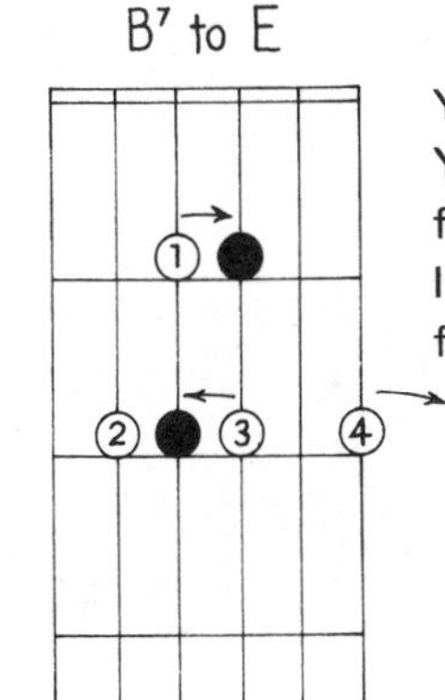

Your second finger *doesn't move.* Your third finger goes back to the fourth string and your fourth finger lifts off. This is in the second fret. In the first fret your first finger goes back to the third string.

FIGURE 10-3 *Changing from E to B^7 to E*

will move at the same time, when changing chords. All you've got to do to make that happen is to keep on practicing the changes until your fingers begin to fall into place naturally.

I'M GONNA SING

Adapted and arranged by R.T. Jacobs (Based on a spiritual)

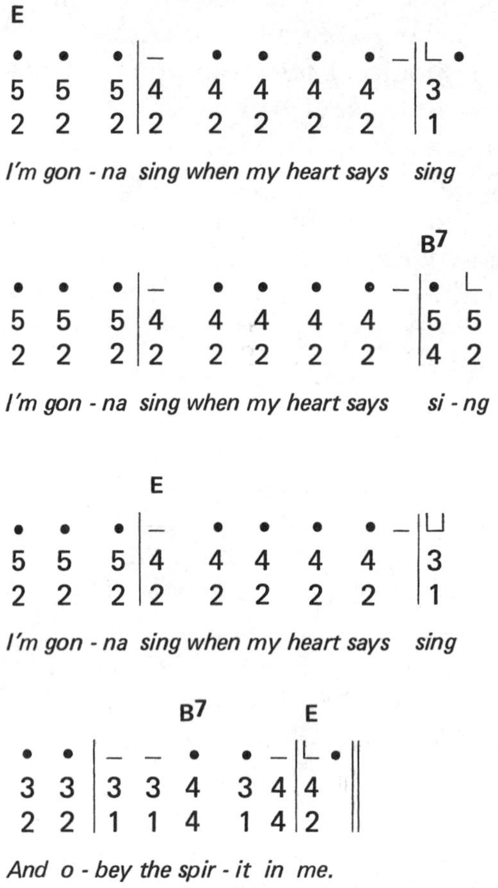

```
E
•  •  • | _   •  •  •  •  _ | L •
5  5  5 | 4   4  4  4  4    | 3
2  2  2 | 2   2  2  2  2    | 1
```

I'm gon - na sing when my heart says sing

```
                              B7
•  •  • | _   •  •  •  •  _ | •  L
5  5  5 | 4   4  4  4  4    | 5  5
2  2  2 | 2   2  2  2  2    | 4  2
```

I'm gon - na sing when my heart says si - ng

```
          E
•  •  • | _   •  •  •  •  _ | ⊔
5  5  5 | 4   4  4  4  4    | 3
2  2  2 | 2   2  2  2  2    | 1
```

I'm gon - na sing when my heart says sing

```
             B7       E
•  • | _  _  •    •  _ | L •  ||
3  3 | 3  3  4    3  4 | 4    ||
2  2 | 1  1  4    1  4 | 2    ||
```

And o - bey the spir - it in me.

If you're singing too low for comfort, you can sing higher up in the same key by starting off with the following sets of numbers:

```
•  •  • | _  •  •  •  •  _ | L
2  2  2 | 1  1  1  1  1    | 1
0  0  0 | 0  0  0  0  0    | 4
```

When you alternate basses for the E chord, you'll alternate between the sixth string and the fifth string. When you alternate basses for the B^7 chord, you'll alternate between the fifth string and the fourth string. Don't play the sixth string in the B^7 chord accidentally: remember, there's no E note in the B^7 chord. Do the B-fingers down strum with the alternating basses.

E
I'm gonna sing when my heart says sing
B7
I'm gonna sing when my heart says sing
E
I'm gonna sing when my heart says sing
B7 E
And obey the spirit in me.

2 *I'm gonna dance when my heart says dance, etc.*

3 *I'm gonna sway when my heart says sway, etc.*

4 *I'm gonna shout when my heart says shout, etc.*

5 *I'm gonna clap when my heart says clap, etc.*

6 *I'm gonna smile when my heart says smile, etc.*

Repeat the first verse or make up some verses of your own.

Do your fingertips feel sore? Do your wrists ache? Don't forget the charley horse shake.

THE BANJO BRUSH

You remember that the bass–fingers-down was a two-step strum. Here's another two-step version of the B–fingers-down strum. It's called the Banjo Brush. However, on the Bnj B, as we'll call it, the second step is divided. The first step, brushing across the bass string, is exactly the same as the B–fingers-down strum. You start the second step with the fingers down and end with your first finger brushing up across the strings. Don't be concerned about how many strings the first finger

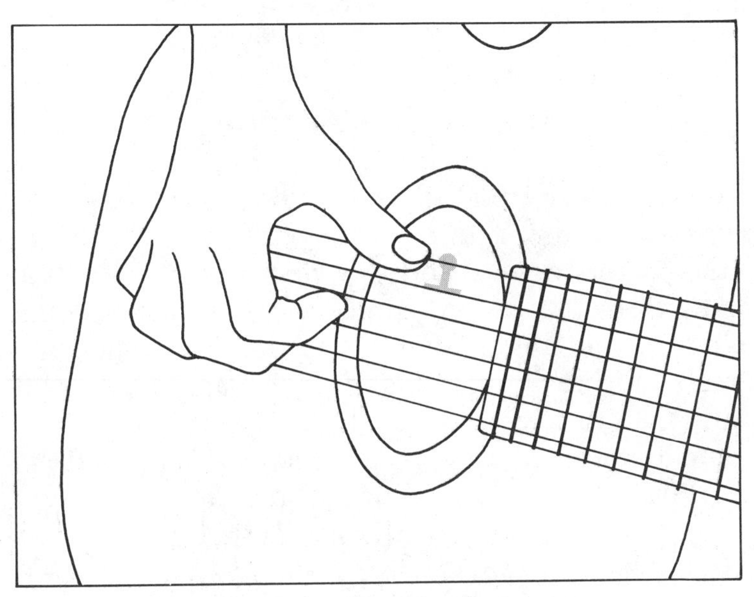

FIGURE 10-4a *Banjo Brush, first step*

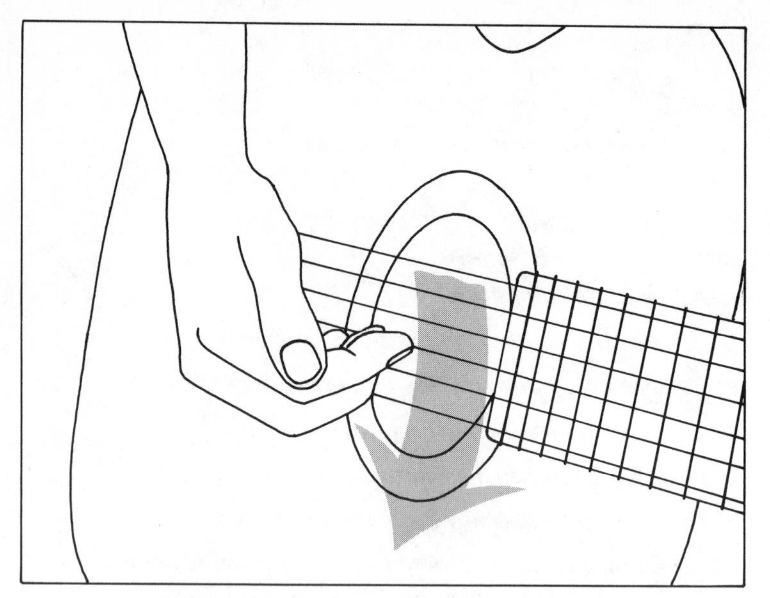

FIGURE 10-4b *Banjo Brush, second step*

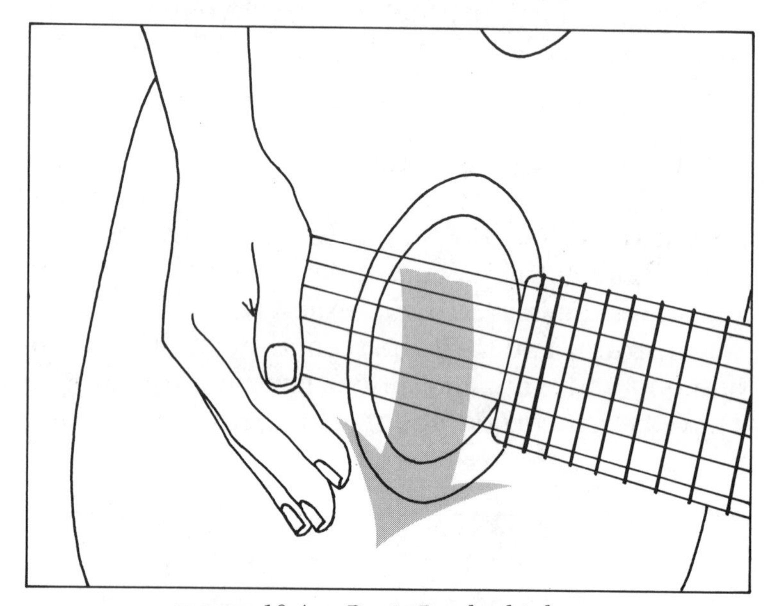

FIGURE 10-4c *Banjo Brush, third step*

brushes across. It doesn't matter. What does matter, though, is that this is a two-step strum, so don't give equal time to the bass, 'the fingers down,' and the 'first finger up' movements. That's three steps. The timing for the bass is equal to the timing for the 'fingers down' *and* the 'first finger up.' It's as though the bass equals 1 and each part of the next step equals 1/2. Visually, it would look this way: — – –. The first line for the bass is twice as long as each of the two shorter lines for the 'fingers down' and the 'first finger up.' Emphasize the bass and do the Bnj B strum pattern so that it sounds like this, *Sooo* ea-sy, *Sooo* ea-sy, *Sooo* ea-sy. The correct timing is important because that's what makes

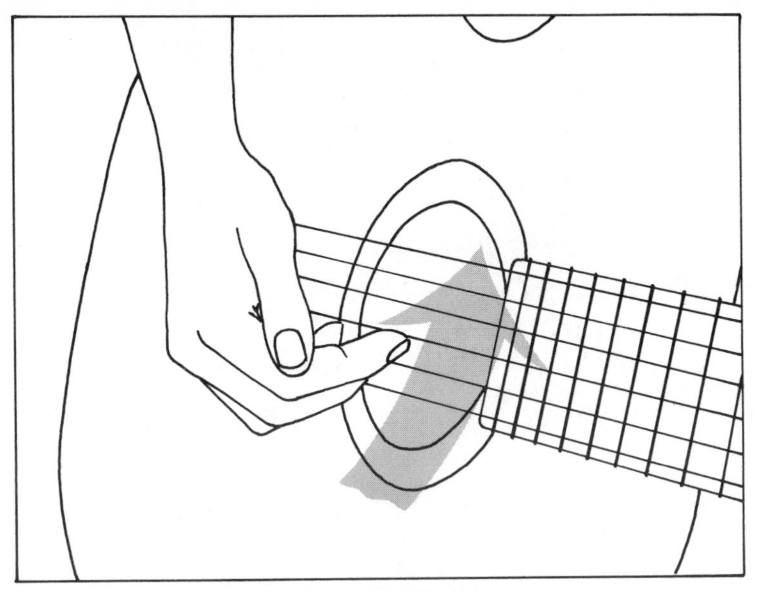

FIGURE 10-4*d* *Banjo Brush, fourth step*

the Bnj B sound full, free, and easy. If you don't have the right timing, it'll sound rigid and choppy. Also, make sure your first finger really *brushes* up across the strings. Don't let it get caught or hooked under the strings as you brush across them. If it does, that means you're not really brushing across casually. Your finger is rigid and tense.

Incidentally, the Bnj B is a basic strum and can be used for countless numbers of songs, as long as they're not in waltz time. The following two steps illustrate its basic pattern.

1. Brush across the bass string of the chord, coming to rest on the very next string.
2. Start with the 'fingers-down' and end with the 'first finger brush-up' across the strings.

You can try out your new Bnj B strum on any of the old songs, except the waltz strum songs (they're three-step strums). The next song, "Rocka My Soul," is a good rocking song to strum and have fun with; go to it using the Bnj B.

ROCKA MY SOUL

Adapted and arranged by R.T. Jacobs (Based on spiritual)

E

•	•	–	–	•	•	•	•	•	–	•	–
3	3	3	4	4	4	3	3	3	2	3	3
1	0	1	2	2	2	1	0	1	0	1	1

Rock - a my soul in the bos - om of Ab - ra - ham

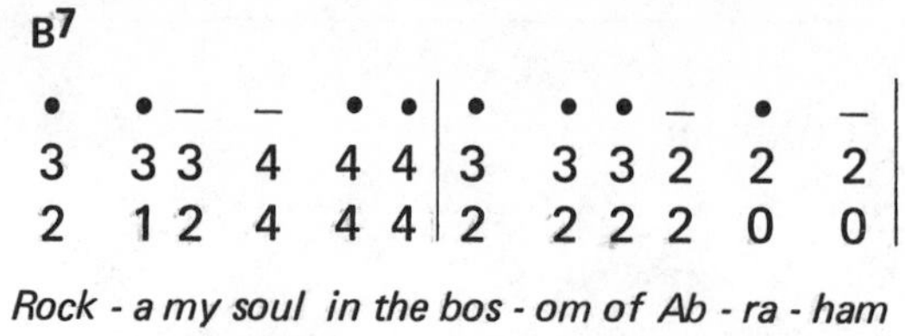

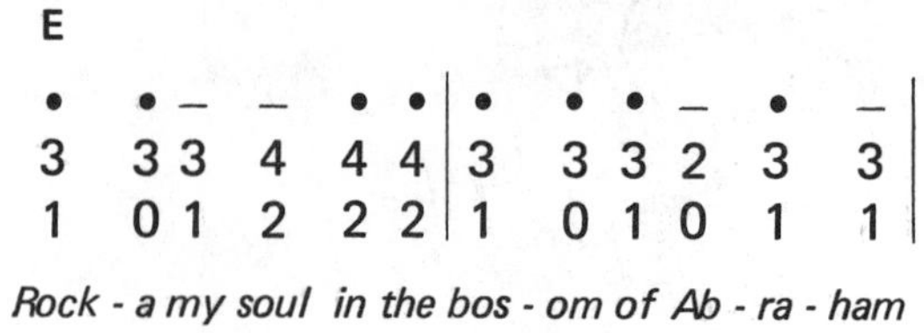

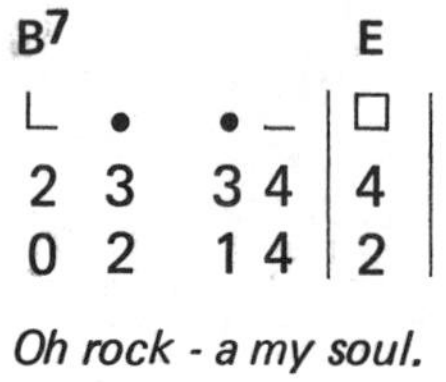

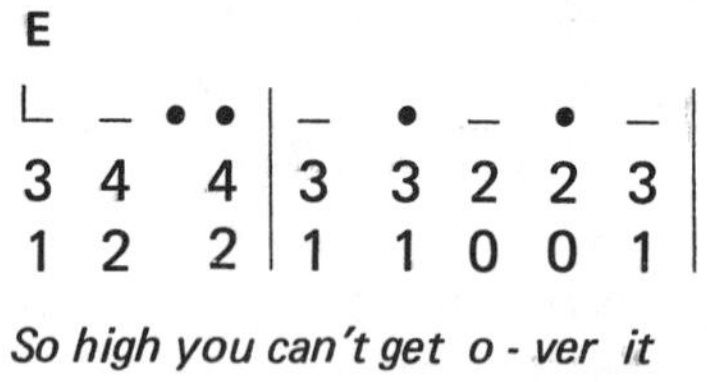

B7

• •_ _ •• | • ••_ • _

3 33 4 44 | 3 332 2 2

2 12 4 44 | 2 222 0 0

Rock - a my soul in the bos - om of Ab - ra - ham

E

• •_ _ •• | • ••_ • _

3 33 4 44 | 3 332 3 3

1 01 2 22 | 1 010 1 1

Rock - a my soul in the bos - om of Ab - ra - ham

B7 E

L • •_ | □ |

2 3 34 | 4 |

0 2 14 | 2 |

Oh rock - a my soul.

E

L _ •• | _ • _ • _ |

3 4 4 | 3 3 2 2 3 |

1 2 2 | 1 1 0 0 1 |

So high you can't get o - ver it

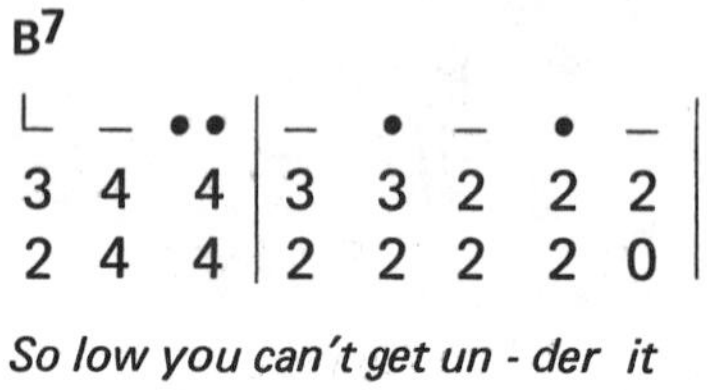

B7

L _ •• | _ • _ • _ |

3 4 4 | 3 3 2 2 2 |

2 4 4 | 2 2 2 2 0 |

So low you can't get un - der it

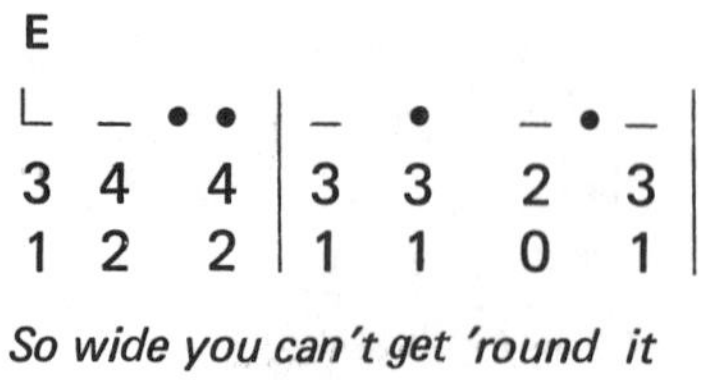

E

L _ •• | _ • _•_ |

3 4 4 | 3 3 2 3 |

1 2 2 | 1 1 0 1 |

So wide you can't get 'round it

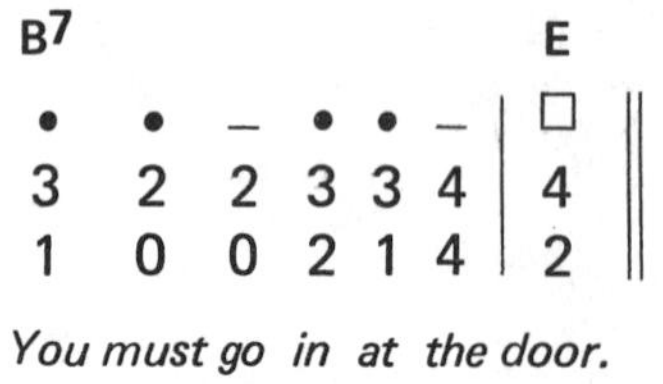

B7 E

• • _ •• _ | □ ||

3 2 2 334 | 4 ||

1 0 0 214 | 2 ||

You must go in at the door.

E

Rocka my soul in the bosom of Abraham

B7

Rocka my soul in the bosom of Abraham

E

Rocka my soul in the bosom of Abraham

B7 **E**

Oh rocka my soul.

E

So high, you can't get over it

B7

So low, you can't get under it

E

So wide, you can't get 'round it

B7 **E**

You must go in at the door.

Repeat the following line.

B7 **E**

Oh rocka my soul.

Don't forget, the strum mark shows you where to play the bass for the Bnj B. The pattern starts there and ends before the next strum mark. It's *Sooo* ea-sy.

At this point, we know the three main chords, the I, IV, and V^7 chords, in the keys of D, G, and A. Now we're ready to add the three main chords in the key of E.

Changing between E and A

You already know how to change between the E and B^7, which are the I and V^7 chords in the key of E. Let's practice changing between E and A. It's not very difficult. In the change from the E chord to the A chord, slide your second and third fingers two strings over in the second fret, moving in the direction of your knees. Your first finger will easily

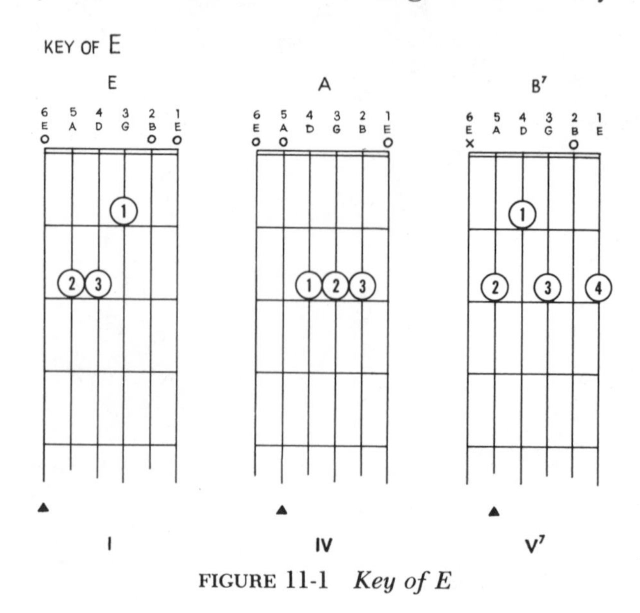

FIGURE 11-1 *Key of E*

find its way to fit in front of them on the fourth string, second fret. Try changing several times, without strumming. Then do it again, strumming across the strings for each chord.

The reason for doing it without strumming at first is to prevent you from being distracted by sounds when you are concentrating on your finger moves.

Changing between A and E

It's easier to slide down than to slide up. So it's going to be a little more awkward to slide the second and third fingers two strings over, moving in the direction of your chin. A better way to change from A to E would be to move your first finger over to the third string, first fret, and then to move your second and third fingers to the fourth and fifth strings, second fret.

Eventually, at the same time that your first finger is moving over, your second and third fingers will move also.

Try out these chord changes with the Bnj B. Then we'll perform the next song, "Worried Man Blues," using the Bnj B as an accompaniment.

WORRIED MAN BLUES

Adapted and arranged with additional words by R.T. Jacobs

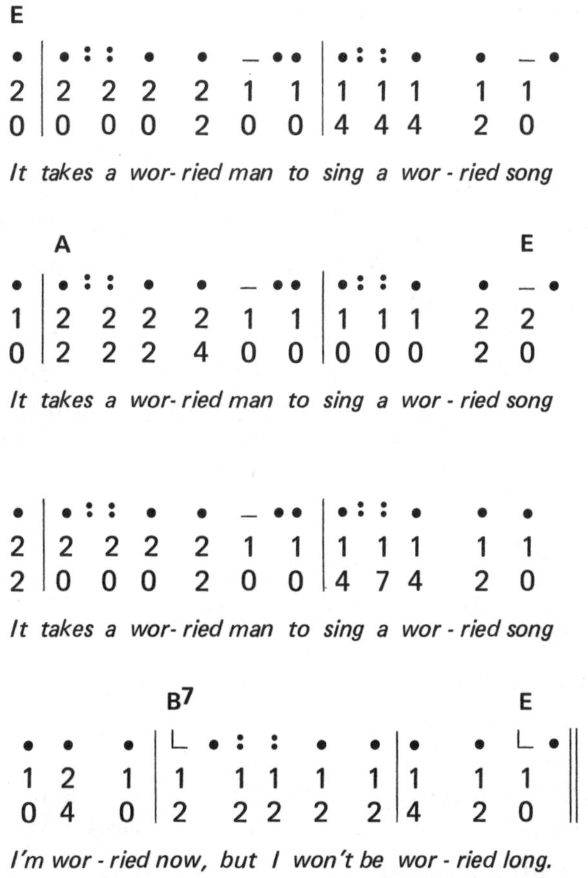

```
E
•  | •  :  :  •  •  _  •  • | •  :  :  •  •  _  •
2  | 2  2  2  2  1  1 | 1  1  1  1  1
0  | 0  0  0  2  0  0 | 4  4  4  2  0
It takes a wor- ried man to sing a wor - ried song

   A                                      E
•  | •  :  :  •  •  _  •  • | •  :  :  •  •  _  •
1  | 2  2  2  2  1  1 | 1  1  1  2  2
0  | 2  2  2  4  0  0 | 0  0  0  2  0
It takes a wor- ried man to sing a wor - ried song

•  | •  :  :  •  •  _  •  • | •  :  :  •  •  •
2  | 2  2  2  2  1  1 | 1  1  1  1  1
2  | 0  0  0  2  0  0 | 4  7  4  2  0
It takes a wor- ried man to sing a wor - ried song

            B7                        E
•  •  •  | L  •  :  :  •  • | •  •  L  • ||
1  2  1  | 1  1  1  1  1 | 1  1  1 ||
0  4  0  | 2  2  2  2  2 | 4  2  0 ||
I'm wor - ried now, but I won't be wor - ried long.
```

E

It takes a worried man/to sing a worried song /

A E

It takes a worried man/to sing a worried song /

It takes a worried man/to sing a worried song

B7 E

I'm worried now/but I won't be worried long. /

2 *I went across the river and I lay down to sleep*
I went across the river and I lay down to sleep
I went across the river and I lay down to sleep
When I awoke, there were shackles on my feet.

3 *Twenty nine links of chain around my feet*
Twenty nine links of chain around my feet
Twenty nine links of chain around my feet
And on each link, an initial of my name.

4 *I asked the judge, what might be my fine*
I asked the judge, what might be my fine
I asked the judge, what might be my fine
"Twenty one years on the R. C. Mountain line."

5 *And now I'm on a chain gang, hammering in the blues*
And now I'm on a chain gang, hammering in the blues
And now I'm on a chain gang, hammering in the blues
Twenty one years, but it feels like ninety nine.

6 *I'm dreaming of the train that hurries down that line*
I'm dreaming of the train that hurries down that line
I'm dreaming of the train that hurries down that line
And takes me home for the very last time.

Repeat first verse

Hammering in the Blues

When you repeat the first verse and come to the last line, here's something you might like to try. After you've sung "I'm worried now . . ." start slowing up. When you get to the last word, "long," each time you do the second step of the Bnj B (fingers down-first finger up), lift your left-hand first finger up. That's the one on the third string, first fret. When you brush the bass to start the pattern again, hammer your first finger down again, very firmly. Play the Bnj B pattern this way, three or four times:

1. Brush the bass with your right hand thumb.
2. While doing the 'fingers-down–first-finger-up,' lift off your left-hand first finger.
3. Hammer it down immediately, in time to brush the bass as you start the pattern again.

If you don't hammer your first finger down very firmly, you won't hear that nice, bluesy sound. Do you wonder why you should be bothering to hammer your first finger down on the third string, when you're only brushing the bass? You're not even strumming across the other strings, at that moment. Here's the reason: When you lifted your left-hand first finger off that string, you lowered the note on the string. That lowered note was what you heard as you strummed the second step of the Bnj B (the 'fingers down–first finger up' movement). When you hammered your first finger down again, you raised the note. You remember when you were exploring the sounds of your guitar, the open string sounds were lower than the fingered string sounds. When you lift your finger, you've got an open string. When you hammer down, you're fingering that string. So even though you're not strumming across the strings at the moment you're hammering down with your first finger, hitting or hammering the third string produces a sound which raises the note on that string. At the same moment that you're brushing the bass, the hammer is giving you the raised note sound. The bluesy effect comes from lowering and raising certain notes. Hammering down on a string is one of the ways to do it.

Warming Up. If you're getting absolutely no sound when your first finger hammers down on the string, make sure you're not hammering down too quickly. That'll cut off the sound. If there's no sound, do the following warm-up exercise.

While you're on the E chord, practice raising your first finger up and hammering it firmly down again, over and over. A good way to help you learn to hammer down hard enough is to think of someone you're mad at. Eventually your first finger will go up and down naturally; you won't even have to think about it. Then you'll be hammering in the blues on the Bnj B strum.

THE G♯m CHORD

This is your very first minor chord. The difference between a major chord(which is what all your chords have been up to now) and a minor chord of the same letter name, is this: the minor chord has one note lowered(the third), which gives it a lovely, haunting quality. If a chord is a major chord, it is referred to simply by letter name; a minor chord has a small "m" after the letter name.

In the next couple of songs, we'll use a simplified version of the G♯m chord. (There are more ways than one to play a chord; in fact, there are several.) Your thumb glides across the G♯m chord from the fourth string to the second string and *stops short of the first string* because it's not part of the G♯m chord. In this version, there isn't a primary bass on the lowest sounding string as there has been on all the

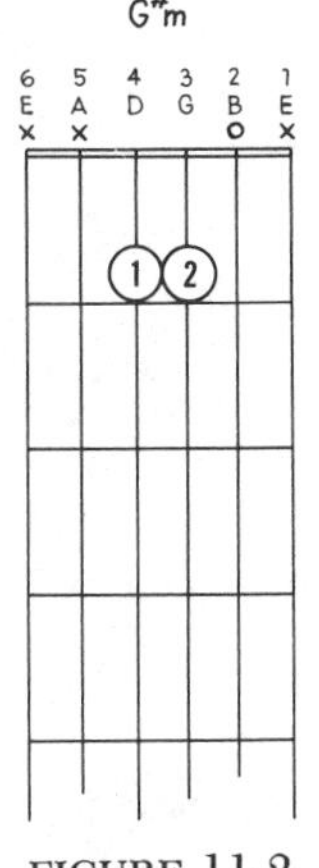

FIGURE 11-2
G sharp minor (G♯ m) chord

chords you've learned so far. The G♯m chord with a primary bass is too difficult for you to finger now.

Changing from A to G♯m

Switching from the A to the G♯m, all you've got to do is slide your first and second fingers from the second fret to the first fret, staying on the same strings; your third finger lifts up. To return to the A from the G♯m, slide your first and second fingers back to the second fret on the same strings and add your third finger to the second string.

Changing from B^7 to G♯m

This change should be easy for you, too. Just move your second finger to the first fret, right behind your first finger, and lift your other fingers off.

SLIDE-AND-GLIDE STRUM

On the next couple of songs, you're going to have a lot of freedom in the strumming, because they're played "rubato," or without strict beats or timing. The slide-and-glide strum works nicely this way. It's simple. All you do is start with the bass string of each chord and slide or glide across each string. When you sing the first three words of "The Water is Wide," play the numbers with it and then start the slide-and-glide strum with the E chord on the word "wide." After that, every time you change chords, start the slide-and-glide again. If you feel like sliding and gliding more than once between some chords, do it. Play the song slowly, and freely.

Be Comfortable. This song might be in a higher-than-comfortable range for some people's voices. In that case, you can lower your starting pitch by beginning the song on the fifth string, instead of the second string as the Numbers Game shows you. Continue the song in this lower range:

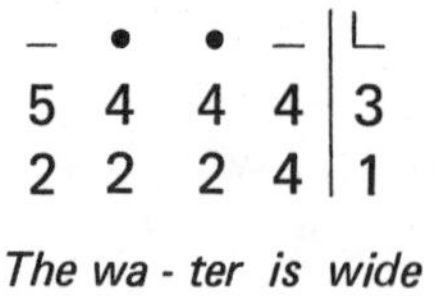

```
—  •  •  — | L
5  4  4  4 | 3
2  2  2  4 | 1
The wa - ter is wide
```

THE WATER IS WIDE

Arranged and adapted by R.T. Jacobs (Based on an English folk song)

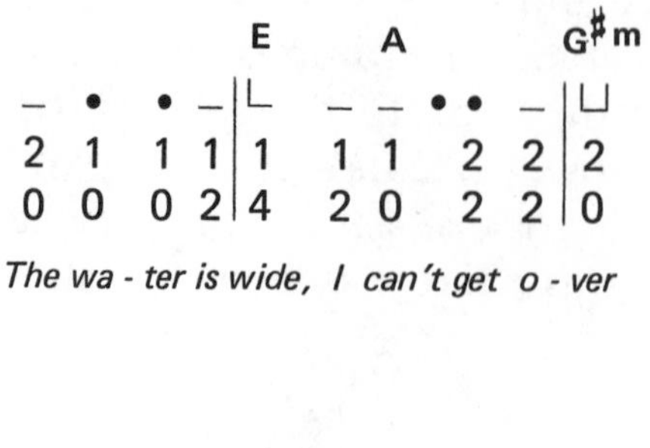

```
               E       A           G♯m
—  •  •  — | L     —  —  •  •  — | ⊔
2  1  1  1 | 1     1  1  2  2  2 | 2
0  0  0  2 | 4     2  0  2  2    | 0
The wa - ter is wide,  I can't get o - ver
```

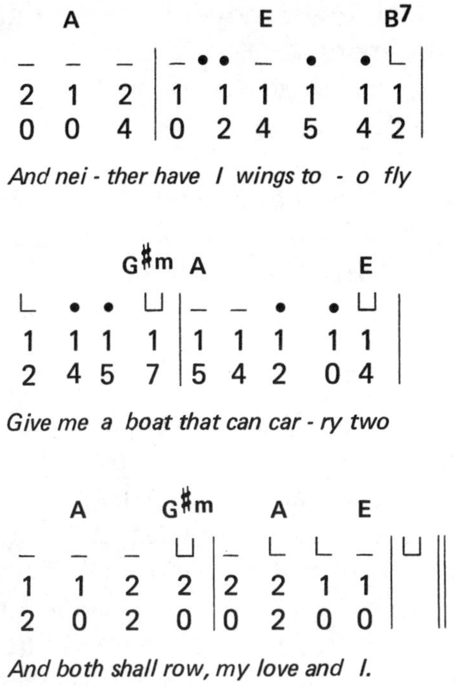

A E B7

– – – | – • • – • • └ |

2 1 2 | 1 1 1 1 1 1 |

0 0 4 | 0 2 4 5 4 2 |

And nei - ther have I wings to - o fly

G♯m A E

└ • • ⊔ | – – • • ⊔ |

1 1 1 1 | 1 1 1 1 1 |

2 4 5 7 | 5 4 2 0 4 |

Give me a boat that can car - ry two

A G♯m A E

– – – ⊔ | – └ └ – | ⊔ ||

1 1 2 2 | 2 2 1 1 | ||

2 0 2 0 | 0 2 0 0 | ||

And both shall row, my love and I.

E A G♯m
The water is wide, I can't get over
A E B7
And neither have I wings to fly
G♯m A E
Give me a boat that can carry two
A G♯m A E
And both shall row, my love and I.

2 *Oh love is tender and seems so fine*
Bright as a star when first it is new
But love grows old and then it grows cold
And fades away like summer dew.

3 *Oh if I'd have known the pain love brings*
I'd have locked my heart with a golden key
And tied it up with silver chains
And never know how love could be.

4 *Oh love it is a painful thing*
Like flowers trampled all in vain
But flowers grow once more each spring
And so my love can grow again.

Remember to stretch and squeeze in longer or shorter lines of other verses in order to fit the lines to the tune. That could mean squeezing two or more words in on one set of numbers, or stretching one word for two or more sets of numbers.

Changing from E to G♯m In this chord change, your first finger moves from the third string, first fret, to the fourth string, first fret. Your second finger goes right behind it, to the third string, first fret. Of course, you must lift up your third finger.

Changing from G♯m to B⁷ This change is just as easy as the change from B⁷ to G♯m. Again, your first finger doesn't move. Your second, third, and fourth fingers go to the second fret, on every other string: the fifth, third, and first strings. Now you're playing a B⁷ chord.

Changing from A to B⁷ This change is less common than the changes from E to B⁷ or even from E to A. Did you notice that most of your songs usually contain changes from V⁷ to I chords?

When you're changing from A to B⁷, slide your first finger over from the fourth string, second fret, to the fourth string, first fret. Then your second finger moves along the second fret from the third string to the fifth string. Your third finger moves from the second string to the third string, in the second fret. Add your fourth finger to the first string, second fret.

All this new instruction, plus one new, easy chord, the AM⁷ (A major seventh), are to prepare you to play the next song, "Wandering."

Changing from E to AM⁷ to A The change from E to AM⁷ couldn't be easier. Your first finger doesn't move. Your second finger goes from the fifth string to the fourth string in the second fret, and at the same time, your third finger moves from that fourth string to the second string in the same fret.

In changing from AM⁷ to A, the third finger doesn't move. The second finger goes from the fourth string to the third string in the second fret. The first finger lines up in front of them, on the fourth string.

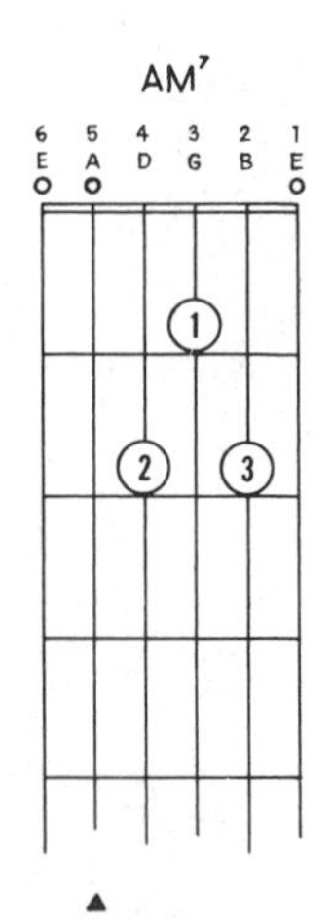

FIGURE 11-3
A major seventh (AM⁷) chord

Rubato, Again. Since the next song is rubato also, play it the way you feel it. The strum marks are only a loose guide. You could use the Easy Strum in places where there are quick chord changes and then try sliding and gliding. Make sure you don't slide and glide down to the first string on the G♯m.

WANDERING

Arranged and adapted with new words by R.T. Jacobs (Based on a traditional song)

```
E                          G#m
— | —  —   — — | —  L  | —  —   —  — | — L
2 | 1  1   1 1 | 1  1 R| 1  2   2  2 | 2 2 R |
0 | 0  0   0 0 | 0  0  | 0  4   4  4 | 4 4   |
```

My fa - ther's an en - gi - neer, my moth - er drives a cab

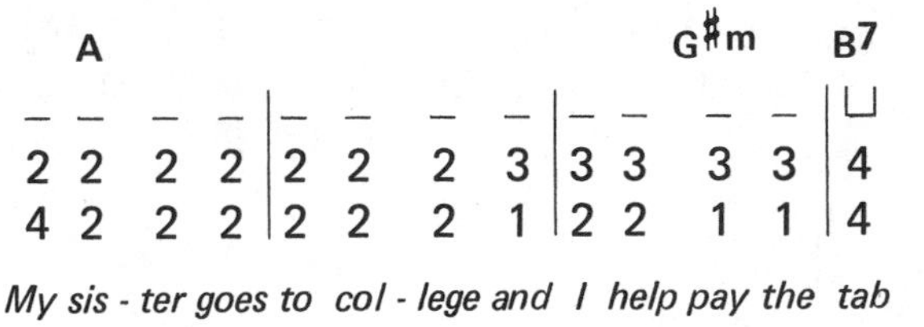

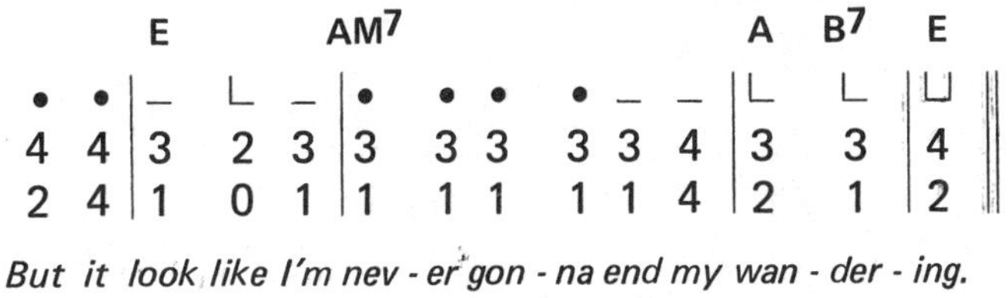

```
A                                    G#m     B7
— —  — — | — —   — — | — —   — — | ⊔
2 2  2 2 | 2 2   2 3 | 3 3   3 3 | 4
4 2  2 2 | 2 2   2 1 | 2 2   1 1 | 4
```

My sis - ter goes to col - lege and I help pay the tab

```
      E        AM7                       A    B7   E
• • | —  L  — | •   • •   • — — | L    L  | ⊔ ||
4 4 | 3  2  3 | 3   3 3   3 3 4 | 3    3  | 4 ||
2 4 | 1  0  1 | 1   1 1   1 1 4 | 2    1  | 2 ||
```

But it look like I'm nev - er gon - na end my wan - der - ing.

```
E                   G#m
```
My father's an engineer, my mother drives a cab
```
A                          G#m   B7
```
My sister goes to college and I help pay the tab
```
E              AM7                  A B7 E
```
But it looks like I'm never gonna end my wandering.

2 *They all want me home, I've often heard it said*
They'd like for me to have a roof above my curly head
But it looks like I'm never gonna end my wandering.

3 *I've wandered long and I've wandered late*
Never ever knowing what's to be my fate
But it looks like I'm never gonna end my wandering.

4 *Snakes in the ocean, eels in the sea*
Who would ever dare to make a fool outa me
But it looks like I'm never gonna end my wandering.

5 *Heaven's up above and hell's down below*
No one's ever sure where they're gonna go
But it looks like I'm never gonna end my wandering.

FOLK-ROCK STRUM

I call this the folk-rock strum because it sounds a lot like the background music you hear in today's popular songs. It's very easy and can be used as a basic strum to lots of songs requiring a good strong beat. The action is down-down-up, down with the thumb and up with the first finger. The thumb brushes all the way across the strings, starting from the bass string of whatever chord you're on, just as you do in the Easy Strum. The second step is really two actions: down with the thumb again (same as in the first step) and then brush up with the first finger. However, the two actions of the second step are performed in the same time it takes to do the first step. The rhythm is the same as for the Banjo Bass strum. Visually, it looks like this: down-down-up — – –. We're going to do this strum in the next song, "Careless Love."

CARELESS LOVE

Adapted and arranged with new words by R.T. Jacobs (Based on a traditional song)

```
E              B7     E
⊔  _ | _  _  _    _ | □ | □ |
3  3 | 3  4  4    4 | 4 |   |
1  2 | 1  2  1    4 | 2 |   |
```

Love, oh love oh care - less love

```
       B7
⊔  _ | _  _  _    _ | □ | □ |
3  3 | 2  2  2    2 | 4 |   |
1  2 | 0  0  2    0 | 4 |   |
```

Love, oh love oh care - less love

```
E      E7   A
⊔  _ | L  L | L    L | □ ||
3  3 | 2  2 | 2    3 | 4 ||
1  2 | 0  1 | 2    2 | 2 ||
```

Love, oh love oh care - less love

```
E                B7   E
⊔    _ | _  _  _  _ | □ | □ ||
3    3 | 3  4  4  4 | 4 |   ||
1    2 | 1  2  1  4 | 2 |   ||
```

Look what love has done to me.

```
E            B7    E
Love, oh love oh careless love / /
        B7
Love, oh love oh careless love / /
E      E7    A
Love, oh love oh careless love
E               B7    E
Look what love has done to me. / /
```

2 *I wrote a letter to you dear*
I wrote each word down with a tear
I waited long for your reply
I've waited now almost a year.

3 *Last night I dreamed of you again*
I dreamed o how it used to be
When we first loved so long ago
You loved me long and tenderly.

4 *Why did I once believe in love*
Why did I once believe in you
Believe the things you said were true
You left me sad and lonely too.

Repeat first verse

The Name of the Game. This ends the first section of the book. Let's stop and take inventory of what you've learned so far. You know how to play the Numbers Game, how to play chords in four different keys, and you know lots of songs to sing them with. You've learned some strumming styles and techniques and something about rhythm. You've learned how to tune your guitar; if you've been practicing your tuning all along, you should be getting better at it. Your ear has begun to really hear, in spite of your doubts. More than all of that, I hope you've learned how to relax and to enjoy yourself with the guitar. If you've practiced sufficiently and kept reasonably close to the progression of learning outlined in this book (that means *no skipping around*), then I'm sure you have.

The idea behind any game is to reach a goal. That goal, whatever it is, satisfies something in you. I hope the *E-Z Numbers Game* helped you experience some fulfillment by realizing a dream that you may have thought impossible: You're playing the guitar!

2
PLAYING THE NOTES

Up to Now. If you never went any further than the first section of this book, where would you be with your guitar? You'd know about a dozen chords and as many strums. You could use them to accompany lots of songs inside of, and many outside of, this book. You could accompany other people on your guitar, if they sang songs you knew. You might even try to find songs elsewhere that you're familiar with and you could sing those songs with any of the chords in the four keys that you know. *But* if you weren't familiar with the tunes of the songs, you couldn't do that.

If you've decided that all you want to know about the guitar is some tunes, some chords to accompany the songs you sing, and a few strums, then you're finished. Fine. Nobody knows better than you just what you want and would like to do.

For those of you who'd like to pick countless new songs to play and sing, though, there's one thing you must pick up first: Notes. Without learning how to play notes, you'll only be able to sing and play songs you either know the tune to, or can play the Numbers Game with. (Unless of course, all music everywhere is converted to the Numbers Game.) If you know how to play notes, you can learn to play anything. Actually, you've been playing notes all along. The Numbers Game is merely a simpler form of musical notation. You're now ready to learn how to read and play notes as they're more commonly written.

NOTATION: WHY BOTHER?

Notation! What's that? Well, a note is a single sound, something you can hear. Notation is written music, something you can see. So, notes are the sounds of music as well as the written musical symbols for those sounds. A note has a particular pitch, which is the high or low quality of its sound. It also lasts for a certain amount of time. If you can read notation and play it on your guitar, you'll be able to play the tunes of any songs you'd like to learn.

If you've set up some barriers in your own mind about not being able to concentrate on what follows, here's a suggestion. Take the time to do your E-Z Relaxation before you start. It may clear away those barriers so you can concentrate more easily.

THE STAFF: A FRAMEWORK

These notes are written on a framework of lines and spaces. The lines and spaces have the same purpose as the markings on your radio dial. The only difference is that with your radio, you turn to a certain number on the dial for a particular station you want to tune into, or hear. In written music, the lines and spaces tell you where certain pitches are that you want to play, or hear. This framework is called a staff. There are five lines on a staff, with four spaces between those lines. Both the lines and the spaces are counted from the bottom to the top of the staff. Music for the guitar (or for any other musical instrument) is written on a staff (see Figure 12-1). That strange-looking curly symbol is called a G clef, or treble clef. (It actually used to be the letter G.) Its presence provides a basis from which the notes on the lines and spaces can be given specific names.

FIGURE 12-1 *G clef*

FIRST STRING NOTES

Notation has tighter guidelines to follow than the Numbers Game. For instance, when you play the notes on the first string, you must use your left hand first finger for the F on the first fret and your left hand third finger for the G on the third fret.

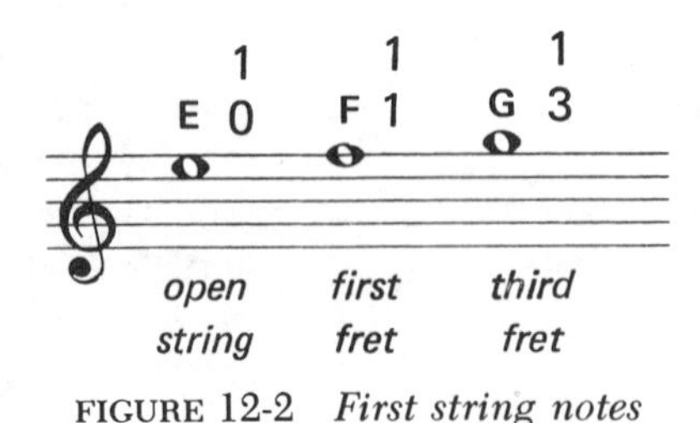

FIGURE 12-2 *First string notes*

Never lift your fingers too far from the fingerboard, otherwise it will be hard to control them. Also, you should do something you haven't done before with your right hand when it plucks the strings your left hand is fingering: alternate the first and second fingers of your *right* hand. It doesn't matter whether you start off with your first or second finger, as long as you alternate them. If you started off with your right-hand first finger when you played the E on the open first string, then use your right-hand second finger to pluck the string when your left hand fingers the F note on the first fret. Then, use your right hand first finger again when your left hand fingers the G note on the third fret. Alternating the fingers creates a connected rather than a separated sound. You brush your right-hand first or second finger tip across the first string and rest it against the second string (the next lower string). Remember our discussion about high and low in space and sound, in part 1 (see page 30)? When we speak of the second string here as being lower, we're speaking of sound.

If you start off with your right-hand second finger for the E note on the open first string, use your first finger for the F and your second finger again for the G. Play these notes and memorize their names, so that you can recognize them instantly by seeing what lines and spaces they're on. This is learning how to read music.

RHYTHM: THE LONG AND SHORT OF IT

When we played the Numbers Game, we had rhythm marks that indicated when to hold a number longer or to play it more quickly. It gave you an idea of the rhythm, but it isn't quite as accurate as notes are. That's because every note will tell you exactly how long to hold it by the way it looks. For instance:

- The whole note (Figure 12-3a) is held for four counts, like your four-hum rhythm mark,□.
- The half note (Figure 12-3b) is held for two counts, like the two-hum rhythm mark,└.
- The quarter note (Figure 12-3c) is held for one count, like the one-hum rhythm mark,–.
- The eighth note (Figure 12-3d) gets one half count, like the quick count rhythm mark,•.
- The sixteenth note (Figure 12-3e) gets one quarter count, like the very quick count rhythm mark,**:**.

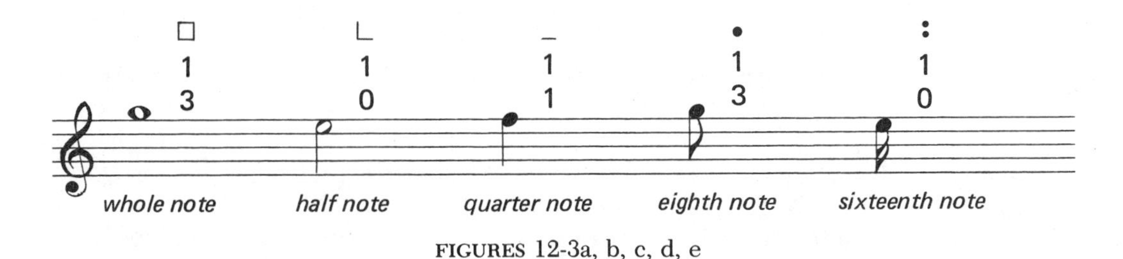

FIGURES 12-3a, b, c, d, e

Note Power

You've come a long way up to now, but you sure can go a lot further if you understand *Note Power* (see Figure 12-4). The Note Power chart shows that you hold one whole

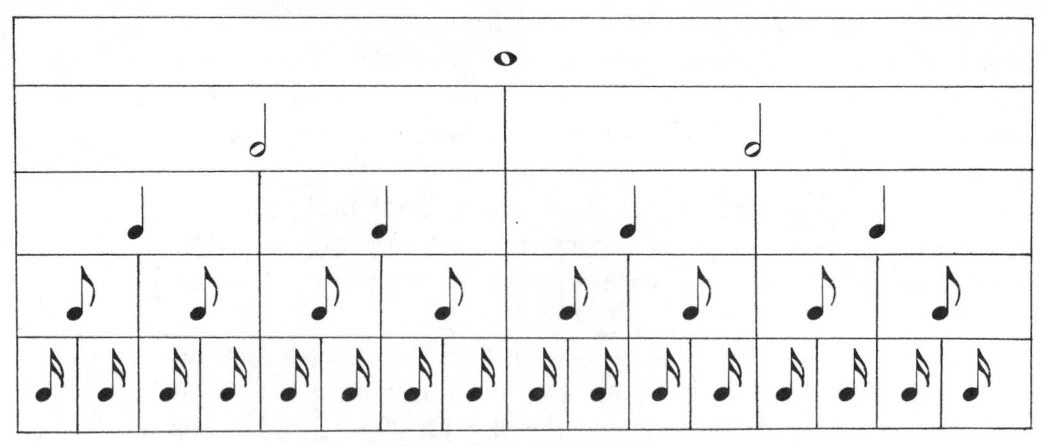

FIGURE 12-4 *Note Power*

note for the same space of time as you hold two half notes, or four quarter notes, or eight eighth notes, or sixteen sixteenth notes. If you have one measure with one whole note, another measure with two half notes, and another measure with four quarter notes, you must give equal time to each one of these measures. For instance, it shouldn't take you any longer to play the measure with four quarter notes than it does to play the measure with one whole note. If you hold a quarter note for less time than a whole note, how many quarter notes do you play in the same space of time as one whole note? The answer is four.

Just as notes represent the duration of sound, rests represent the duration of silence.

- A whole rest (Figure 12-5a) equals four counts of silence.
- A half rest (Figure 12-5b) equals two counts of silence.
- A quarter rest (Figure 12-5c) equals one count of silence.
- An eighth rest (Figure 12-5d) equals a half of a count of silence.
- A sixteenth rest equals a quarter of a count of silence.

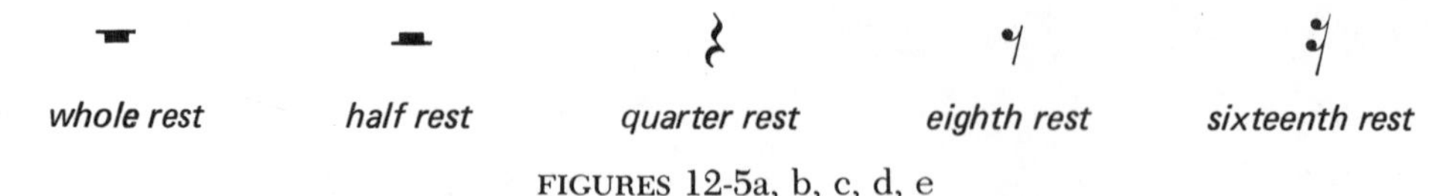

FIGURES 12-5a, b, c, d, e

Hold counts of silence for rests for the same length of time as you play the equivalent notes. It's accepted in musical language to write a whole rest if four counts of silence are needed. You won't see two half rests together, or four quarter rests. However, hold the half rest for half the count of silence that you hold the whole rest.

Did you notice something missing? It wasn't in Note Power and it wasn't included in the rests. There were no notes or rests that had three counts. That's because that involves dotted rhythms, which we'll get to later.

What's the Time?

When music is written on a staff, there's something at the beginning of the musical piece that's called a time signature (see Figures 12-6a, b, and c). There are also other time signatures, but that doesn't concern us now.

The lower number tells us that a quarter note gets one beat, or a count of one. The upper number tells us that there are four beats, three beats, or two beats to a measure. What's a measure? It's a group of beats set off by bar lines. In fact, measures are also referred to as bars. (You had them in your Numbers Game.)

The right timing is very important. If you're timing is wrong, it just won't sound like the right tune, even if you're playing the right notes.

Go back and look at the first string notes again. Make sure you've memorized their names and places (lines and spaces). Then, play the first string notes in the measures. Notice the double bar lines at the end. You'll always see that at the end of a piece of music. Don't forget to alternate the first and second fingers of your right hand, allowing them to come to rest on the string below. Remember not to lift your left-hand fingers too far away from the strings. In fact, whenever you need to play an F note, a G note, and then an F note again, you can leave your left-hand first finger down on the F note while you put your left-hand third finger down for the G note. When you pluck the string with your right hand for the G note, that's all you'll hear. You won't hear the F note that your first finger is still covering because you've shortened the string. Anything that you touch down the neck from the place where you're fingering won't be heard. Practice playing those F and G notes.

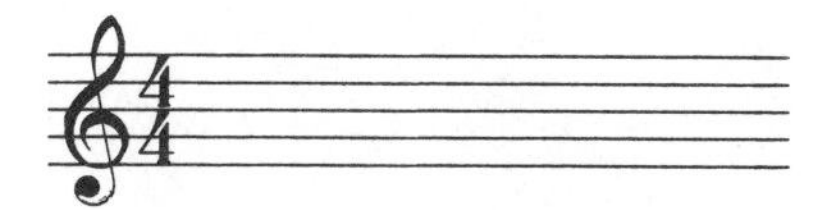

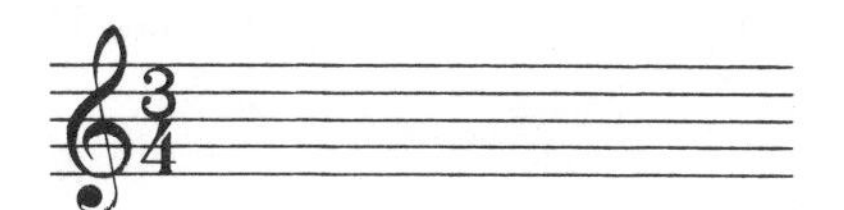

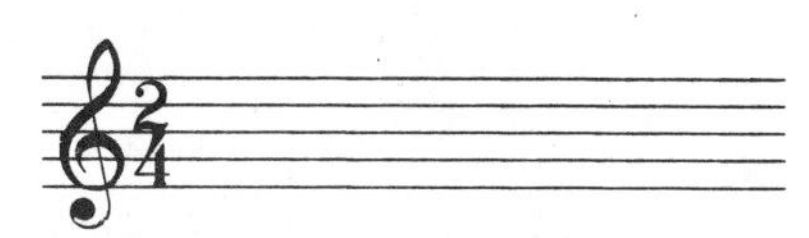

FIGS. 12-6a, b, c *Time signatures*

About Other Games. How'd you do? Lots of people get scared at the sight of, or even the idea of notes. They're sure it's impossible for them to read, much less, play those notes. Yet, many of these same people can learn the most complicated rules for playing all kinds of games of skill. If

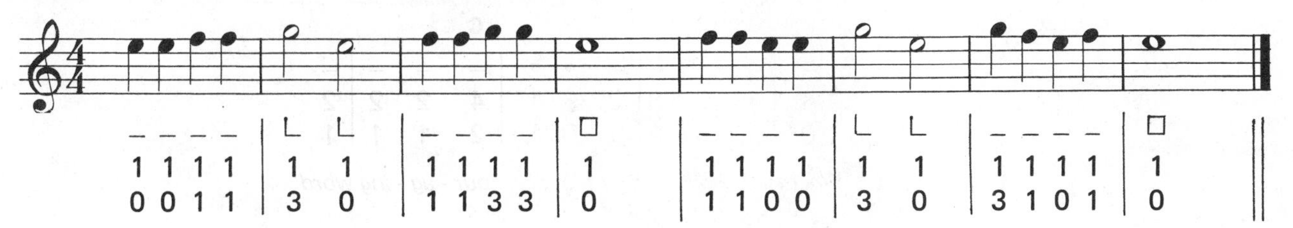

FIGURE 12-7 *Notes to practice on the first string*

you're intimidated by notes, you've got to turn your thinking around. Think of it as a game with certain rules, which you've got to learn in order to play.

Meanwhile, here's a song to review some chords with, "Home on the Range." Why don't you try using the Double bass-down strum on the verses and the B-down-down, on the chorus? Don't forget they're both waltz strums, and each pattern has three steps.

Changing from G to A^7 to D^7

If you're using your first, second, and third fingers on the G chord, going from G to A^7, move your first finger from the fifth string to the fourth string, in the second fret. Your second finger goes from the sixth string, third fret, to the second string, second fret.

Going from the A^7 to the D^7, move your first finger from the fourth string, second fret, to the second string, first fret. Your second finger goes from the second string to the third string, in the second fret. Put your third finger on the first string, second fret.

If you finger the G chord with your second, third, and fourth fingers, when going to the A^7 chord, put your first finger on the fourth string, second fret. Move your second finger from the fifth to the second string, in the second fret. Lift off your other fingers. Change from A^7 to D^7 as you would if you played the G with your first three fingers.

HOME ON THE RANGE

Adapted and arranged by R.T. Jacobs (Based on a traditional cowboy song)

	G		C	
—	— — —	L • •	— — —	L
4	4 3 3	2 3 4	4 2 2	2
0	0 0 2	0 0 4	2 1 1	1

Oh give me a home where the buf - fa - lo roam

	G	A^7	D^7	
• •	— •• —	— — —	⊔	L
2 2	2 3 3	3 4 3	3	
0 1	3 0 0	0 4 0	2	

Where the deer and the an - te - lope play

	G		C	
—	— — —	L • •	— — —	L
4	4 3 3	2 3 4	4 2 2	2
0	0 0 2	0 0 4	2 1 1	1

Where sel - dom is heard a dis - cour - ag - ing word

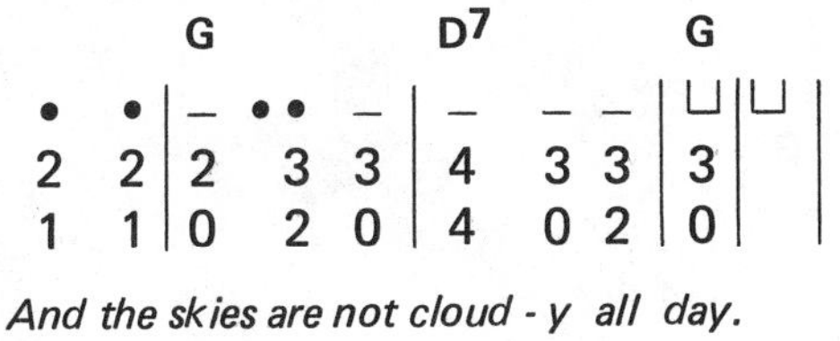

G D7 G

2 2 | 2 3 3 | 4 3 3 | 3 | |
1 1 | 0 2 0 | 4 0 2 | 0 | |

And the skies are not cloud - y all day.

Chorus

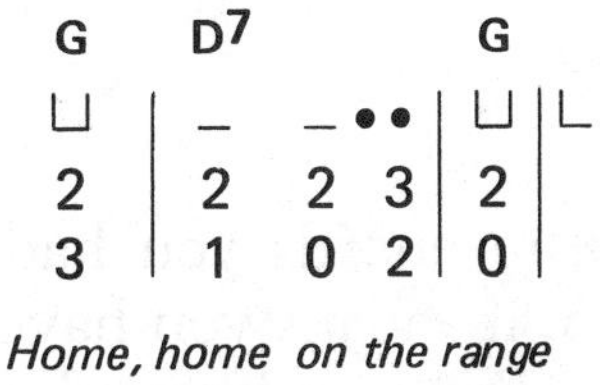

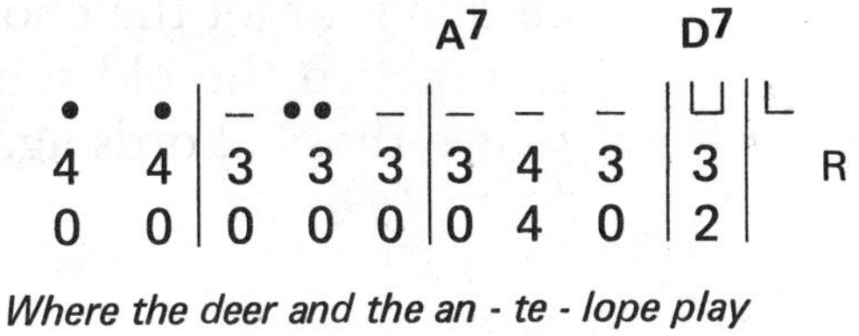

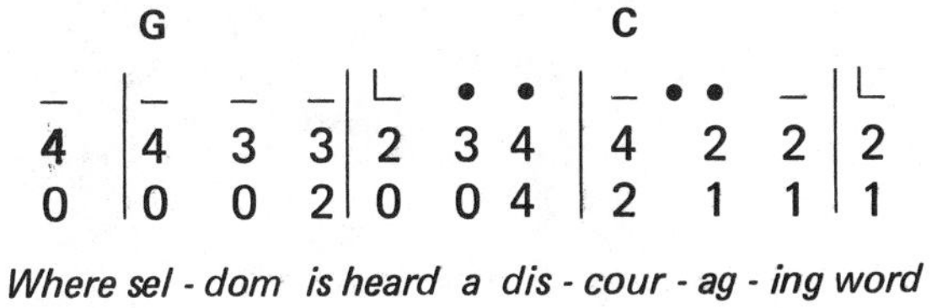

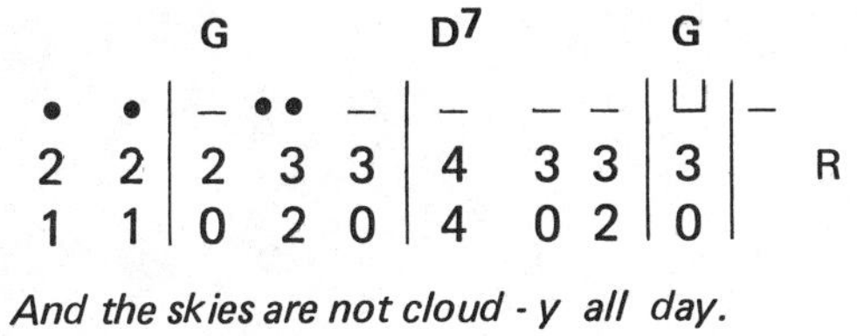

G D7 G

2 | 2 2 3 | 2 |
3 | 1 0 2 | 0 |

Home, home on the range

A7 D7

4 4 | 3 3 3 | 3 4 3 | 3 | R
0 0 | 0 0 0 | 0 4 0 | 2 |

Where the deer and the an - te - lope play

G C

4 | 4 3 3 | 2 3 4 | 4 2 2 | 2
0 | 0 0 2 | 0 0 4 | 2 1 1 | 1

Where sel - dom is heard a dis - cour - ag - ing word

G D7 G

2 2 | 2 3 3 | 4 3 3 | 3 | R
1 1 | 0 2 0 | 4 0 2 | 0 |

And the skies are not cloud - y all day.

G C
Oh give me a home where the buffalo roam
G A7 D7
Where the deer and the antelope play /
G C
Where seldom is heard a discouraging word
G D7 G
And the skies are not cloudy all day. /

Chorus

G D7 G
Home, home on the range /
A7 D7
Where the deer and the antelope play /

G C

Where seldom is heard a discouraging word

G D7 G

And the skies are not cloudy all day. /

2 *Where the air is so pure and the land is so sure*
Where the people are friendly and free
Oh I would not exchange my home on the range
For all of the cities I see.

Chorus

Confess. Did you forget some of the chords you had to use with "Home on the Range"? If so, it means you haven't bothered to go over the earlier songs, after you learned new songs and chords. Make sure that you don't forget the chords by going back from time to time to practice the old songs. You never know when you've got to use those chords again.

thirteen

SECOND STRING NOTES

Don't feel foolish if you're counting out loud to help keep time on the notes. The most skilled musicians count aloud when they need to. Whatever method you use to keep the timing going is fine.

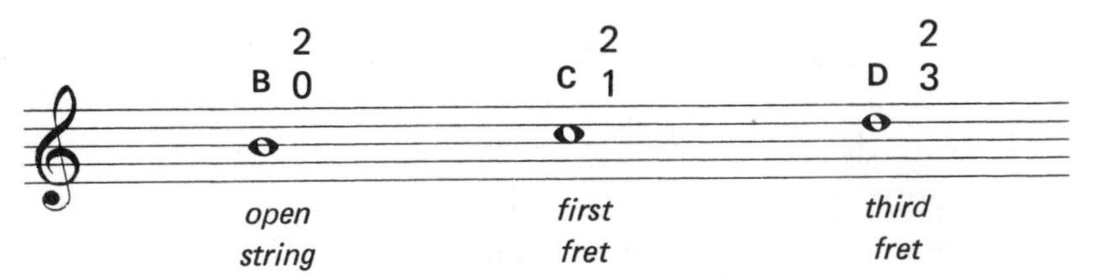

FIGURE 13-1a *Second string notes*

FIGURE 13-1b *Notes to practice on the second string*

Remember, in playing notes, the first finger of the left hand goes in the first fret, the second finger in the second fret and the third finger in the third fret. The first and second finger tips of your right hand alternate in brushing the second string and coming to rest on the string below (the third string). The left-hand fingers remain in the same frets as the notes just played.

Memorize the names of the notes, so that you can recognize them by sight. If you don't undertake this responsibility, you're being foolish. Knowing all the notes is essential to your progress.

First and Second String Notes—All Together Now

Play the tune in Figure 13-2. If your timing is right and you've played the right notes, it may sound familiar. It's a calypso folk song called "Maryann." We'll come back to "Maryann" later on. Now, you've got two strings to play around with.

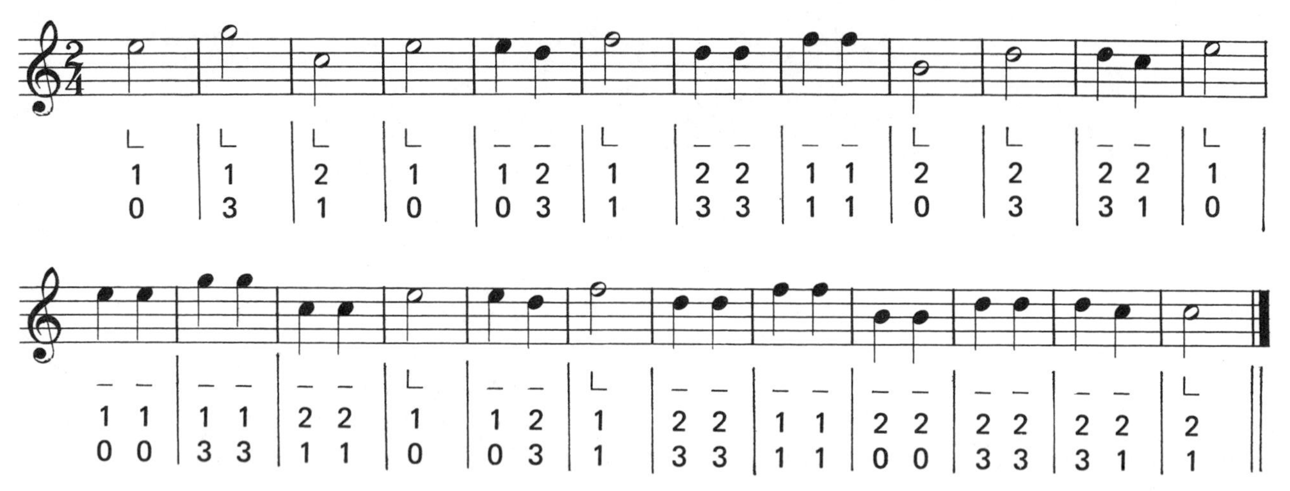

FIGURE 13-2 *First and second string notes*

THE Am CHORD

Here's your third A chord. You started with the A^7 chord, then you went on to the A, and now, you're playing the Am (your second minor chord). Can you guess which string is the bass? All A chords are strummed down from the fifth string bass, or A string. The bass is also called the "root" of the chord. Strum the Am a few times and see how the rest of the chord "grows" from the bass.

Changing from C to Am

This is the easiest change you've had to make so far. The first and second fingers never move and the third finger sneaks behind the second finger onto the third string, second fret. Practice this change a few times. Of course, if you need to change from Am back to C simply reverse the moves.

Changing from Am to G

This change isn't quite as easy as the C to Am change. However, if you've been using the second, third, and fourth fingers for the G chord, you'll find this change somewhat easier. When going from Am to G, move your second finger from the fourth string to the fifth string in the same second fret. At the same time, move your third finger to the sixth string, third fret, and your fourth finger to the first string, in the third fret. Continue to work towards changing all your fingers at the same time.

The next song, "Michael Row the Boat Ashore," has three fast chord changes at the end of the chorus and each verse. It's convenient and practical to go a bit slower when changing from G to D⁷ to G. Do the Bnj B strum with this song. The tune is the same for the chorus and verses.

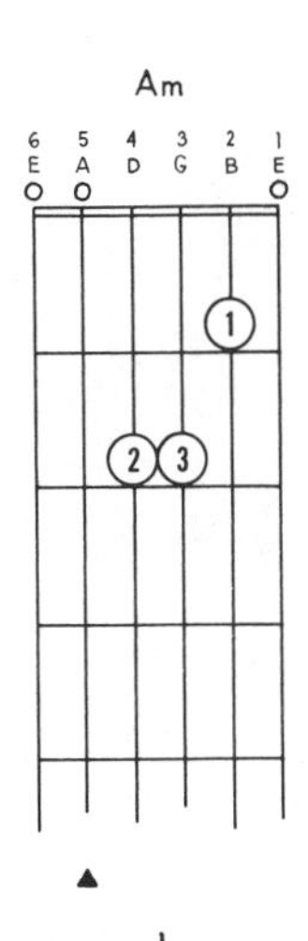

FIGURE 13-3
A minor (Am) chord

MICHAEL ROW THE BOAT ASHORE

Chorus

```
G                                     C   G
—   —  | —  ••  —   —  | L   —   — | □ | L
3   2  | 2   2  2   1  | 2   2   2 | 1 | 2
0   0  | 3   0  3   0  | 3   0   3 | 0 | 3
Mi - chael row  the boat  a - shore hal - le - lu - yah
```

```
                 C       Am          G  D7   G
—   —  | —  ••  —   —  | L   —   — | L   L | L  ||
2   2  | 2   2  2   2  | 3   3   3 | 2   3 | 3  ||
0   3  | 3   0  1   0  | 2   0   2 | 0   2 | 0  ||
Mi - chael row  the boat  a - shore hal - le - lu - u - yah.
```

Chorus

G   C   G
Michael row the boat ashore hallelu / yah
C   Am   G D7 G
Michael row the boat ashore, hallelu - u - yah.

G   C   G
2 *Michael's was a music boat hallelu /yah*
C   Am   G D7 G
Michael's was a music boat hallelu - u /yah.

Chorus

3 *Sister helped to trim the sails, hallelu-yah*
Sister helped to trim the sails, hallelu-u-yah.

Chorus

4 *River Jordan is chilly and cold hallelu-yah*
Chills the body but not the soul hallelu-u-yah.

Chorus

5 *River Jordan is deep and wide hallelu-yah*
Milk and honey on the other side hallelu-u-yah.

Chorus

6 *If you get there before I do, hallelu-yah*
Tell the people I'm coming too, hallelu-u-yah.

Chorus

Having Your Relatives Around. Incidentally, the Am chord is a relative of the C chord. The reason that the two chords are related is because they share two notes in common; of the three notes each chord has, only one of the notes is different. That was easy to see in the change between the C and Am chords because only one finger moved. Experiment occasionally, substituting an Am chord for a C chord, but there's no need to overdo it.

Incidentally, "Michael Row the Boat Ashore" is a good song to sing with those friends of yours who love to harmonize.

Changing from Am to E^7 to Am

On the next song, "House of the Rising Sun," we'll be changing from Am to E^7 to Am. Going from Am to E^7, your first finger moves from the second string to the third string, in the first fret. Your second finger moves from the fourth string to the fifth string, in the second fret. Your third finger lifts off. Switching from E^7 to Am, reverse the moves, putting your third finger down last.

In "House of the Rising Sun," play the numbers from home base chord positions. Use the double bass-down strum pattern (B-B-down) for the accompaniment. Remember, that's a three-step strum, so each bass movement and down movement count for one step of the pattern.

Play the first bass with your thumb wherever you've got a strum mark; often, you'll be thumbing the second bass on the same word, if that word aligns under a two-hum mark. (Each step of the pattern is equal to one hum.) The following example of the first few measures will serve as an illustration:

```
B-B-down B-B-   down B-B- down B-B-  down B-B-down
There i-s a     house in  New Or  -  leans they  call the
```

Try to see if you can play the numbers from home base chord positions. Whenever you change chords, strum the chord instead of playing the numbers below. Of course, play the numbers to hear the tune, first.

HOUSE OF THE RISING SUN

Adapted and arranged by R.T. Jacobs (Based on a traditional song)

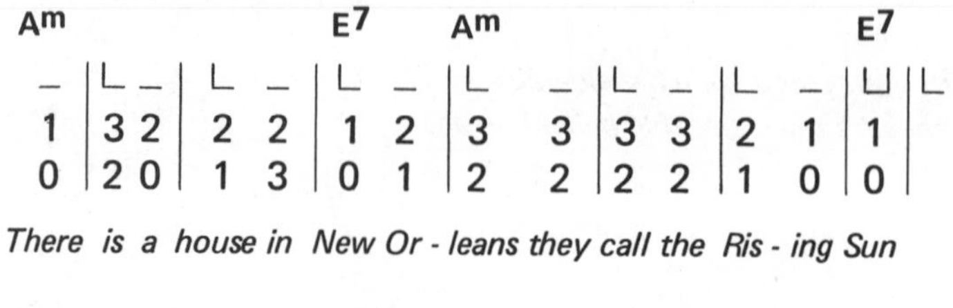

```
Am                      E7       Am                          E7
_  | L  _ | L    _ | L    _ | L      _ | L    _ | L    _ | ⊔ | L
1  | 3  2 | 2    2 | 1    2 | 3      3 | 3    3 | 2    1 | 1 |
0  | 2  0 | 1    3 | 0    1 | 2      2 | 2    2 | 1    0 | 0 |
There is a house in New Or - leans they call the Ris - ing Sun
```

Am E7 Am E7 Am

• • | L _ | L _ | • • _ • • | L _ | L _ | _ _ _ | ⊔ ||
1 1 | 3 3 | 2 2 | 1 1 2 2 2 | 3 3 | 2 2 | 2 2 2 | 3 ||
0 0 | 2 2 | 1 3 | 0 0 0 1 0 | 2 2 | 0 0 | 0 1 0 | 2 ||

It has been the ruin of man - y a po - or girl and me oh Lo - rd was one.

Am E7 Am E7

There is a house in New Orleans, they call the Rising Sun

Am E7 Am E7 Am

It has been the ruin of many a poor girl, and me oh Lord was one.

2 *If I had listened to my dear mom, I wouldn't be here today*
But I was so young and so foolish oh Lord, and so I had my way.

3 *And now I am a drunkard Lord, drink down in New Orleans*
And booze has taken all I had, except these cold, cold beans.

4 *So listen hard you dreaming girls, don't do what I have done*
Please grow and look to find your way, and stay out of that Rising Sun.

Changing from Am to D7

This change will probably be as easy for you as the one from Am to C. Here also, the first finger never leaves the second string, first fret. The second and third fingers simply move over in the same second fret. The second finger transfers from the fourth string to the third string, while the third finger moves from the third string to the first string. Remember, the first finger never moves.

Let's use the folk-rock strum as the accompaniment in the following song:

DEEP BLUE SEA

G C G

L L | L • _ • | L L | □ |
2 2 | 2 3 3 | 3 4 | 4 |
0 1 | 0 2 0 | 0 2 | 0 |

Deep blue sea ba - by, deep blue sea

Am D7

L L | L • _ • | L L | □ |
2 2 | 2 3 3 | 2 2 | 3 |
0 1 | 0 2 0 | 1 0 | 2 |

Deep blue sea ba - by, deep blue sea

G C G

L L | L • _ • | L L | □ |
2 2 | 2 3 3 | 3 4 | 4 |
0 1 | 0 2 0 | 0 2 | 0 |

Deep blue sea ba - by, deep blue sea

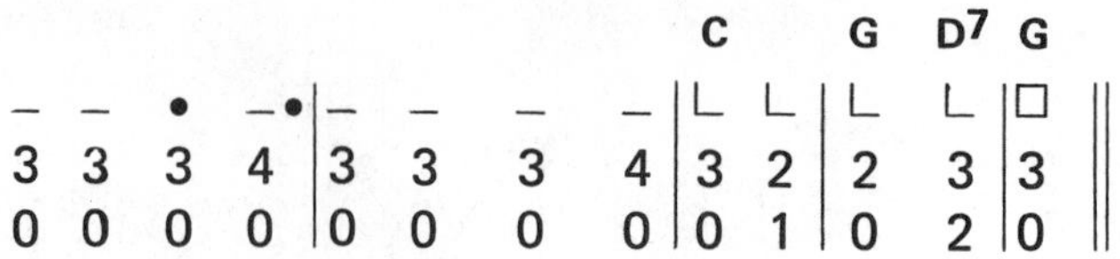

```
                                    C      G   D7  G
 –  –  •  –•| –  –   –   – | L  L | L   L | □ ||
 3  3  3  4 | 3  3   3   4 | 3  2 | 2   3 | 3 ||
 0  0  0  0 | 0  0   0   0 | 0  1 | 0   2 | 0 ||
```

It was Wil - lie what got drown-ded in the deep blue sea.

```
 G                 C       G
Deep blue sea baby, deep blue sea
                  Am      D7
Deep blue sea baby, deep blue sea
 G                 C       G
Deep blue sea baby, deep blue sea
                              C       G    D7 G
It was Willie what got drownded in the deep blue sea.
```

2 *Lower him down with a golden chain*
Lower him down with a golden chain
Lower him down with a golden chain
It was Willie what got drownded in the deep blue sea.

3 *Dig his grave with a silver spade, etc.*

4 *Golden sun bring him back again, etc.*

Repeat first verse

This is a good point at which to go back and review earlier songs and strum techniques to see if you've made reasonably adequate progress and can continue adding new skills. If you're in doubt about your playing, slow down. Practice more than you did before. Eventually, you *will* be playing reasonably well.

THIRD STRING NOTES

Review your first and second string notes. When you're really sure of their names and positioning on the staff, start on the third string notes. The first note you learn on the third string is the G. It's played on the open string and is located on the second line of the staff. That explains how the G clef symbol got its name. Its curly end circles around the G note staff line.

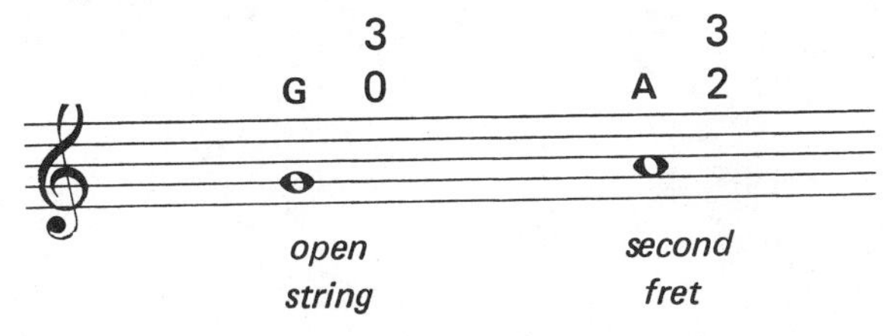

FIGURE 14-1a *Third string notes*

Tied Notes

A curved line that joins two notes of the same pitch means that you should not sound the second note. Hold the first note for its required amount of counts *plus* the count of the tied note. This is similar to holding a set of numbers for its required amount of hums plus the amount indicated by the next rhythm mark without numbers below it. Play the third string notes again; hold the tied A's (in the seventh and eighth measures) and the tied G's (in the last two measures) for four counts each.

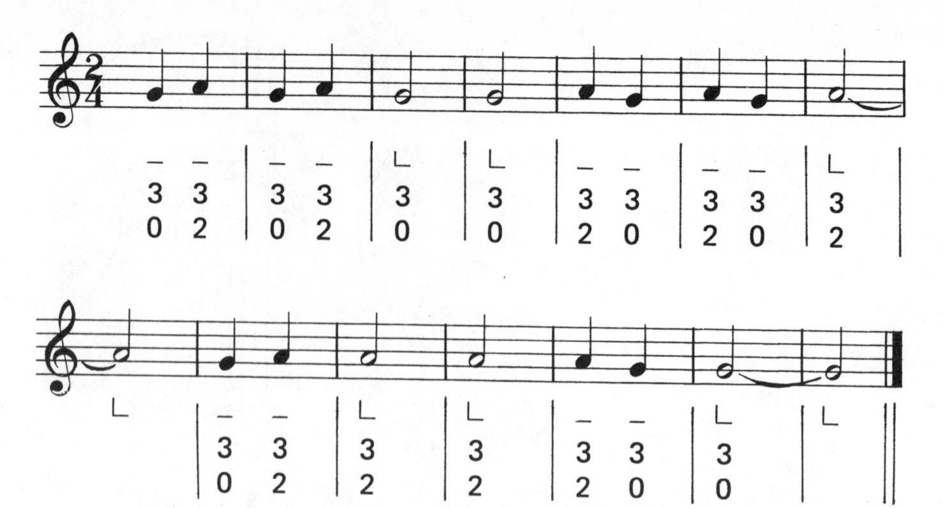

FIGURE 14-1b *Notes to practice on the third string*

Stems Up or Stems Down? All notes below the third line of the staff have stems going up on the right side of the note; all notes above the third line have stems going down on the left side of the note. The B note on the third line can have its stem going up or down. Although this is the style that's usually followed, occasionally you'll see music where it isn't.

Figure 14-2 is a very simple arrangement of "Michael Row the Boat Ashore." You played a much more complicated Numbers Game version for the introduction to this piece in chapter 2; Figure 14-3 is the musical notation for that earlier arrangement.

FIGURE 14-2 *First, second, and third string notes*

FIGURE 14-3 *Simple arrangement of "Michael, Row the Boat Ashore"*

Dotted Rhythms

A dot next to a note adds half the time value to that note. For instance, a half note gets two counts, but if it has a dot next to it, it gets three counts, the equivalence of three hums. The dotted half note is the three-count note missing from Note Power (Figure 12-4, page 112). A dotted half rest indicates three counts of silence.

Incomplete Measures. You may notice that the following piece of notation has only one beat instead of three beats in the first measure, as the time signature shows it should. This is called an incomplete measure; the first measure beat is the missing beat from the last measure, which has only two beats (one for the note and one for the rest). Incomplete measures appear often in notation. If you add the number of beats in the incomplete beginning measure to the last measure of the piece, you'll get the right number of beats, as required by the time signature.

Yes, you just played the tune to "On Top of Old Smoky." Now, you can go back to the version you played in chapter 9 (page 80) and play the introduction by playing music instead of numbers. How about that?

FIGURE 14-4 *More notes on the first three strings*

THE Em CHORD

The Em is your third E chord: you've already learned the E^7 and the E. The Em is very easy isn't it? The fingering is optional; you can use either the first or second finger on the fifth string, second fret, and either the second or third finger on the fourth string, second fret. It's easier to change to a B^7 chord, when you use your second and third fingers, though.

Em is the relative minor of the G chord. If you'd like to try substituting Em for G occasionally, go right ahead. Feel free to experiment with your growing knowledge of the guitar's many sounds.

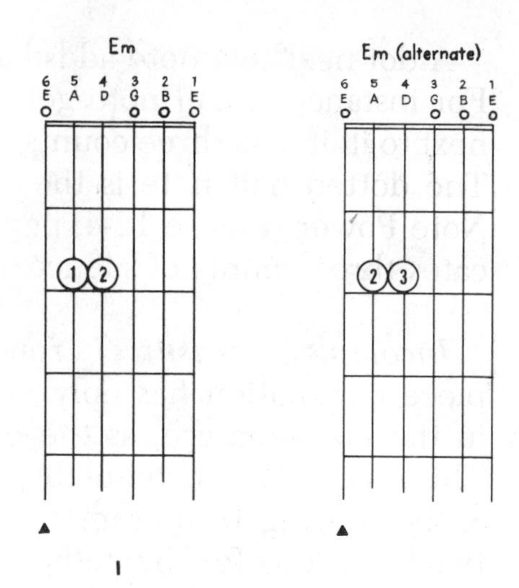

FIGURE 14-5a, b *Two versions of the E minor (Em) chord*

By now you must know that the bass string for the Em chord is the sixth or E string. Since the E minor is probably the easiest chord you've learned up to now, why not use it to review all the strums you know?

Changing from Em to B^7 to Em

If you've chosen to use your second and third fingers to play the Em chord, your second finger won't move when you change from Em to B^7. Your first finger will go to the fourth string in the first fret, your third finger will move from the fourth string to the third string in the same second fret and your fourth finger will move to the first string in the second fret. When changing back to Em, reverse these actions.

When changing to a B^7, it's easier to use the second and third fingers on the Em. There may be times though, when you'll be changing from a G chord to an Em. If you're using the second, third, and fourth fingers on the G chord, it's easier to use your second and third fingers on the Em. If you use your first, second, and third fingers for the G chord, then it's easier to change to the Em chord using your first and second fingers.

THE PULL-TOGETHER STRUM

In this strum, the first finger tip is slightly curled under the third string, the second is slightly curled under the second string, and the third is slightly curled under the first string. Always think that the first three fingers of the right hand

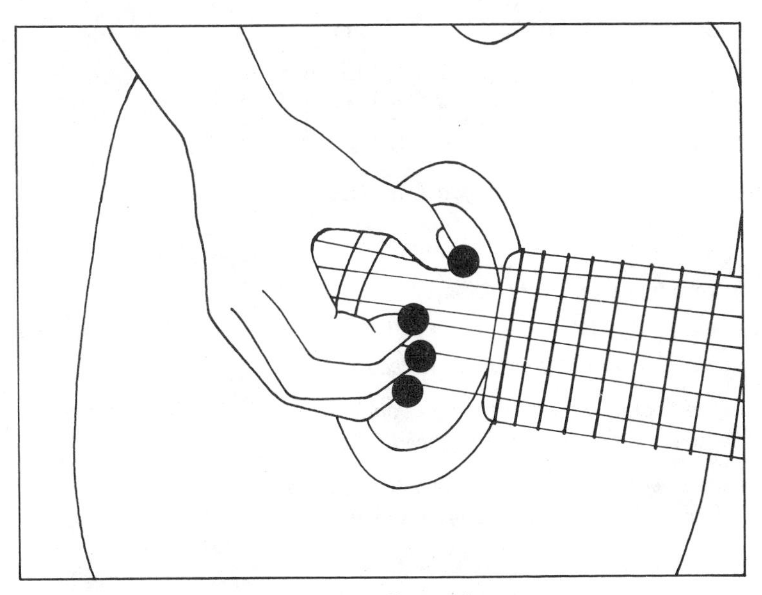

FIGURE 14-6 *Pull-together strum*

correspond with the first three strings, because in this strum and in some others we'll do, the only thing that changes when you change chords is the bass string. The first three strings and the bass are all plucked at the same time. The thumb plucks the bass string while the first three fingers pluck the first three strings. Let the thumb and first three fingers pull up or lift the strings slightly as they pluck.

The pull-together strum, like the Easy Strum, is a one-step strum. After plucking the strings, the finger tips naturally curl in very slightly towards the palm of your hand. *The first three fingers should hover closely above the first three strings, ready to curl under them when you get to the next chord position.* If you get into the habit of plucking the strings and moving your fingers away, it'll be harder for the fingers to find their way back to the first three strings for the next chord.

Now practice the pull-together strum with the Em and B^7 chords. The chords sound nice by themselves, without singing, but we'll use them to accompany the next song.

AUNT RHODY

Em					B7			Em		
L	_	_	L	L	L	_	_	_	_	L
3	3	4	4	4	4	4	3	3	4	4
0	0	4	2	2	4	4	2	0	4	2

Go tell Aunt Rho - dy, go tell Aunt Rho - o - dy

						B7				Em
L	_	_	L	_	_	_	_	_	_	□
2	2	3	3	3	3	4	4	4	3	4
0	0	2	0	0	0	4	2	4	0	2

Go tell Aunt Rho - dy, her old grey goose is dead.

Em B7 Em

Go tell Aunt Rhody, go tell Aunt Rhody

B7 Em

Go tell Aunt Rhody, her old grey goose is dead.

2 *It died in the mill pond, it died in the mill pond*
It died in the mill pond, standing on its head.

3 *It's the one she's been saving, the one she's been saving*
The one she's been saving, to make a feather bed.

Repeat first verse

The haunting quality of the Em chord seems to suit this sad little ditty very well.

THE BASS–PULL-TOGETHER STRUM, B-(3)

The position of the right hand's first three fingers, in relation to the first three strings, is exactly the same as in the pull-together strum. Since this is a two-step strum, brush the bass string first. *The number enclosed in parentheses indicates the number of strings to be plucked, beginning with the first string; so (2) means the first two strings, (3) means the first three strings, and so on.*

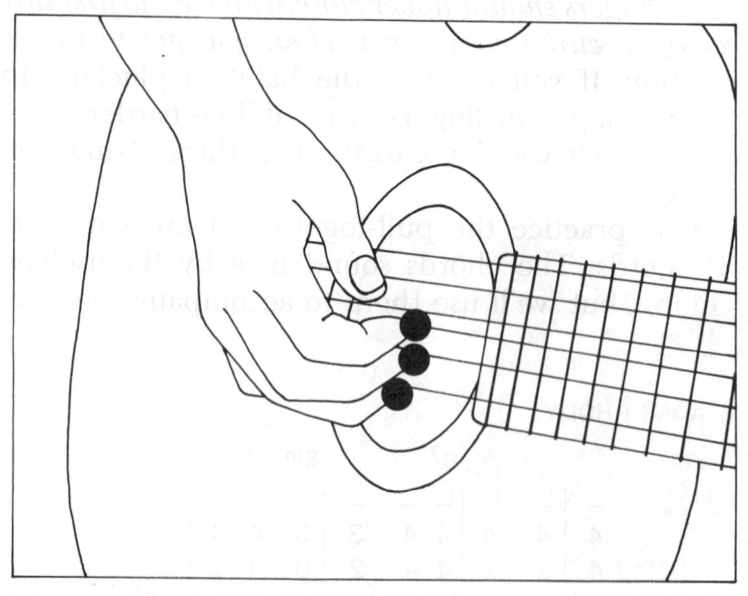

FIGURE 14-7 *Bass–pull-together strum: B-(3)*

1. Brush the bass string with your right hand thumb.
2. Curl the first three finger tips of your right hand slightly under the first three strings and pluck them simultaneously.

Changing from G to Em to G

When going from the G chord to the Em chord, no matter how you play the G, the finger on the fifth string, second fret, doesn't move, the finger on the sixth string, third fret moves behind it, and the finger on the first string, third fret, lifts off. Now you're on an Em chord. To go back to G from Em, don't move the finger that's on the fifth string, second fret, move the finger behind it back to the sixth string, third fet, and return your finger to the first string, third fret. Do this several times without strumming, always making sure that in either change, whichever finger is on the fifth string, second fret, *doesn't move.* After you've mastered this, try the changes with the Bass–pull-together strum. We'll use it on the next song.

THIS LITTLE LIGHT OF MINE

Adapted and arranged with additional words by R.T. Jacobs (Based on a spiritual)

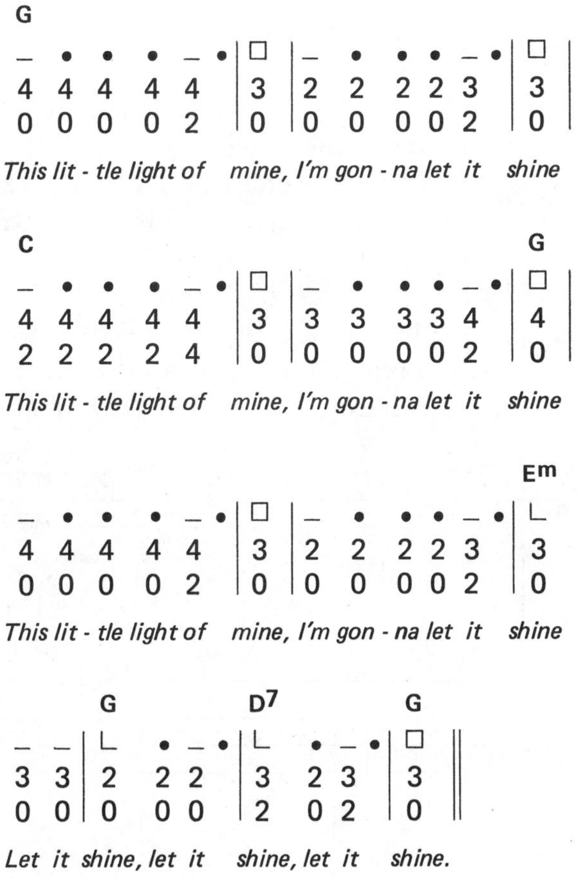

```
G
—  •  •  •  —  • | □ | —  •  •  •  —  • | □ |
4  4  4  4  4    | 3 | 2  2  2  2  3    | 3 |
0  0  0  0  2    | 0 | 0  0  0  0  2    | 0 |
This lit - tle light of   mine, I'm gon - na let it   shine

C                                          G
—  •  •  •  —  • | □ | —  •  •  •  —  • | □ |
4  4  4  4  4    | 3 | 3  3  3  3  4    | 4 |
2  2  2  2  4    | 0 | 0  0  0  0  2    | 0 |
This lit - tle light of   mine, I'm gon - na let it   shine

                                           Em
—  •  •  •  —  • | □ | —  •  •  •  —  • | L |
4  4  4  4  4    | 3 | 2  2  2  2  3    | 3 |
0  0  0  0  2    | 0 | 0  0  0  0  2    | 0 |
This lit - tle light of   mine, I'm gon - na let it   shine

        G               D7              G
—  — | L     •  —  • | L     •  —  • | □ ||
3  3 | 2     2  2    | 3     2  3    | 3 ||
0  0 | 0     0  0    | 2     0  2    | 0 ||
Let  it  shine, let it   shine, let it   shine.
```

For this song, brush the bass string on the first step of the pattern and pluck your first three strings simultaneously in the second step of the pattern. Continue, playing the entire song this way.

B- (3) B-(3) B- (3) B-(3)
G
This little light of mine, I'm gonna let it shine
C G
This little light of mine, I'm gonna let it shine
Em
This little light of mine, I'm gonna let it shine
G D^7 G
Let it shine, let it shine, let it shine.

2 *Gather 'round good friends, I'm gonna let it shine*
Gather 'round good friends, I'm gonna let it shine
Gather 'round good friends, I'm gonna let it shine
Let it shine, let it shine, let it shine.

3 *Go and tell the people, I'm gonna let it shine, etc.*

4 *I'll light up all the darkness, I'm gonna let it shine, etc.*

5 *All 'round this great big world, I'm gonna let it shine, etc.*

Repeat first verse

Listen to what you're playing. Do you recognize it? It's "House of the Rising Sun." You know what to do. Return to the previous numbered version in chapter 13 (page 120) and substitute this new notation in Figure 14-8a for the introduction.

The notes in Figure 14-8b are called eighth notes. In Note Power (Figure 12-4, page 112) they looked like the notes in Figure 14-8c. These are single eighth notes and the line jutting out from the stem is called a flag. When *two or more*

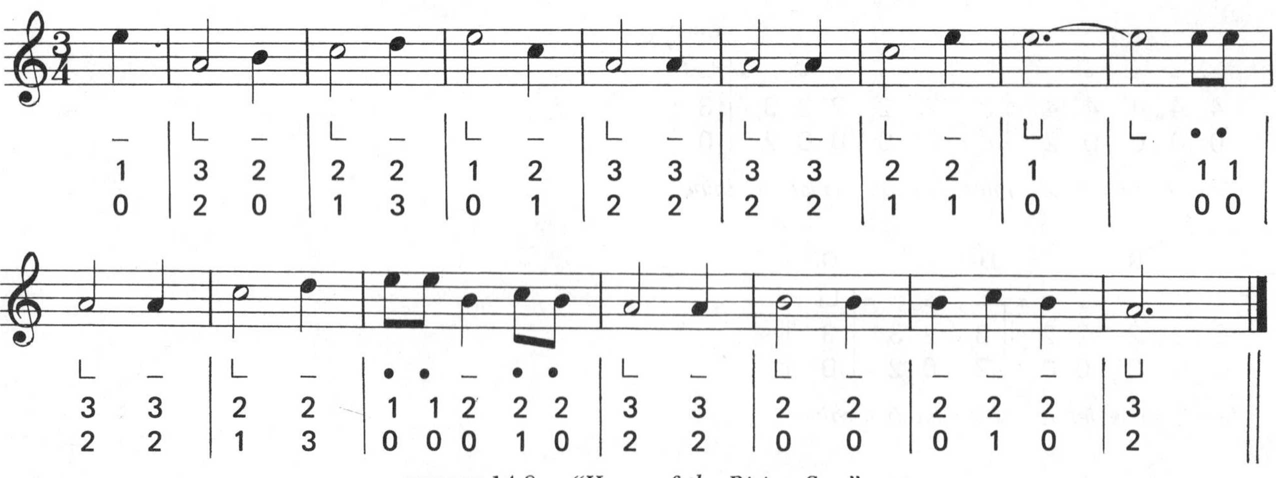

FIGURE 14-8a *"House of the Rising Sun"*

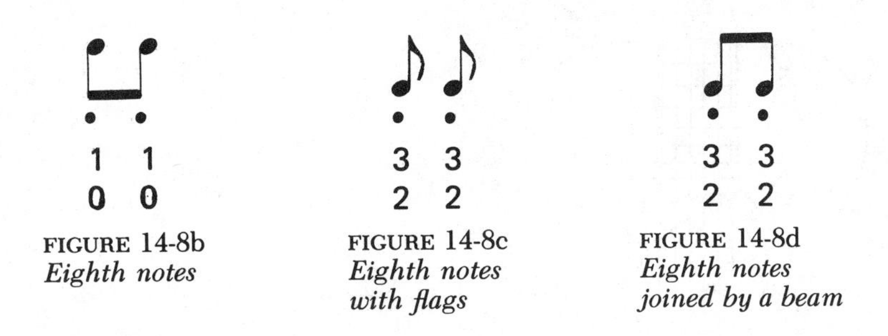

FIGURE 14-8b
Eighth notes

FIGURE 14-8c
Eighth notes with flags

FIGURE 14-8d
Eighth notes joined by a beam

eighth notes are joined together, as in Figure 14-8d, the line joining them is called a beam. Eighth notes are played twice as fast as quarter notes. It's equivalent to the timing of the single dot rhythm mark in the Numbers Game.

fifteen

Keep memorizing your notation so that there's no chance of forgetting any notes. If you forget, it'll just hold you back until you relearn it. Go over all the notes on the first three strings. Then, when you're absolutely sure of them, go on to the fourth string.

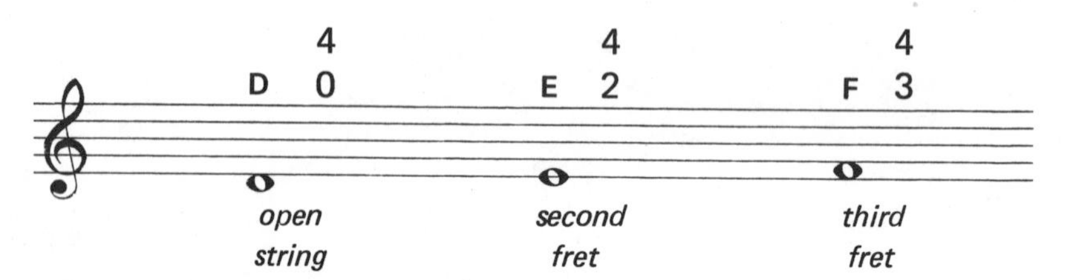

FIGURE 15-1a *Open string, second fret, and third fret on the fourth string*

The fourth, fifth, and sixth strings are bass strings. So, starting with the fourth string, instead of alternating the first two fingers of your right hand to play the notes, use your thumb only. Also, instead of coming to rest on the string below, as you did when you played notes on the first three strings, let your thumb glide freely *over* the adjacent string after playing the note. On the fourth string, after your thumb plays the note, it should glide over the third string. Continue alternating the first and second fingers for the first three strings, however. When you're playing a tune that includes notes on any of the first three strings as well as on the fourth, fifth, or sixth strings, alternate your first and second fingers on the first three treble strings and use your thumb on the last three bass strings.

I've simplified the timing on the following tunes and left out something called a key signature, which we'll take up later.

FIGURE 15-1b *Notes to practice on the fourth string*

FIGURE 15-2a *Notes to practice on the first four strings*

FIGURE 15-2b *"Deep Blue Sea"*

Did you recognize the tune in Figure 15-2b? It's "Deep

Blue Sea," with the numbers converted to notes. Compare it and you'll see (page 121).

Are you convinced now that you can read music, something you probably thought you could never do?

No Surprise. If there's anything at all that you were always absolutely sure you couldn't do, maybe now's the time to try it. Maybe it was singing in tune or playing an instrument, swimming, or riding a bike? There must be several things you've *really wanted* to do your entire life; maybe now is the time to attempt those "impossible" tasks. You'll be happier if you do, especially when you discover they're not as impossible as you thought.

Changing from G to D

If you're using the first, second, and third fingers on the G chord, you've got the easier change this time. When going from G to D, move your first finger from the fifth to the third string in the second fret. Move your second finger from the sixth string, third fret to the first string, second fret. Move your third finger from the first string to the second string, in the third fret.

If you use your second, third, and fourth fingers, move your unused first finger to the third string, second fret, your second finger from the fifth string to the first string, second fret, and your third finger from the sixth string to the second string, third fret. Lift your fourth finger.

Changing from D to Em to C

When going from D to Em, slide your first and second fingers from the third and first strings to the fifth and fourth strings, in the second fret. Lift your third finger. When going from Em to C, your third finger goes on the fifth string, third fret, your second finger *doesn't move,* and your first finger transfers to the second string, first fret.

If you use the second and third fingers on the Em, in switching from the D, move your second finger from the first to the fifth string, second fret, and put your third finger right behind it. When going to the C, your third finger goes to the fifth string, third fret, your second finger moves from the fifth string to the fourth string, second fret, and your unused first finger plays the second string, first fret.

SOME MORE DOTS

In the next piece of music, "The Riddle Song," there are dotted quarter notes. Since a dot next to a note adds on half the time value of that note, the dotted quarter note gets one-and-a-half counts. (The quarter note gets one count and the dot next to it adds on half its value.) The count is

FIGURE 15-3a *Dotted quarter notes*

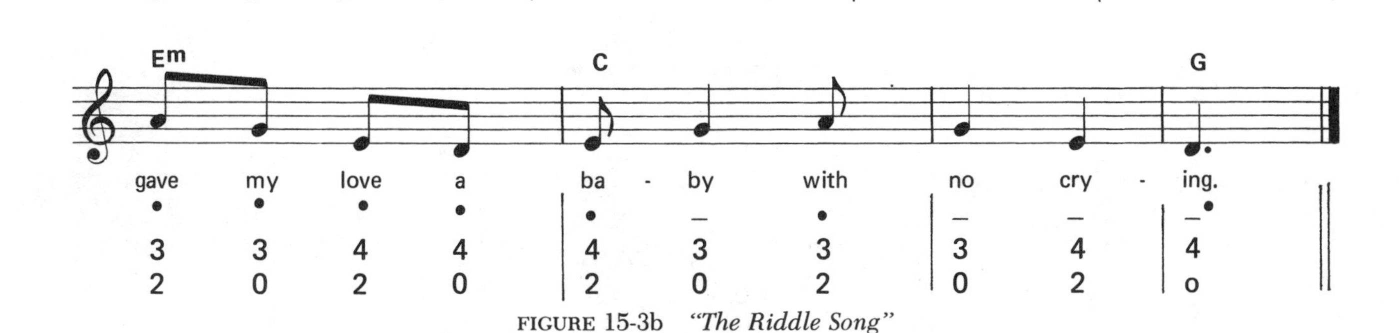

FIGURE 15-3b *"The Riddle Song"*

the same as when you had a set of numbers with a single-line rhythm mark over it, and next to it, a single dot with no numbers below. You held that set of numbers for one-and-a-half counts or hums. In the measures with a dotted quarter note and then an eighth note, this is how you'd count (since the time signature of the music shows you that there are two beats to a measure): ONE, TWO–OO. ONE for the first note, which is a quarter note, TWO beginning the count of two, for the dot, and OO, finishing the count of two, on the next eighth note. That gives you the two beats to a measure that the time signature indicates you should have for each measure.

It might be nice to accompany yourself with the B-down strum on the first two verses of "The Riddle Song." On the last verse, you can do the slide-and-glide strum, really slowing up on the last line. Make sure, for both strums, to begin the bass part wherever you have a strum mark. On the slide-and-glide strum, brush the bass string where there's a strum mark and then continue sliding and gliding across the strings.

THE RIDDLE SONG

Adapted and arranged by R.T. Jacobs (Based on a traditional)

```
  G              C              G
I gave my love a cherry that has no stone
  D7             G              D7
I gave my love a chicken that has no bone
                 G              D
I told my love a story that has no end
  Em             C              G
I gave my love a baby with no crying.
```

2 *How can there be a cherry that has no stone?*
How can there be a chicken that has no bone?
How can there be a story that has no end?
How can there be a baby with no crying?

3 *Well, a cherry when it's blooming it has no stone*
And a chicken when it's pippin, it has no bone
And the story of our love, it has no end
And a baby when it's sleeping there's no crying.

Changing from Em to Am

In "The Cruel War" you have some more dotted rhythms and a change from Em to Am. Also, for now I left out something called a key signature. If you use your first and second fingers on the Em, your second finger doesn't move. Your third finger goes right behind it to the third string and your first finger goes to the second string, first fret. If you use your second and third fingers on the Em, slide them from the fifth and fourth to the fourth and third strings, second fret, and add your first finger to the second string, first fret.

Use the slide-and-glide strum and do one slide and glide for each measure.

THE CRUEL WAR

Adapted and arranged by R.T. Jacobs (Based on English folk song)

G Em Am G

The cruel war is raging and Johnny has to fight

Em C D7 G

I so want to be with him from morning till night.

2 *I'll go to your captain, get down on my knees*
I'll plead and I'll beg him for your release.

3 *I'll give all I own, it grieves my heart so*
Won't you let me go with you? Please don't say no.

4 *Tomorrow is Sunday and Monday is the day*
That your captain will call you, and you must obey.

5 *Your captain will call you, it grieves my heart so*
Won't you let me go with you? Please don't say no.

6 *Your years are not many, your courage is not small,*
Your face is too fair to face the cannonball.

7 *Your face is too fair, it grieves my heart so*
Won't you let me go with you? Please don't say no.

8 *I'll pull back my hair, men's clothes I'll put on*
I'll pass for your comrade as we march along.

9 *I'll pass for your comrade and none will ever know*
Won't you let me go with you? Please don't say no.

10 *Johnny, oh Johnny, why are you so unkind?*
I love you far better than all of mankind.

11 *I love you far better than I ever can express*
Won't you let me go with you? Oh yes, yes, yes, yes.

FIGURE 15-4 *"The Cruel War"*

THE G^7 CHORD

The bass string for the G^7 chord is the sixth or E string. This chord has the toughest stretch of any chord you've played so far. Practice stretching your fingers into this position. You may think right now that it's impossible for you to stretch that far, but you'll do it, eventually.

Changing from C to G^7 to C

Although both the C and G^7 chords are long stretches, changing between them is easy. When you're switching from the C to the G^7 chord, your third finger moves from the fifth string to the sixth string, third fret; your second finger moves from the fourth string to the fifth string, second fret; and your first finger moves from the second string to the first string, first fret. That's pretty easy, isn't it? All the moves are just one string over. Don't lift your fingers off the fingerboard when changing, just slide them over. It's important to keep this in mind. You're wasting movement and time, and making the change more difficult, if you lift your fingers. That will only force your fingers to stray; they'll have to find their places all over again for the next chord. Practice sliding back and forth between both chords, silently at first, and then while strumming.

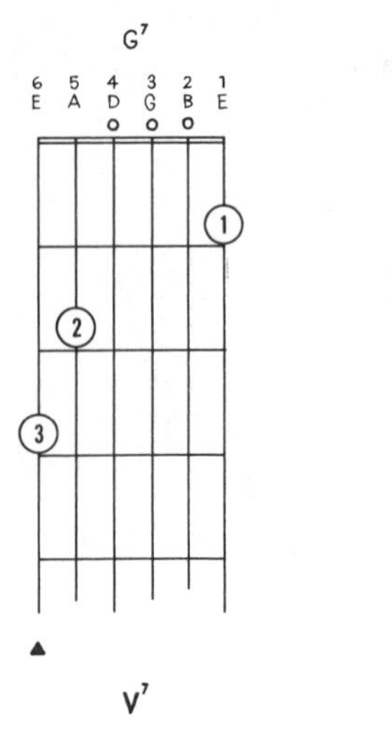

FIGURE 15-5 *G seventh (G^7) chord*

B–FINGERS-DOWN–DOWN-UP–DOWN-UP STRUM

This is another wonderful, basic strum that you can play with lots of songs utilizing strong rhythms. You start the pattern with the B–Fingers-down and continue, using your first finger to brush down with the flat part of the finger nail and then brush up. End the strum pattern by brushing down and up again with your first finger. This is a four-step strum.

1. Brush the bass string with your thumb.
2. Fingers down.
3. Brush down across the strings with the flat side of the first finger nail. Brush up. Don't worry about what strings you brush. It doesn't matter.
4. Repeat third step.

If you saw the four steps of the strum pattern in the Numbers Game rhythm and timing marks, it would look like this:

1. Bass
2. fingers down
3. down up
4. down up

Each of the four steps is equal in time. The down-ups in the third and fourth steps each get the same single combined count as do each of the first and second steps.

Practice this strum for a few minutes with your C and G^7 chords. Then use it to accompany yourself with the next song, "Tom Dula." Each step of the strum counts for one beat. In the music notation, each measure or bar of music gets the full pattern of the strum. Use the music notation as well as the strum marks to guide you with fitting in the pattern. There's a full pattern between each strum mark.

FIGURE 15-6 *"Tom Dula"*

Here's an example of how you'd fit the pattern in.

C

B- Fingers down-down up-down up B- Fingers down-down up-down up

Bow down your h-e-a-d T-o- m D - u - l - a

TOM DULA

Adapted and arranged by R.T. Jacobs (Based on a Traditional Cowboy Song)

C

Bow down your head Tom Dula

G7

Bow down your head and cry

Bow down your head Tom Dula

C

Poor boy, you're gonna die.

2 *I walked her to the mountain*
And there I took her life
Walked her to the mountain
And stabbed her with my knife.

3 *I wish I'd a never seen her*
Or that she'd never been born
Then I'd be free tomorrow
And see another morn.

4 *This time tomorrow*
Reckon where I'll be
Down in some lonesome valley
A-hangin' from a white oak tree.

Repeat first verse

Here's "Maryann." When you played the first and second string notes together (Figure 13-2, page 118), you played a simple version of the tune. Why don't you try playing the notes from home base chord positions now? When you change chords, don't play the note underneath; just strum the chord.

FIGURE 15-7 *"Maryann"*

We're going to do the down-up–damp strum. Each measure of the music gets one full pattern of the strum, even the measures that have rests. The first of each two strum marks gets the down-up movement of the pattern and the next strum mark gets the 'slap damp.' *Every two strum marks comprise a full pattern of this strum.* Every two strum marks in the verses equal a measure in the music. Play "Maryann" and you'll see what I mean.

MARYANN

Adapted and arranged with new words by R.T. Jacobs (Based on a calypso folk song)

C G7
All day, all night Maryann / /
C
Sitting by the seashore sifting sand / /
G7
Even little children love Maryann / /
C
Sitting by the seashore sifting sand. / /

2 *When I first saw Maryann*
She was at the seashore sifting sand
Even little children know Maryann
Always will be down there sifting sand.

3 *Sweet girl, shy girl, Maryann*
Won't you come with me now, here's my hand
I will take you far far, Maryann
To a place where there's no sifting sand.

4 *Morning, evening, every day*
Maryann will never go away
Everybody knows that Maryann
Always will be down there sifting sand.

Repeat first verse

BASS–PULL-TOGETHER–PULL-TOGETHER STRUM, B-(3)-(3)

It's waltz time again. This is another variation of the B-down-down strum. You brush the bass string of each chord and simultaneously pluck the first three strings, twice. This is a three-step strum. You already played the first two steps of this strum in "This Little Light Of Mine."

1. Brush the bass string.
2. Pluck the first three strings simultaneously.
3. Repeat the second step.

Don't forget to keep your first three finger tips hovering closely over the first three strings. As you brush the bass string of a chord, curl your finger tips under the first three strings and pluck them. We're going to be doing this strum in the next song, "Streets of Laredo," so practice it with the C and G7 chords.

FIGURE 15-8 *"The Streets of Laredo"*

The Slur The curved line you see in the notation of "The Streets of Laredo" is called a slur. When two or more notes are played and sung on one syllable of a word, those notes are joined by a slur. Although the slur looks like the tie, don't confuse them. A tie is used to join two notes of the same pitch, and remember, the second note isn't sounded. (A tie can have more than two notes, but still, all will have the same pitch and only the first note will be sounded. You sound *all* the notes that are joined with a slur.)

Lining Out the Strum. In the next song, "The Streets of Laredo," be sure to play the strum exactly as I've lined it out. This will give you step-by-step directions on when to strum while singing.

THE STREETS OF LAREDO

```
    C           G7          C         G7
(3) B-(3)-(3)    B-(3)-(3)   B-  (3)-(3) B-(3)-
As I   walked out in the streets of Laredo
    C           G7        C        G7
(3) B-(3)-(3)    B-(3)-(3) B-(3)-(3) B-(3)-
As I   walked out in Laredo one day
    C           G7               C          G7
(3) B - (3)-(3)  B-(3)-(3)         B-(3)-(3)    B-(3)-
I spied a young cowboy wrapped up in white linen
           C            G7                C
(3)        B-(3)  -  (3)  B-(3)-(3) B-(3)-(3)   B-(3)-
Wrapped up    in white linen, as cold as the clay.
```

2 *I see by your outfit that you are a cowboy*
These words he did say as I boldly stepped by
Come sit down beside me and hear my sad story
I was shot in the breast and I know I must die.

3 *Go gather around you a crowd of young cowboys*
And tell them the story of this, my sad fate
Tell one and the other before they go further
To stop their wild roving before it's too late.

4 *My friends they live scattered all over this nation*
They know not where their poor friend has gone
He first came to Texas and hired to a ranchman
Oh I'm a poor cowboy and know I've done wrong.

5 *Then swing your rope slowly and rattle spurs lowly*
And give a wild whoop as you carry me along
And in the grave throw me and roll the sod o'er me
For I'm a poor cowboy and know I've done wrong.

6 *Bury beside me my knife and six shooter*
Spurs on my heel and rifle by my side
And over my coffin put two bottles of brandy
That the cowboys may drink as they carry me along.

7 *Go fetch me a cup, a cup of cold water*
To cool my parched lips, the cowboy then said
Before I returned his spirit had left him
And gone to the roundup, the cowboy was dead.

Taking Time. This chapter, like chapter 9 in the first section, has been full of new strings, strums, and changes to work on. If you want to take more time with this chapter than you took with others, by all means, do it.

While we're speaking of time, have you taken time out to do your E-Z Relaxation?

Extensions on the Ladder. Since there are only five lines and four spaces in the framework of the staff, when notes go below or above that framework, we've got to add ledger lines to put them on. They're really just extensions of the staff, like the extensions on a ladder. Ladder extensions allow you to reach up higher. On the music staff, you can use the extensions to reach down lower, also.

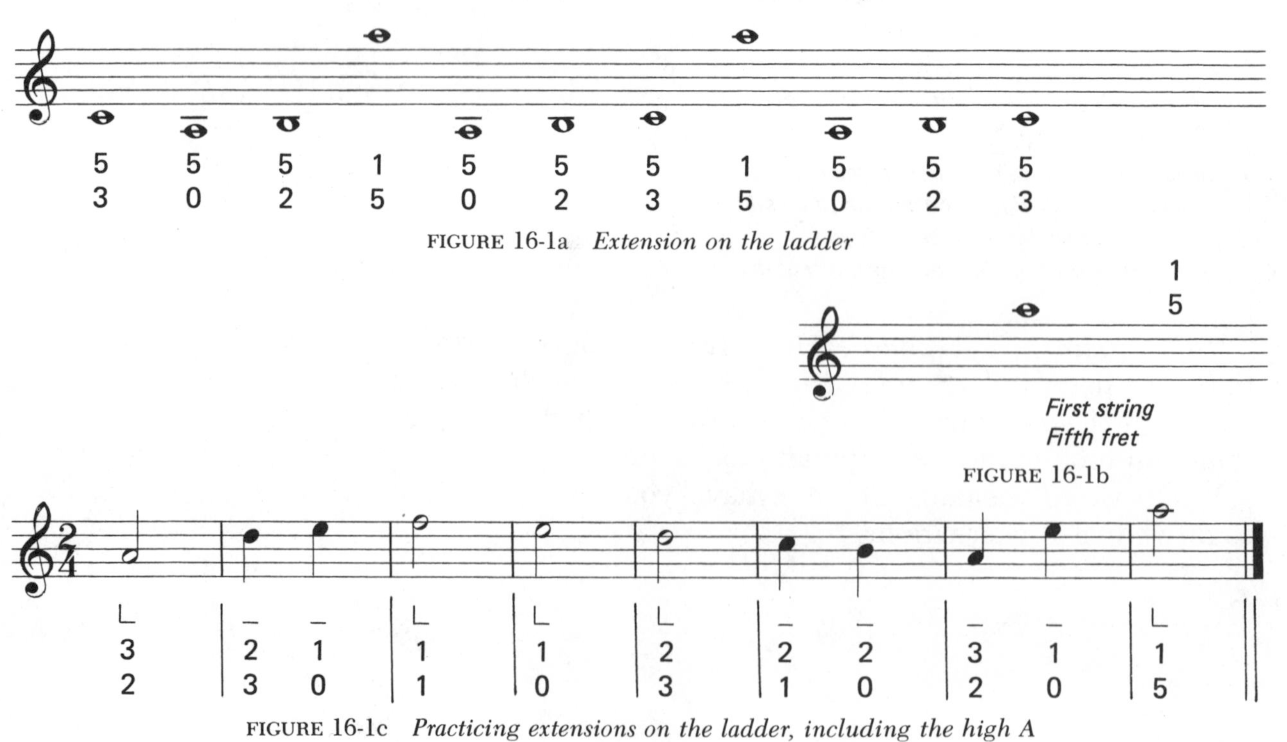

FIGURE 16-1a *Extension on the ladder*

FIGURE 16-1b

FIGURE 16-1c *Practicing extensions on the ladder, including the high A*

Before we begin learning the notes on the fifth string, which are played with your thumb, go over all the notes on the first four strings. Do you know them well? Half-learned notes only get more confusing as you progress. If you've taken the time to really know them well, you'll be surprised to find yourself reading music almost as easily as you read a book.

Now you're ready for the notes on the fifth string. After all this time, you're about to learn your ABC's.

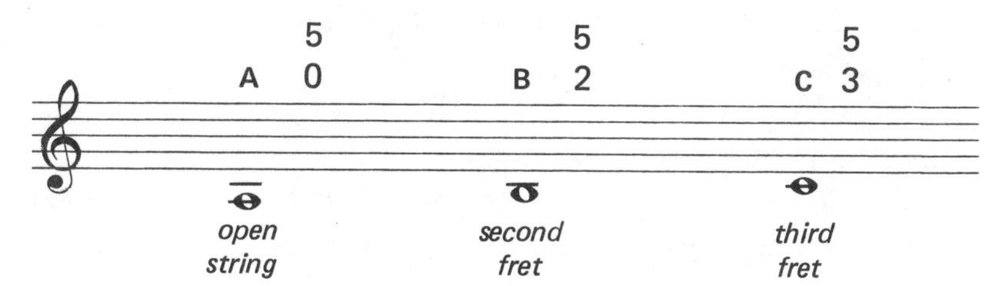

FIGURE 16-2a *Fifth string notes*

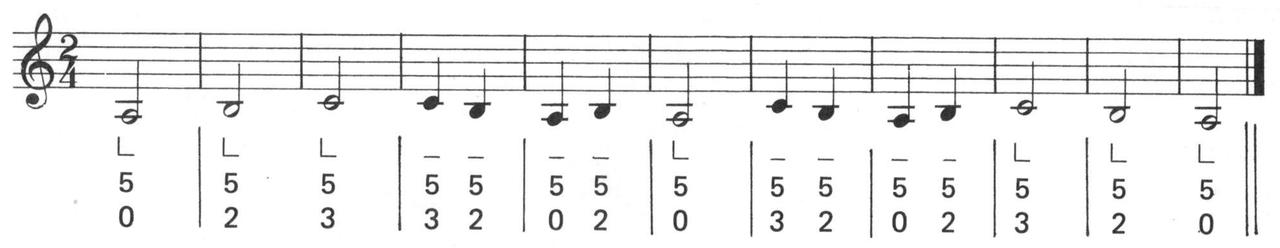

FIGURE 16-2b *Notes to practice on the fifth string*

FIGURE 16-3a *Notes to practice on the second, third, fourth, and fifth strings*

FIGURE 16-3b *Notes to practice on the fourth and fifth strings*

FIGURE 16-3c *More notes to practice on the fourth and fifth strings*

In *Silent Night,* dotted quarter notes are followed by eighth notes, just as in "The Riddle Song." Since the time signature tells you that there are three beats or counts to a measure or bar, count ONE, TWO-OO, THREE: ONE for the first note, which is a quarter note; TWO beginning the count of two for the dot next to it; OO finishing the count of two for the eighth note; and THREE for the last note in the measure, which is a quarter note. That gives you three beats to the measure.

Incidentally, *Silent Night* was sung for the very first time on Christmas Eve 1818 in Bavaria with a *guitar* accompaniment. For teaching purposes I've simplified the traditional timing and changed the time signature.

FIGURE 16-4 *"Silent Night"*

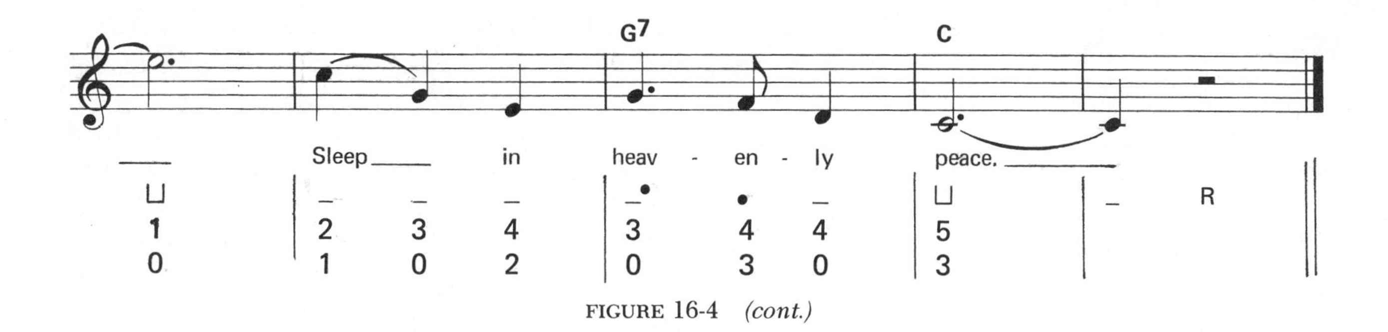

FIGURE 16-4 *(cont.)*

THE CHEATER'S F CHORD

This chord is almost, but not quite, an F chord. Many students feel that the F chord is the most difficult of all the basic beginner's chords. The cheater chord will help prepare you to play the F chord, which we'll take up in the next chapter. This chord will serve as a temporary substitute for the F.

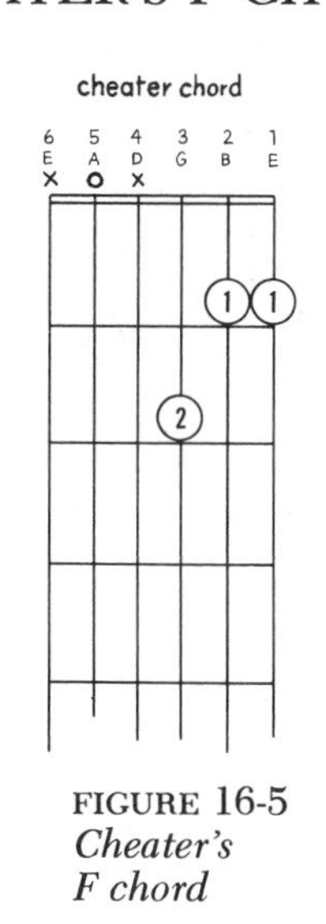

FIGURE 16-5 *Cheater's F chord*

The greatest difficulty in playing this chord comes from trying to get a clear sound out of the first two strings, which are pressed down (barred) by the first finger. If you've already tried playing the cheater chord, you've found that out already. If not, do this test on yourself.

Place your left-hand first finger on the first string, first fret, and pluck that first string. Listen to the sound carefully. Play it a few times, always listening to the F note sounded. Now, take the cheater chord position. Strum across the first three strings. (A note of warning here: since this is a cheater chord, don't get tricked into touching the fourth string. If you do, you'll be playing another chord that doesn't belong in *Silent Night.* You can play a secondary bass on the fifth or A string, when using the cheater chord correctly.) Now pluck the first string individually, while still holding the cheater chord position. What do you hear? If it's a dull or muffled sound, you're not pressing down hard enough. If you hear a sound that seems alright, make sure it's the sound of the F note on the first string, first fret. Do this by taking your finger off the chord position. Then, place your left-hand first finger on the first string, first fret again, and pluck the string. Is the sound the same one you heard when you were fingering the chord and plucking the first string individually? If not, experiment with the way your first finger is pressing down on the string until you find a position that gives you a clear sound.

Changing from C to Cheater Chord to C

This change is easy in both directions. When going from C to the cheater chord, your third finger lifts off, your second finger moves from the fourth string to the third string, second fret, and your first finger lays down (and presses hard) across the first two strings, first fret.

When going from the cheater chord back to C, reverse the moves. Your first finger stands up, so that just the finger tip is pressing on the second string, first fret; your second finger returns to the fourth string, second fret; and your third finger comes down again on the fifth string, third fret.

To accompany yourself for "Silent Night," do the variation of the waltz strum, the B—pull together—pull together strum. When you come to a place where you have to use an F chord, substitute the cheater chord, for now.

SILENT NIGHT

C G7 C
Silent night, holy night, All is calm, all is bright
F C
Round yon Virgin Mother and Child
F C
Holy Infant so tender and mild
G7 C G7 C
Sleep in heavenly peace, sleep in heavenly peace.

Noche de paz, noche de amor
Todo duerme en rededor
En la altura resuena un cantar
Os anuncia una dicha sin par
Brilla la estrella de paz, brilla la estrella de paz.

Stille nacht, heilige nacht
Alles ruht, einsam wacht
Nur das traute hoch heilige Paar
Holder Knabe mit lockigen Haar
Schlaf in himmlischer Ruhe, schlaf in himmlischer Ruhe.

In "Nine Hundred Miles," you'll notice a double bar preceded by two vertical dots: this is called a repeat sign. When you see it at the end of a piece, go back to the point where the previous repeat sign appears, and play everything between the two signs again.

You remember from Note Power (page 112) that the note with two flags on the stem is a sixteenth note and that it gets one quarter of a count. It's played twice as fast as the eighth note and it's treated the same as the double dots in the Numbers Game.

Since there are so few chord changes in this song, if you haven't been playing from home base chord positions, why don't you try again here? Strum the chord whenever there's a chord change and whenever the word "strum" appears above a note. When you strum the chord, don't play the note.

FIGURE 16-6 *"Nine Hundred Miles"*

After this song, I'm not going to include the Numbers Game under the notation. I've brought you around from playing numbers to playing notes. Maybe reading music is not as scary or impossible a task as you once thought.

We'll do the Bnj B for "Nine Hundred Miles" with alternating basses. On the Am chord, alternate between the primary bass string and the fourth string. On the E chord, alternate between the primary bass and the fifth string. After you become a bit familiar with the song, I'm going to add a little flourish that you can do at the end. Play two Bnj B strum patterns to each measure.

NINE HUNDRED MILES

Adapted and arranged with new words by R.T. Jacobs (Based on a traditional)

Am
I'm a-riding on that train, I've got tears in my eyes
Tryin' to read a letter from my home
If that train runs me right, I'll be home Saturday night
E7 Am
'Cause I'm nine hundred miles from my home.

Chorus

E7 Am
And I hate to hear that lonesome whistle blow
E7 Am
Oh that long lonesome train a-riding down.

2 *Well, I'll pawn you my chain, that's been worn near my heart*
I'll pawn anything that I've got
If that train runs me right, I'll be home Saturday night
'Cause I'm nine hundred miles from my home.

Chorus

3 *Oh, I hope that there's still time and my mom's at the gate*
That she's waiting for me now to come home
If that train runs me right, I'll be home Saturday night
'Cause I'm nine hundred miles from my home.

Chorus

4 *Yes, that letter made me cry, for they say that she may die*
I've got to get to see her one more time
If that train runs me right, I'll be home Saturday night
'Cause I'm nine hundred miles from my home.

Chorus

Repeat first verse

Try this: the last time you sing the word "down," do the Bnj B four or five times, hammering in the blues with your first finger just as you did at the end of *Worried Man Blues* (page 97). Then, start slowing up as you do the Bnj B three or four more times. End with one Easy Strum. With a little imagination, it'll sound like train wheels on a track, slowing up, and then coming to a full stop.

If your hammer has gotten rusty, polish it up again, because if you don't hammer down hard enough, you won't hear it. Also, make sure your left-hand fingers are curved, so that your third finger isn't leaning against the second string. If your finger touches that string, you'll muffle the hammer.

THE F CHORD

The F chord has quite a reputation with beginners. It can be frustrating when you think you'll never get it right, but you will if you give it persistence rather than resistance.

Knowing the cheater chord should make it easier for you to go on to the F chord. The bass string for the F chord is the fourth string; your third finger is on the F note on the fourth string, so you're strumming from its root. (Actually, you've been strumming from the root on all the chords with fingered bass strings that you've learned.)

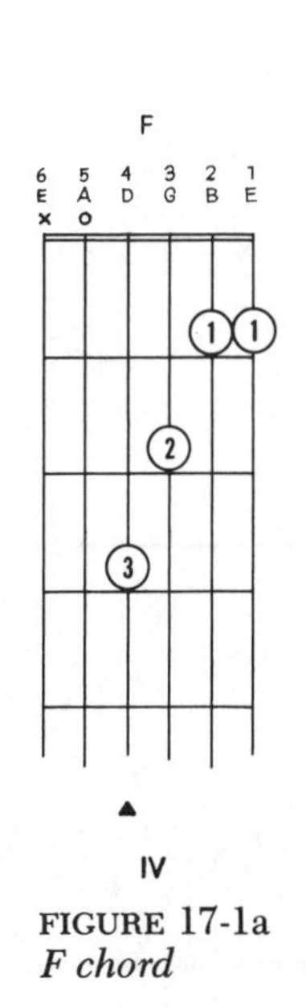

FIGURE 17-1a
F chord

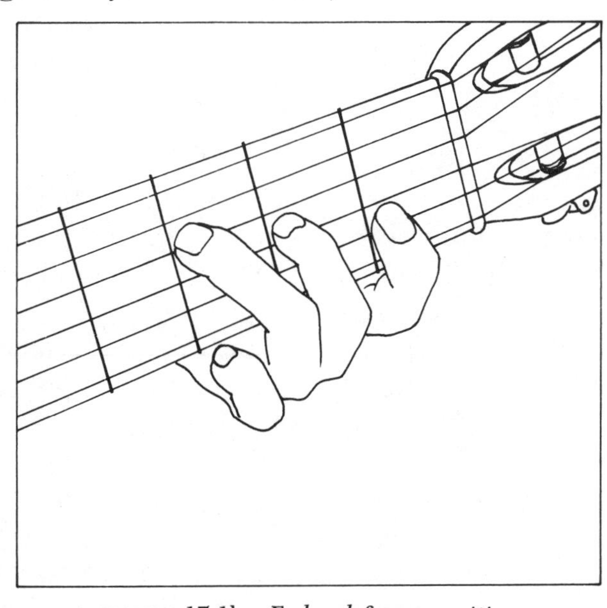

FIGURE 17-1b *F chord finger position*

All the steps for testing the clarity of the first two strings of the cheater chord apply to the F chord also. However, it's a bit trickier getting those first two strings to sound clearly when you're fingering the fourth string as well. You may have to readjust the position of your first finger. The ideal position is to keep your first finger as straight as possible across the first two strings of the first fret. Nevertheless, your position will be influenced by the size and shape of your fingers. For instance, in order for me to get a better sound from those strings barred by my first finger, my finger is in a slightly diagonal position. I get a pressure mark from the first string on the right side of my finger, the side that's closer to my thumb. Of course, that string pressure mark continues around on the flat underside of the finger, about halfway between the first joint and the top of the finger. The string pressure mark from the second string shows up on the tip of my finger.

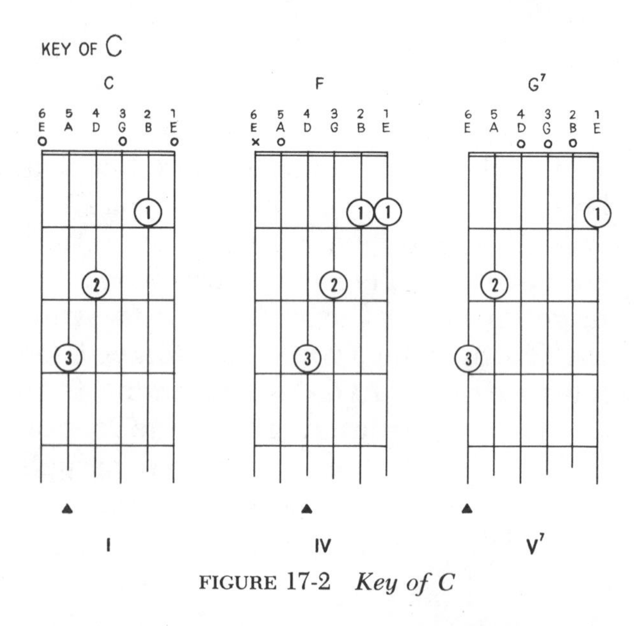

FIGURE 17-2 *Key of C*

That position works for the size and shape of *my* fingers. If it doesn't allow *you* to sound the chord clearly, try moving your first finger into slightly different positions, always testing the first string sound. Yes, learning the F chord can be a frustrating experience.

When you finally do master the F chord, and that'll probably take awhile, you'll have learned yet another key family. You now know the key of C.

Changing from C to F to C

This is an easy change. Going from C to F, your second and third fingers move down one string towards your knees in the same frets. Your first finger adjusts its position to barre, or fret, the first two strings. The reverse is a slightly more awkward, but still, uncomplicated change. Your third finger moves from the fourth string to the fifth string in the third fret. Your second finger moves from the third string to the fourth string in the second fret. And your first finger, which was fretting the first two strings, simply stands up so that just the tip is pressing down on the second string, first fret. Practice these changes for awhile. Then we'll try a new technique for a song in the key of C.

Bass Runs

Bass runs are single notes leading from one chord to another, usually substituting for the last two or three beats of the chord. This bass run is made up of four notes. The first note will be the bass note of the chord you're playing and the fourth note will be the bass note of the chord to which you're changing. Understand that the bass note is the lowest note in the chord and that you play that note on the bass string of the chord. The second and third notes are passing notes (passing notes don't belong to a chord) in between the two chords. For example, in the next song, "Down by the Riverside," when you're going from the C chord in the verse to the F chord in the chorus, strum down on the first beat of the measure, and as you sing "I aint gonna," this is what you do:

1. Pluck the bass of the C chord (second beat of that measure).
2. Pluck the open D or fourth string.
3. Finger the D string in the second fret and pluck the string.
4. Pluck the bass of the F chord.

That ends the bass run. This is also called a walking bass, or a bass progression. The progression of notes in the run from C to F are C, D, E, F. Pick the bass run notes with your right hand thumb. Since you'll be doing the Bnj B strum (at two patterns to a measure) to accompany the song, when you get to the F (the bass for the Bnj B), you'll be beginning the strum again on the word "study."

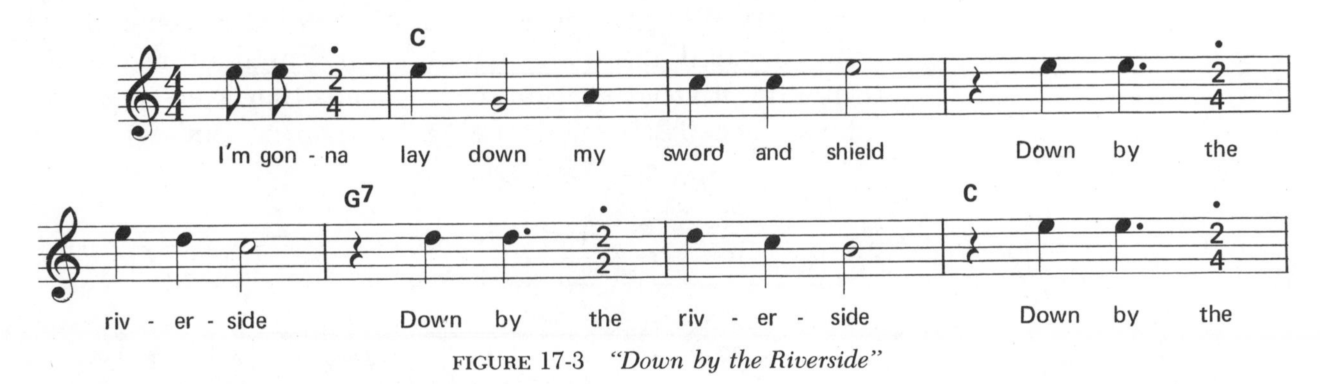

FIGURE 17-3 *"Down by the Riverside"*

FIGURE 17-3 *(cont.)*

I want you to notice several things in the notation for "Down by the Riverside." The first thing to notice is that I've substituted the Numbers Game for some of the notes because of something called "accidentals." We'll take that subject up at the beginning of Chapter 20.

The second thing to notice is that in one measure, you'll see a slur over a tie. The definitions of the terms haven't changed. A tie still joins two or more notes of the same pitch and only the first note is sounded; a slur joins two or more notes that are sung to the same syllable. Those two situations happen to be in the same place here.

The third thing I want you to notice is that in the chorus, at the very end, there are two brackets. You'll often see this at the end of a piece of music. It means that there are two endings. The first time you sing the chorus, end with the

FIGURE 17-4 *Second chorus ending for "Down by the Riverside"*

number 1 ending; the second time you sing the chorus (when you go back to the repeat sign), skip the number 1 ending and end with the number 2 ending.

DOWN BY THE RIVERSIDE

C
I'm gonna lay down my sword and shield,/down by the riverside
G7
/Down by the riverside
C
/Down by the riverside
I'm gonna lay down my sword and shield,/down by the riverside
G7 C
And study war no more.

Chorus

bass run F
I ain't gonna study war no more
C
I ain't gonna study war no more
G7 C
I ain't gonna study war no more.

Repeat chorus

2 *I'm gonna shake hands with everyone, down by the riverside*
Down by the riverside
Down by the riverside
I'm gonna shake hands with everyone, down by the riverside
And study war no more.

Chorus

3 *I'm gonna walk with my friends in peace, down by the riverside*
Down by the riverside
Down by the riverside
I'm gonna walk with my friends in peace, down by the riverside
And study war no more.

Chorus

4 *I'm gonna meet up with all you folks, down by the riverside*
Down by the riverside
Down by the riverside
I'm gonna meet up with all you folks, down by the riverside
And study war no more.

Chorus

It's common practice and lots of fun to add verses to this song that you've made up yourself.

THE C^7 CHORD

This is hardly a new chord. It's really a C chord with your fourth finger added to the third string, third fret.

When you change from C to C^7 and back to C, can you see that you simply lift off and put back your fourth finger for the changing?

B-3-(2) STRUM

This bass–three–pull-together strum is still another variation of your original waltz strum. It's in three steps. First, you brush the bass string of whatever chord you're on. Then, you pluck the third string with your first finger, as you see in Figures 17-6a. Last, you pluck the first and second strings at the same time, as you see in Figure 17-6b.

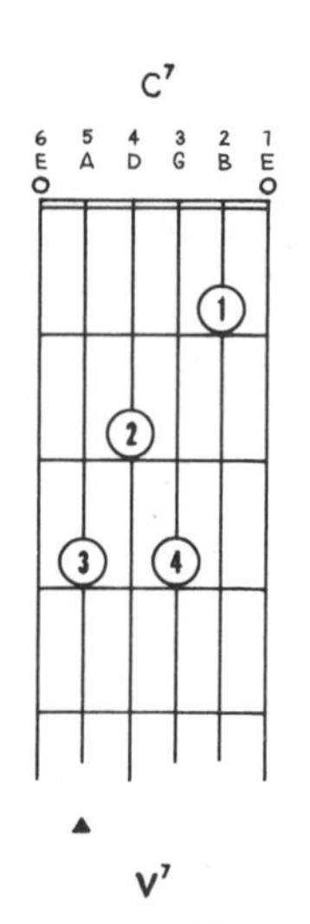

FIGURE 17-5 *C seventh (C^7) chord*

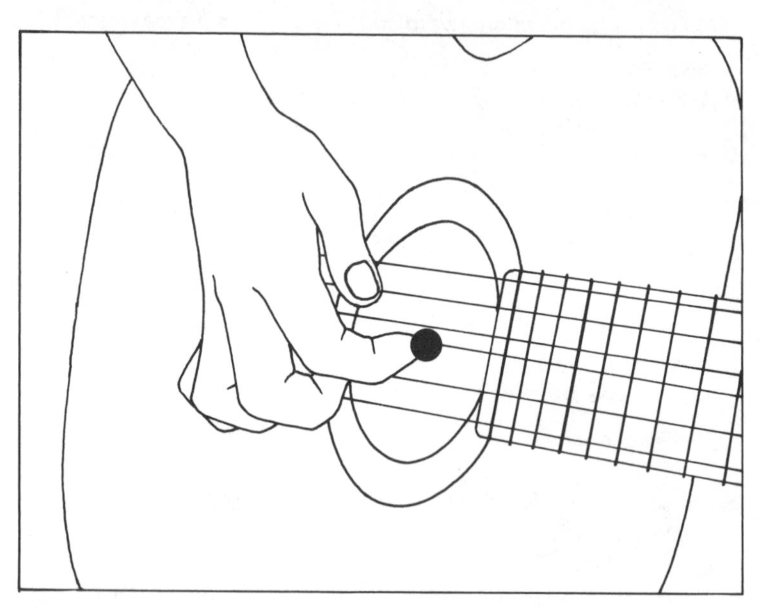

FIGURE 17-6a *Second step of the bass–three–pull-together strum: B-3-(2)*

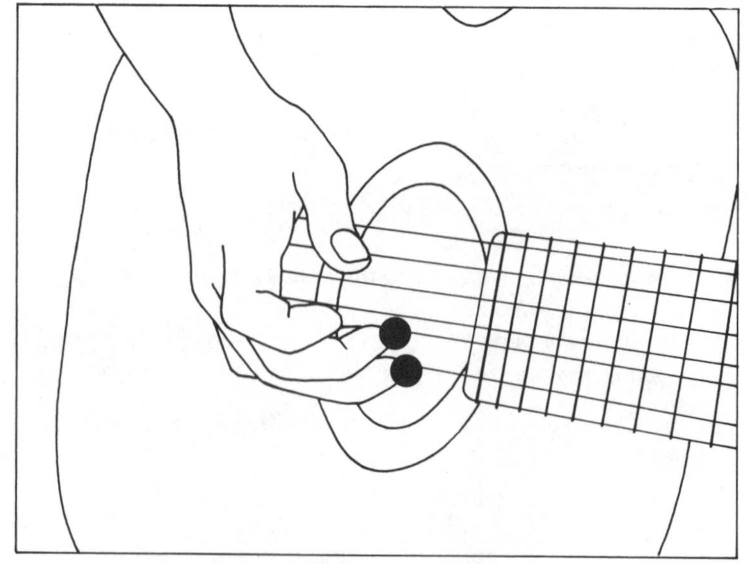

FIGURE 17-6b *Third step of the bass–three–pull-together strum: B-3-(2)*

1. Brush the bass string.
2. Pluck the third string.
3. Pluck the first and second strings simultaneously.

Practice this strum with the chords in the next song, the C, G^7, F, and C^7.

You can alternate basses with a waltz strum. Try it on "Who's Gonna Shoe Your Pretty Little Foot." On the C, C^7, and G^7 chords, you can alternate between the fourth, fifth, and sixth strings. On the F chord, you can alternate between the fourth and fifth strings. Whenever you change to a new chord, you must play the primary bass string first.

FIGURE 17-7 *"Who's Gonna Shoe Your Pretty Little Foot?"*

You can play these notes from home base chord positions. Try it. What do you think you should do in the last measure? Would you believe that's the C chord you've been playing all along, but didn't see in notation until now? If you strum down from the bass of the C, that's what you'll be playing in the last measure. You can also play that C chord by doing the C note with your thumb and the other four notes with your first, second, third, and fourth fingers plucking together as in the pull together strum. When you sing the song and accompany yourself with the B-3-(2) strum, play one pattern to each measure, and vary that strum with the B-down-down or any of the other waltz strums.

WHO'S GONNA SHOE YOUR PRETTY LITTLE FOOT?

C
Who's gonna shoe your pretty little foot
F C
Who's gonna glove your hand
F C
Who's gonna kiss your red ruby lips
G^7 C
Who's gonna be your man?
C^7 C
Who's gonna be your man, love
F C
Who's gonna be your man
F C
Who's gonna kiss your red ruby lips
G^7 C
Who's gonna be your man? /

2 *Papa's gonna shoe my pretty little foot*
Mama's gonna glove my hand
Sister's gonna kiss my red ruby lips
I don't need no man
I don't need no man, love
I don't need no man
Sister's gonna kiss my red ruby lips
I don't need no man.

3 *The longest train I ever did see*
Was a hundred coaches long
The only one I ever did love
Was on that train and gone
On that train and gone, love
On that train and gone
The only one I ever did love
Was on that train and gone.

Repeat first half of first verse (the first four lines)

More Bass Runs

In the following song, in addition to the bass runs from C to F, we'll add a bass run from G^7 to C. The principle is the same. There are four notes, the first and last being the basses of the chords you're coming from and going to. The two notes in between are passing notes. The bass note of the G^7 chord is G, which you sound when you brush the

FIGURE 17-8 *"This Land is Your Land"*

bass string on the Bnj B as you sing the word, "made" on the last line. This time, complete the Bnj B pattern, the fingers down—first finger up, on the word "for." The next two steps of the run are the notes A and B, on the open fifth string and on the fifth string, second fret; play those steps on the words "you and," completing the fourth step of the run on the note C. The C note is sounded when you brush the bass for the Bnj B, which you've started again for the C chord over the word "me." After each verse, when you begin the chorus, strum down on the Easy Strum and then play the bass run from the C chord to the F chord as you did in "Down By The Riverside" (Figure 17-3, page 153). Begin the run by sounding the bass of the C chord on the word "this," then perform the next step on the open fourth string when singing the word "land," do the third step on the fourth string, second fret, for the word "is," and complete the run with the bass of the F chord on the word "your."

Bass runs from the C chord to the F chord are called I to IV bass runs. These include all bass runs going from a I chord to a IV chord in any key. The bass run from G^7 to C is called a V to I bass run and includes all bass runs going from the V chord to the I chord in any key.

A few years ago, I was at a party where some people visiting from Sweden were present. Several of us sat around, singing

THIS LAND IS YOUR LAND*

Chorus

C bass run F C
This land is your land,/this land is my land /
G7 C
From California/to the New York Island /
F C
From the Redwood forest/to the Gulf Stream Waters / /
G7 bass run C
This land is made for you and me. /

(Same tune for verses)

F C
2 *As I was walking/that ribbon of highway /*
G7 C
I saw above me/an endless skyway /
F C
I saw below me/that golden valley / /
G7 C
This land was made for you and me. /

Chorus

3 *I roamed and I rambled, and I followed my foot steps*
From the sparkling sands of her diamond desert
And all around me, a voice came calling
This land was made for you and me.

Chorus

4 *The sun came shining and I was strolling*
Through the wheat fields waving and the dust clouds rolling
And all around me, a voice was chanting
This land was made for you and me.

Chorus

and playing guitars. The Swedes seemed to be enjoying it all; they were listening and smiling quietly. But when we sang "This Land Is Your Land," they all knew and sang the song with us. We were delighted to hear that they loved the song and thought of it as our national anthem.

* British Commonwealth, Ireland, and South Africa rights granted by TRO-Essex Music Limited; Australian rights courtesy of Essex Music of Australia Pty. Limited.

eighteen

KEY SIGNATURES, KEY OF C

In the last three songs, "Down By The Riverside," "Who's Gonna Shoe Your Pretty Little Foot?," and "This Land Is Your Land," you heard the tune when you played the introduction by notation. Each one of these tunes is in the key of C. When you look at a piece of written music, one of the ways you can tell which key it's in, is to look at the beginning of the piece. If there are no sharps or flats between the G (or treble) clef and the time signature, then it's in the key of C or its relative, Am. Whatever you *do* see in that space is called the key signature. A key signature gives you direction: It tells you whether you should play all the notes in the piece natural (which is how you've been playing all your notes, so far), or whether you should play certain notes flat or sharp.

FIGURE 18-1
Key signature of G

sharp.

That's and that's

flat

THE KEY OF G KEY SIGNATURE

In Figure 18-1, you'll see a sign on the upper right-hand side of the G clef; this is a sharp sign, and when it appears in the key signature, it means that music will be in the key of G. (There's an identical key signature for the relative minor key of G, but we won't take that up now.)

Notice what line of the staff the sharp is on. If you saw a note on that same top line of the staff, you'd know that it's an F. What does that mean? It means that every F note high and low, in that piece of music is to be played as F sharp (F♯). A sharp raises a note one half step. On the guitar, it raises the note from one fret to the next highest fret because the frets are a half step apart.

You know that if you wanted to play an F note, you'd play it on the first string, first fret. If you wanted to play an F♯ note, you'd play it on the first string, second fret. Try that. Play F, then F♯. Do you hear that the F♯ is slightly higher in sound? Again, that's because a sharp raises a musical note (or tone) a half step.

All the F notes, high and low, have got to be played F♯ in the key of G. You already know two F notes: one on the first string, first fret, and one on the fourth string, third fret. The F on the first string would be played F♯ in the second fret, instead of the first fret and the F on the fourth string would be played F♯ in the fourth fret, instead of the third fret.

Let's take a look at a couple of songs in the key of G. On the first one, "Grandfather's Clock," accompany yourself with the bass–pull together strum, B-(3), for the entire song, except when you reach the words "stopped," "short," and "tick." There, do the pull together strum.

Remember, all F's in this song must be played F♯ according to the key signature.

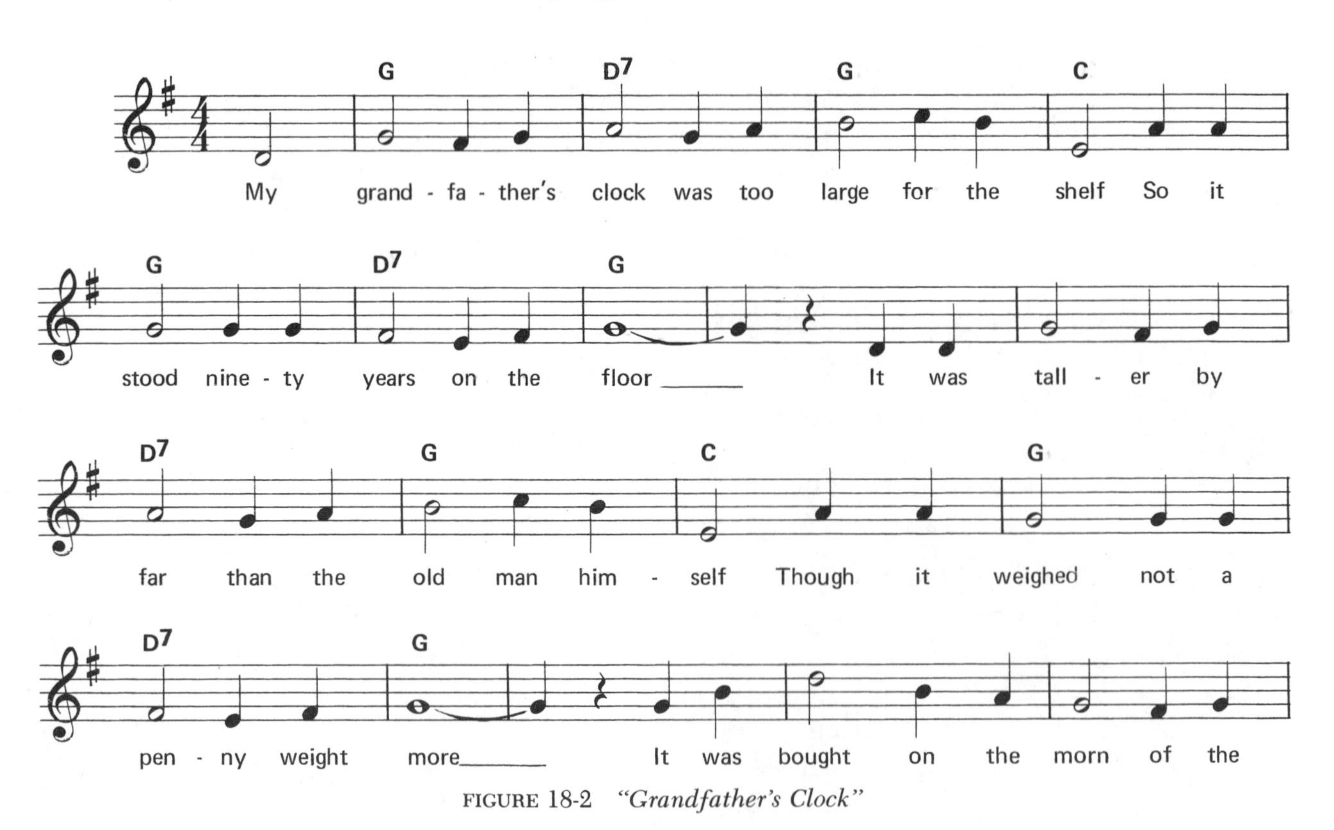

FIGURE 18-2 *"Grandfather's Clock"*

FIGURE 18-2 *(cont.)*

GRANDFATHER'S CLOCK

G D7 G C
My grandfather's clock was too large for the shelf
G D7 G
So it stood ninety years on the floor /
D7 G C
It was taller by far than the old man himself
G D7 G
Though it weighed not a penny weight more. /
G C G
It was bought on the morn of the day that he was born
A7 D7
And was always his treasure and pride /

G D7 G C
But it stopped short never to go again
G D7 G
When the old man died. /

Chorus

G
Ninety years without slumbering, tick, tock, tick, tock
His life seconds numbering, tick, tock, tick, tock
D7 G C
It stopped short never to go again
G D7 G
When the old man died. /

2 *In watching its pendulum swing to and fro*
Many hours had he spent while a boy
And in childhood and manhood the clock seemed to know
And to share both his grief and his joy
For it struck twenty four when he entered at the door
With a blooming and beautiful bride
But it stopped short never to go again
When the old man died.

Chorus

3 *My grandfather said that of those he could hire*
Not a one so faithful he found
For it wasted no time, and had but one desire
At the close of each week to be wound
And it kept its pace, not a frown upon its face
And its hands never hung by its side
But it stopped short never to go again
When the old man died.

Chorus

4 *It rang an alarm in the dead of the night*
An alarm that for years had been dumb
And we knew that his spirit was planning its flight
That his hour of departure had come
Still the clock kept the time, with a soft and muffled chime
As we silently stood by his side
But it stopped short never to go again
When the old man died.

Chorus

What about Strum Marks? All along, I've shown you where to strum by inserting the strum marks or slashes in the music. By this time, you've begun to develop a sense of timing and rhythm. Rhythm is the beat or pulse in music. From now on, I'm going to count on you to instinctively feel that beat and to know, on your own, where to strum your accompaniments. Trust yourself to feel the pulse of the music.

Perhaps you've already been doing the strumming on your own. A simple guideline is to strum on the strong beats of each measure. In $\frac{4}{4}$ time, that's on the first and third beats; in $\frac{2}{4}$ time and $\frac{3}{4}$ time, it's on the first beat of the measure. Play the bass of your strum pattern on all the strong beats.

Notice the broken circle where the time signature is in "Red River Valley." That's an often-used time signature that means to play in $\frac{4}{4}$ time. Formerly, it was the most commonly used time signature. The broken circle is actually a C, which stood for "common time" or $\frac{4}{4}$ time.

Don't forget to play all the F's sharp.

FIGURE 18-3 *"Red River Valley"*

BROKEN CHORD STRUM, B-3-2-1

This new strum really breaks up and spreads out each note of the chord into individual sounds. These sounds come one after the other in succession, starting with the lowest or bass note and ending with whatever note is on the first string of each chord. Just as you do in each of the pull together strums, you keep your first three fingertips slightly curled under the first three strings. Only the bass string changes. The first three strings are plucked the same way for each chord.

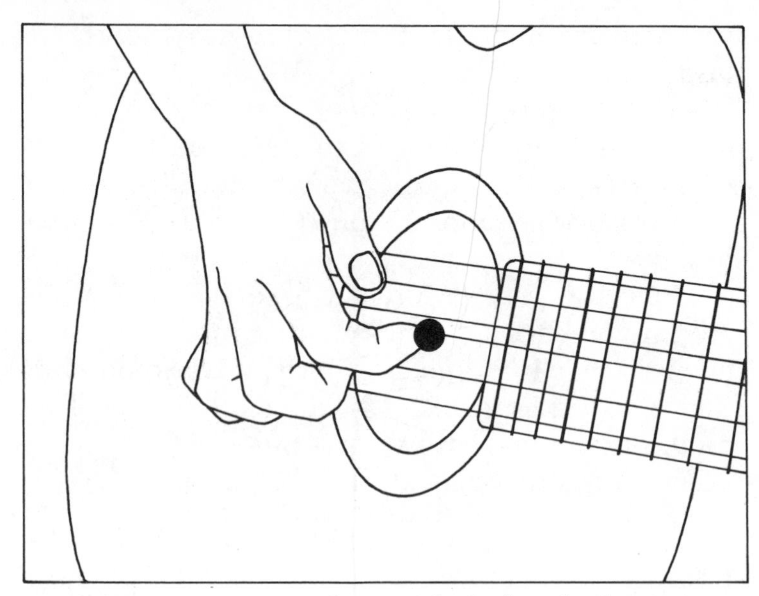

FIGURE 18-4a *Second step of the broken chord strum*

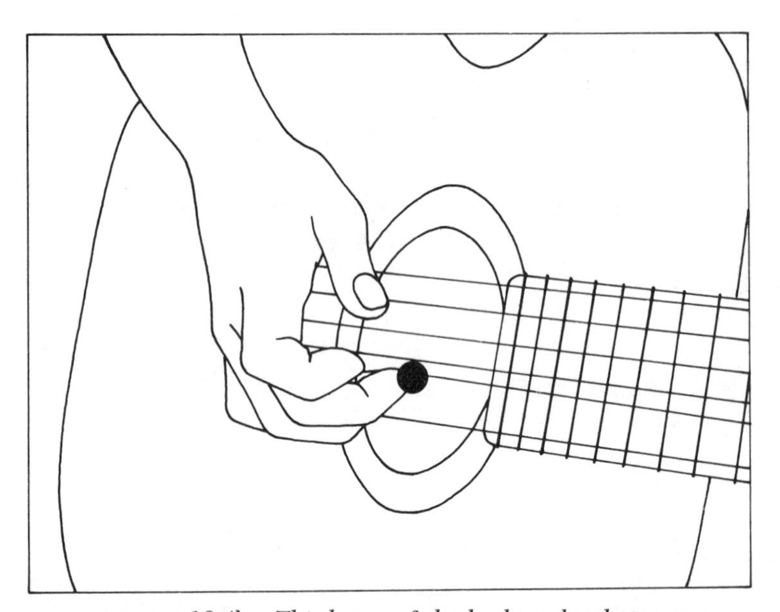

FIGURE 18-4b *Third step of the broken chord strum*

It's a four-step strum:

1. Brush the bass string of whatever chord you're on.
2. Pluck the third string with your first finger.
3. Pluck the second string with your second finger.
4. Pluck the first string with your third finger.

Each step of the pattern gets one beat or count. Practice this broken chord strum with the chords in the key of G. Then we'll do the next song with that B-3-2-1 pattern, the broken chord strum.

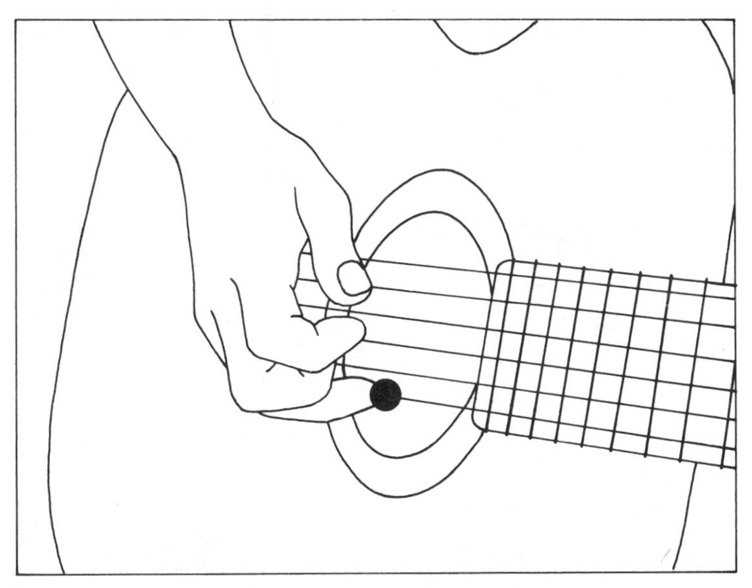

FIGURE 18-4c *Fourth step of the broken chord strum*

Start the song this way. Play one whole pattern, B-3-2-1. On the second pattern, play B-3, then start singing the song as you continue the pattern with 2-1. On the first syllable of the word "valley," start all over again with the bass movement of the B-3-2-1. Continue the strum pattern for the rest of the song.

RED RIVER VALLEY

```
         G
From this valley they say you are going
                                      D7
We will miss your bright eyes and nice smile
        G                 C
For they say you are taking the sunshine
        G          D7       G
That has brightened our pathway awhile.
```

2 *Won't you think of the valley you're leaving?*
Oh, how lonely and sad it will be
Think of this heart that you're breaking
And the grief you are causing to me.

3 *From this valley they say you are going*
When you go may I go with you too?
Would you leave me behind unprotected
When I love no one else but you?

4 *As you go to your home by the ocean*
May you never forget those sweet hours
That we spent in the Red River Valley
And the love we exchanged 'mid the flowers.

On the song that follows, "Plaisir D'Amour," we're going to do the B-3-(2) strum that we did with "Who's Gonna Shoe Your Pretty Little Foot?" Remember, that's a three-step strum. Each one of the steps gets one beat or count. You'll do a full pattern for each measure of music. Start singing on the pull together, the third step of the strum.

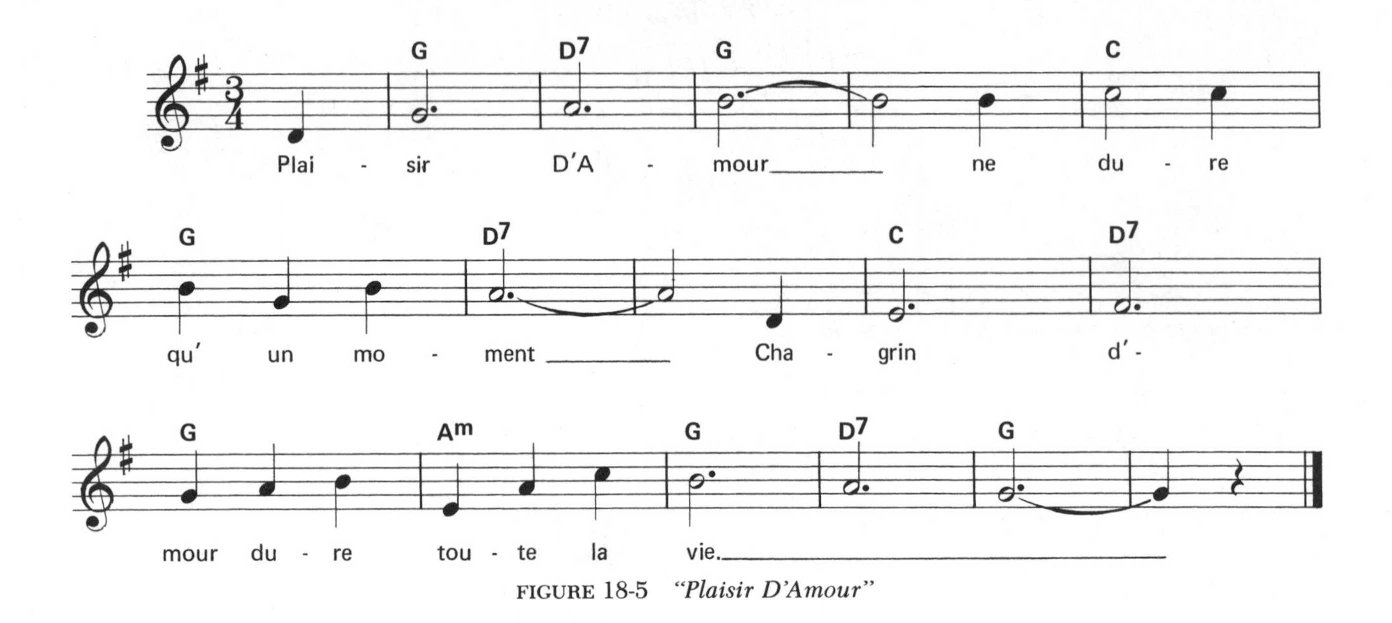

FIGURE 18-5 *"Plaisir D'Amour"*

PLAISIR D'AMOUR

Adapted and arranged with new words by R.T. Jacobs (Based on an old French song)

G D7 G C G D7
Plaisir d'amour, ne dure qu'un moment
C D7 G Am G D7 G
Chagrin d'amour dure toute la v - i - e.

2 *The joy of our love was only a moment to be*
The sorrow of parting lasting so painfully.

3 *My love loved me, and now, no love can I see*
The memory stays locked in my heartstrings so faithfully.

4 *Our love once shone and lit up the wonders around*
It now is lost in the darkness and never again to be found.

Repeat first verse

Notice that all the songs you played in the key of G end on the G note. That's the key of G *name note.* You'll find that, except for rare instances, any key that you play in will end on its key name note. That'll be another way to tell you what key a piece of music is in. Can you now guess the missing key signatures from "The Riddle Song" and "The Cruel War"?

OCTAVES

The two F notes that you already know are an octave apart. The F note on the first string, first fret, is one octave higher than the F note on the fourth string, third fret. Accordingly, the F♯ on the first string, second fret, is one octave higher than the F♯ note on the fourth string, fourth fret.

An octave is the same note sounded eight tones higher or eight tones lower. You remember that the musical alphabet has seven letters: A, B, C, D, E, F, G. If you wanted to sing the A an octave higher, you'd count your original A as one, then count up seven tones to get to the next A. Try it on the guitar.

FIGURE 18-6 *An octave*

If your guitar's in tune, you should hear that the two A's are really the same note. It's just that one is pitched higher than the other: they're an octave apart.

When you first learned the E-Z Numbers Game, I gave you two choices from which to play the numbers for "Three Blind Mice." The first choice was on the first and second strings; the second choice, played and sung an octave lower, was on the fourth string. And when you played the numbers for "The Water Is Wide" you may have felt uncomfortable singing along with the second string numbers, so I gave you the option of starting to sing with the fifth string numbers. If you chose the latter, you sang an octave lower.

Figure out octaves for the entire musical alphabet. You can make octaves with the notes that you know now, on all five strings.

Here's some information to keep in mind for future recall, even if you don't quite understand it now. All the written notes that you've been reading and playing on your guitar are written an octave higher than they're actually sounded. In other words, when you play an E on the open first string, because that's what you see written in the music, what you and everybody else actually hears is the E on the fourth string, second fret. The reason is probably this: If the highest-sounding, open first string on the guitar was to be written on the lowest line of the staff (because that's the sound you really hear), imagine what you'd have to do to write the notes for the fifth and sixth strings. There'd be so many ledger lines for the very low notes, it would be an impractical mess.

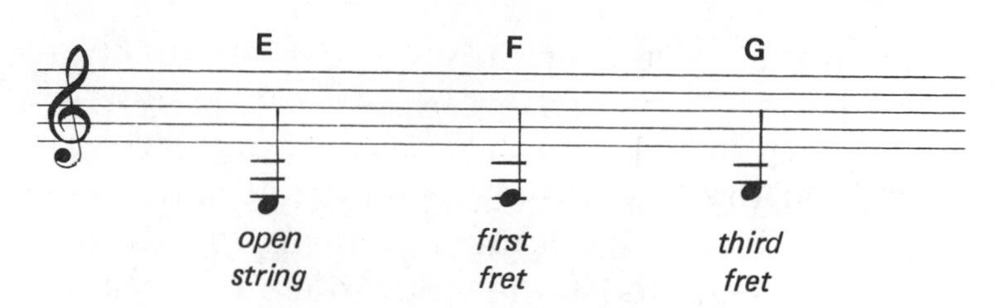

FIGURE 18-7a *Sixth string notes*

FIGURE 18-7b *Notes to practice on the sixth string*

SIXTH STRING NOTES

With the addition of the sixth string notes, you now know the E, F, and G notes in three octaves. (The sixth string notes are really low down. Can you sing that low?) Now that you know the notes on all six strings and you know about octaves, you can play some songs an octave lower or higher than you played them before. Try playing "Michael Row the Boat Ashore" in two octaves. Now, you can read the music notation of the more complicated arrangement of this song and play it just as you did in the Numbers Game.

In the next song, "The Swinger," see if you can find the two notes that you sing and play in both octaves. The strum you can do for this is the B–fingers-down–down-up–down-up strum. Remember, that's a four-step pattern and each step of the pattern gets one beat or count. Since the time

FIGURE 18-8a, b *"Michael, Row the Boat Ashore" in two different octaves*

signature tells you there are four beats to each measure, play a full pattern for each measure. Each beat in the measure gets one step of the strum pattern; in other words, the time signature tells you that each quarter note or quarter rest will get one beat, and that each quarter note or quarter rest will get one of the steps of the strum pattern.

The particular step of the pattern that you'll do for a note or a rest depends on where it is in the measure. For instance, there is an A in "The Swinger" that comes in the middle of the fourteenth measure. You have two options there. You can do the B-down for the first two beats of the measure on an Em chord and finish the pattern, down-up–down-up on the A^7. If that's too tricky, play the B-down on the Em chord, change to the A^7, and do another B-down. That'll give you the four beats you need in the measure.

FIGURE 18-9 *"The Swinger"*

FIGURE 18-9 *(cont.)*

If you'd like to try a real twangy introduction, play two patterns of the strum on the G before you start singing. When you do the third and fourth steps of the pattern, the down-up-down-up, lift your finger off the first string, third fret, then return it for the B-down when you begin the pattern again.

Now let's have some fun with this tongue twister.

THE SWINGER


```
G            C              G
  Remember when I took your hand and married you
                            D7
  You said you loved me and always would be true
                C        G
  I gave you everything a man could give in life
Em                 A7    D7
  But in return you gave to me a faithless cheatin' wife.

  Chorus

     G
  Oh a ring on the finger doesn't make a clinger
```

C

And when love doesn't linger that's the zinger

D7

'Cause when things start floppin' then there ain't no stoppin'

G

And there ain't no toppin' such a swinger

I won't take your lyin' and so don't start tryin'

C

And don't start cryin' I ain't buyin'

D7

Do I have to tell it, do I have to spell it

G

Do I have to yell—goodbye I'm flyin'.

2 *You had a strange look when I came home from my job*
I was an hour early when I turned that knob
And when I saw the pair of socks he left behind
I knew the fool I'd been and nearly lost my mind.

Chorus

You ain't been straight with me since on the day we met
You keep on lyin' and I swear you'll get yours yet
My good friends warned me that you were the cheatin' kind
The best that I could do for you is paddle you from behind.

Chorus

Repeat the last two lines of the chorus

Now that you're playing the lower notes on your guitar, you can see how important it is to position your thumb on the neck correctly. Where is your left-hand thumb? Is it about halfway down the back of the neck? Leave space between the palm of your hand and the neck of the guitar. Don't squeeze the guitar neck in a death grip. It'll be the death of any real mobility and leverage with your fingers.

THE Dm CHORD This is your third D chord; you've had the D and D^7 chords, and now you're playing the D minor. To review, its bass string is the fourth or D string. Strum it slowly at first, gliding your thumb across the strings, from the bass string to the first string. It has the same haunting quality in its sound as the other minor chords.

Changing from Am to Dm to Am This change isn't too difficult. When going from the Am to the Dm, your first finger moves from the second string to the first string, first fret, your second finger moves from the fourth string to the third string, second fret, and your third finger goes from the third string, second fret, to the second string, third fret. Whether you use your third or fourth finger on the second string, third fret, is optional. Experiment with both fingers and choose whichever position feels more comfortable.

When changing back to the Am, your first finger goes from the first string to the second string, first fret, your second finger goes from the third string to the fourth string, second fret, and your third finger goes right behind your second finger to the third string, second fret. Practice the changes between Am and Dm. Practice changing with the bass–pull together strum. Don't forget, it's in two steps.

1. Brush the bass string.
2. Pluck the first three strings simultaneously.

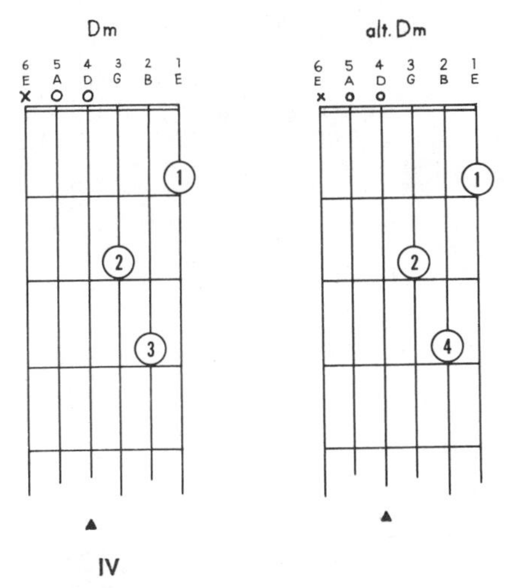

FIGURE 19-1a, b *Two versions of the D minor (Dm) chord*

We're going to accompany the next song, "Dona, Dona," with the bass–pull-together strum. However, on the last three chords of both verse lines, simply strum down with an Easy Strum before returning to the bass–pull-together strum. Alternate the basses on the chorus.

In "Dona, Dona," you'll see four eighth notes joined by a beam. The same half beat count for each eighth note is retained whether they're single eighth notes or eighth notes joined by a beam. Remember, the eighth note gets the same time value as the single dot rhythm mark in the Numbers Game.

FIGURE 19-2 *"Dona, Dona"*

FIGURE 19-2 *(cont.)*

There'll be two patterns to each measure here. You can add variety to the accompaniment by using the B-down strum for the chorus and the bass–pull-together strum for the verses.

DONA, DONA

Am E7 Am E7 Am Dm Am E7 Am
On a wagon bound for market, there's a calf with a mournful eye
Am E7 Am E7 Am Dm Am E7 Am
High above him there's a swallow, flying freely through the sky.

Chorus

G7 C G7 C
How the winds are laughing, they laugh with all their might
G7 C E7 Am
Laugh and laugh the whole day through and half the summer's night.
E7 Am G7 C
Dona dona dona dona, Dona dona dona da
E7 Am E7 Am
Dona dona dona dona, Dona dona dona da.

2 *Stop complaining, said the farmer, who told you a calf to be*
Why don't you have wings to fly with, like the swallow so proud and free?

Chorus

3 *Calves are easily bound and slaughtered, never knowing the reason why*
And whoever treasures freedom, like the swallow has learned to fly.

Chorus

Changing from Dm to E⁷

This change is a bit awkward. It'll be easier if you move your second finger before you move the other fingers. Your second finger goes from the third string to the fifth string, second fret. Then, move your first finger from the first string to the third string, first fret, while lifting off your third or fourth finger from the second string, third fret. Practice changing with the Easy Strum and then with the strum we're going to do for the next song. It's the same strum you did for "Who's Gonna Shoe Your Pretty Little Foot?"

On the next song, "Cocaine Bill," we'll do the B-3-(2) strum. It's a three-step pattern and each step gets one beat, or count. Each measure will get a full pattern. To review,

1. Brush the bass string.
2. Pluck the third string.
3. Pluck the first and second string simultaneously.

FIGURE 19-3 *"Cocaine Bill"*

COCAINE BILL

Adapted and arranged with new words by R.T. Jacobs

Am Dm E7 Am
Cocaine Bill and his sweetheart Sue, went walking down the avenue
Dm E7 Am
Said Sue to Bill, "It won't do no harm if we both have a little shot in the arm."

2 *Bill said, "Sue, I just can't refuse 'cause there's no kick in this old booze."*
They walked down Fifth and they turned up Main, looking for any one who had some cocaine.

3 *They got more than they bargained for, I guess you've heard it all before*
Now, in the graveyard on that far hill, lies the cold and dead body of Cocaine Bill.

4 *In a grave right by his side, lies the body of his cocaine bride*
In a dark grave and so cold and pale, are two dead fools and the end of this tale.

KEY OF Am FAMILY

With "Dona, Dona" and "Cocaine Bill" we've completed the three main chords in our first minor key family. It's the key family of Am. The three main chords of a minor key are derived in the same way as the three main chords of a major key; from the first, fourth and fifth letters of its musical alphabet.

Key of Am

A	B	C	D	E	F	G	A
I			IV	V^7			

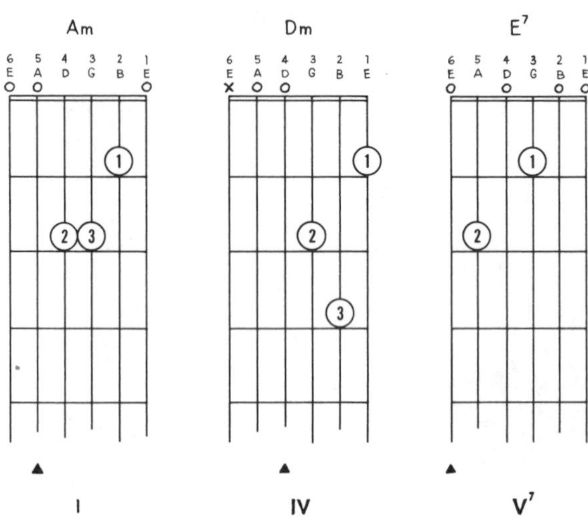

FIGURE 19-4 *Key of A minor*

Changing from Dm to C to Dm

When going from Dm to C, if you're using your third finger on the Dm chord, it goes from the second string to the fifth string, third fret, your second finger goes from the third string to the fourth string, second fret, and your first finger goes from the first string to the second string, first fret.

If you're using your fourth finger on the Dm chord, lift it off and do the same steps. To go from C to Dm, just reverse the moves.

On the next song, *Scarborough Fair,* we're going to do the Bass–pull-together–pull-together strum, B-(3)-(3), on every *other* measure, beginning with the first.

1. Brush the bass string.
2. Pluck the first three strings simultaneously.
3. Repeat the second step.

In the measures between, play the B-3-(2) strum, also a three-step pattern. Each one of the three steps in both patterns gets one beat or count; each measure gets a full pattern.

You'll notice there's a chord change in the middle of the seventh measure. I'm going to give you a very easy way to do it. At the end of the sixth measure, take your fingers off the Dm chord position. Brush the fourth string. Now, finger the first string, third fret, with your third or fourth finger and pluck the first three strings twice. You've completed the pattern for the seventh measure.

On the eighth measure, go back to the Dm chord and continue the accompaniment. Believe it or not, when you fingered the first string, third fret, and plucked the first three strings, you played part of a G chord. If you pluck the fourth string also then you're playing a complete G chord. (Remember that there is more than one way to play a chord.)

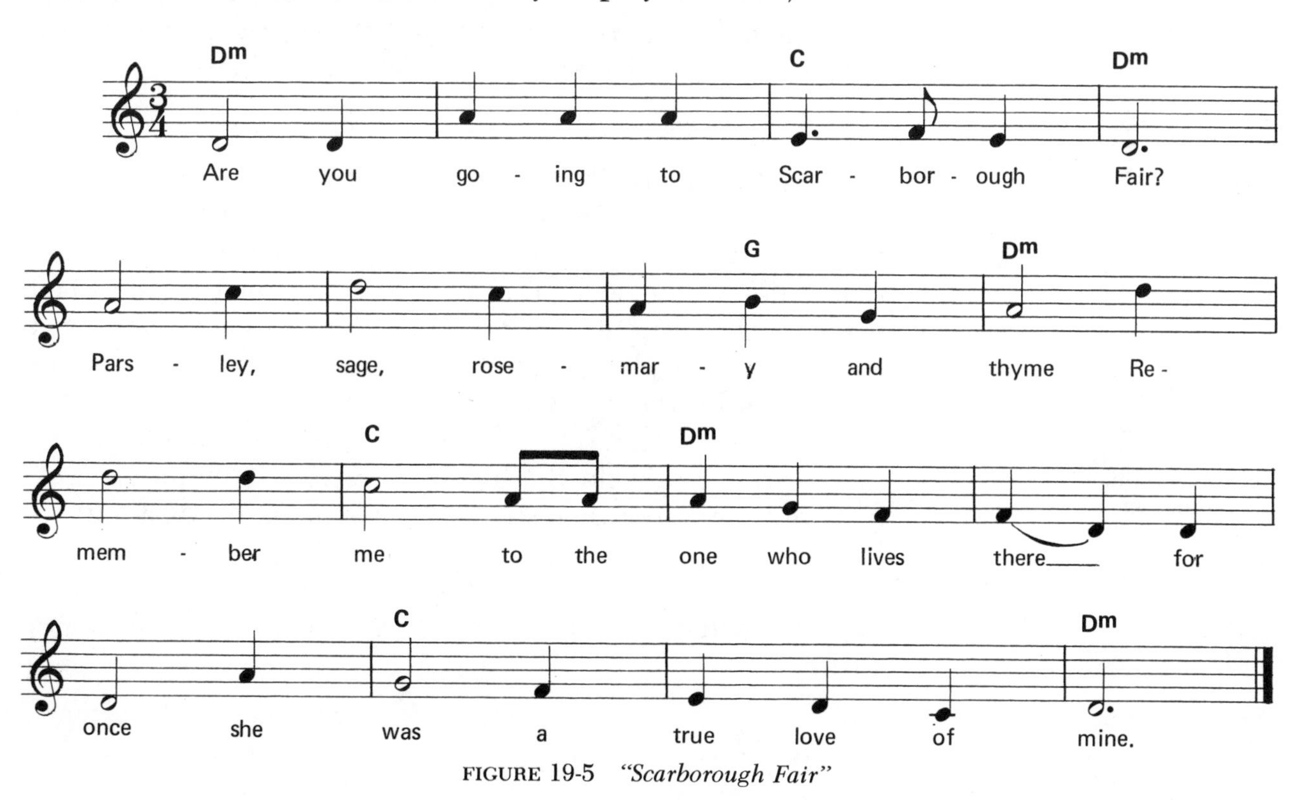

FIGURE 19-5 *"Scarborough Fair"*

SCARBOROUGH FAIR

Adapted and arranged by R.T. Jacobs (Based on an English folk song)

Dm C Dm

Are you going to Scarborough Fair?

G Dm

Parsley, sage, rosemary and thyme

C Dm

Remember me to the one who lives there

C Dm

For once she was a true love of mine.

2 Have her make me a cambric shirt
Parsley, sage, rosemary and thyme
Without a seam of fine needle work
And then she'll be a true love of mine.

3 Have her wash it in yonder dry well
Parsley, sage, rosemary and thyme
There ne'er a drop of water e'er fell
And then she'll be a true love of mine.

4 If she tells me she can't, I'll reply
Parsley, sage, rosemary and thme
Let me know that at least she will try
And then she'll be a true love of mine.

Changing from D to D⁷

This change is a bit awkward, but not very difficult. Your first finger goes from the third string, second fret, to the second string, first fret. Your second finger moves over from the first to the third string, in the second fret. And your third finger goes from the second string, third fret, to the first string, second fret. Now you're on a D^7 chord.

KEY SIGNATURE IN THE KEY OF D

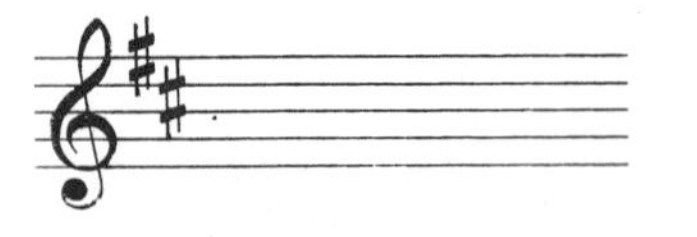

FIGURE 19-6
Key signature of D

Many times, you'll see a key signature that looks like the one in Figure 19-5. What you see is the F♯ and the C♯. When you see those two sharps in the key signature, the music that follows will be in the key of D. So, in the key of D, every F and C note in the piece must be played as sharps. Remember, to play a note sharp, raise it one fret higher. For example, the F note will be played (F♯) on the fourth string, fourth fret; the C will be played (C♯) on the fifth string, fourth fret. You'd do the same thing if you had an F note or C note on any other string, in any piece of music, in the key of D.

In the next song, "Banks Of The Ohio," we'll do the B–fingers-down–down-up–down-up strum. It's a four-step strum:

1. Brush the bass string.
2. Fingers down with the flat side of the finger nails.
3. Scrape down with the flat side of the first finger nail and brush up with the underside of the first finger tip.
4. Repeat third step.

Each measure gets a full pattern of the strum. Begin with one full pattern of the strum, then start the next pattern with the bass movement. Start singing on the "fingers-down," and continue the strum pattern for the rest of the song.

FIGURE 19-7 *"Banks of the Ohio"*

BANKS OF THE OHIO

D A7
I asked my love to take a walk
D
To take a walk, just a little walk
D7 G
Down beside where the waters flow
D A7 D
Down by the banks of the Ohio.

Chorus

D A7
And only say that you'll be mine
D
In no other's arms entwine
D7 G
Down beside where the waters flow
D A7 D
Down by the banks of the Ohio.

2 *I held a knife against her breast*
As into my arms she pressed
She cried, "Oh Willie, don't murder me
I'm not prepared for eternity."

Chorus

3 *I started home 'tween twelve and one*
I cried, "My God, what have I done?
Killed the only woman I loved
Because she would not be my bride."

Chorus

About Changing Chords

At this point, I think you can begin to work out new chord changes on your own. Always do them slowly at first. Notice how your fingers move as they make the changes. Experiment to see which moves seem to be the smoothest. Eventually, try to get all your fingers to make the moves at the same time. The idea is to be able to play without having your eyes constantly watching your fingers move.

On the verses of this next song, "For You," you can use the broken chord strum (B-3-2-1). Here's a new strum that you can use for the refrain.

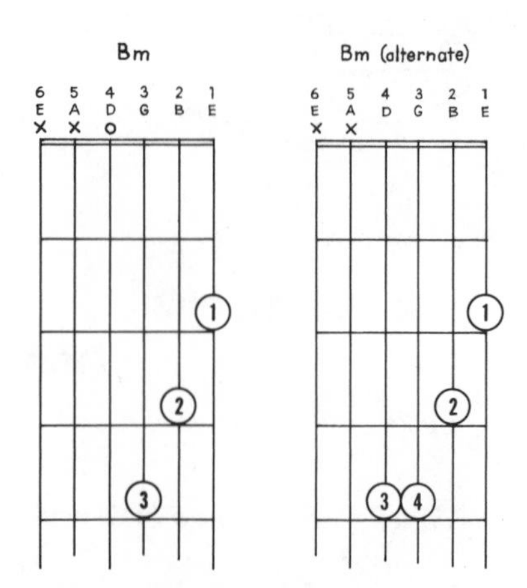

FIGURE 19-8a, b *Two versions of the B minor (Bm) chord*

BASS–3–PULL-TOGETHER–3 STRUM, B-3-(2)-3

This is a four-step strum. Each one of the steps counts as one beat, and each measure of music gets a full pattern.

1. Brush the bass string.
2. Pluck the third string with your first finger.
3. Pluck the second string with your second finger and the first string with your third finger simultaneously.
4. Pluck the third string again.

FIGURE 19-9 *"For You"*

FOR YOU

D Bm
For your tears, there's a circle 'round the sky
G Em A
And for your tears, there's a man who wants to cry

D Bm G
For your tears, there's someone who really tries
Em A
For your tears.

For your smile, there's a flower in my hand
And for your smile, there's a billion grains of sand
For your smile, there's a garden that we planned
For your smile.

Refrain

A D
So here's a simple picture that I drew
Bm E7 A
And here's a song that's written just for you.

2 *Without you, my world is not the same*
And without you, my life is just a game
Without you, inspiration's just a name
Without you.

For your love, there's a new day to begin
And for your love, there's a planet that will spin
For your love, the sunlight's pouring in
For your love.

Accidentals

You know now that when you see a key signature at the beginning of a piece of music, it tells you whether certain notes in the piece should be played sharp or flat. (Of course, if the key is C, there won't be any sharps or flats in the key signature. All the notes in the key of C are played "natural.")

However, there will be times when a sharp or a flat will appear in front of a note without appearing in the key signature: play this note sharp or flat. A sharp, flat, or natural that appears in a line of music, but is not in the key signature, is called an accidental.

It's important to remember that when accidentals show up in a measure, they only apply to that particular measure. In the very next measure and for the rest of the piece of music, play the notes according to the key signature unless, of course, more accidentals pop up.

For instance, if there's an accidental in front of an F in a measure, and another F appears in that same measure, play the second F (and all other F's in the measure) the same as you played the first F. An accidental symbol is never repeated for the same notes in a measure.

Also, if a piece of music is in the key of G, which has F♯ in the key signature, and the composer wants you to play one particular F♯ note in the piece as F natural instead, then that F will have a natural in front of it. This is also an accidental.

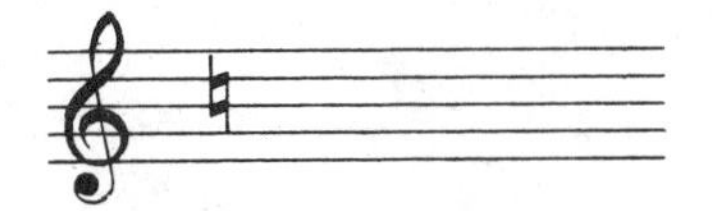

FIGURE 20-1 *Natural sign*

Do you remember that in "Down By The Riverside" you played numbers instead of notes in a couple of places? I said then that it had something to do with accidentals. Go back now and see if you can figure out what those accidental notes are.

In the following song, "John Henry," the key signature tells you the song is in the key of G because it's got one sharp in its key signature, $F^{\sharp}$. Therefore, all the F notes in the song will be played $F^{\sharp}$, unless there's an accidental in front of it. Two kinds of accidentals appear here: one makes an $F^{\sharp}$ an F natural and the other makes a B(B natural) a B flat($B^{\flat}$).

Do the Bass-fingers-down-down-up-down-up strum with this song and try alternating the basses on the G chords since you must hold them for several measures. The following letters will show you how to line the strum: B-fd-du-du. Play one pattern for each measure. For added interest, see if you can lift your first-string finger off the chords *after* you play the B-fingers down movements and return it when you start the pattern again.

FIGURE 20-2 *"John Henry"*

finger up finger up finger up

-d u B-fd- d u-d u B-fd-du - du B- d u- du-du, etc.

When John Henry was a little b a b y sittin' on his daddy's

JOHN HENRY

G D7

When John Henry was a little baby, sittin' on his daddy's knee

G

He grabbed a hammer and a little piece of steel,

Said, "This hammer's gonna be the death of me.
D7 **G**
This hammer'll be the death of me."

2 *Now the captain said to John Henry, "I'm gonna bring that steam drill 'round*
I'm gonna take that steel drill out on the job,
I'm gonna whop that steel on down.
I'm gonna whop that steel on down."

3 *John Henry told his Captain, "A man ain't nothin' but a man*
But before I let that steam drill beat me down,
I'll die with my hammer in my hand.
I'll die with my hammer in my hand."

There was a lot more squeezing than stretching on the second and third verse lines, wasn't there?

For the next song, "Pretty Shacoon," use the broken chord strum on the verses and the Bass-3-(2)-3 on the chorus. Both of them are four-step strums and each of the steps counts as one beat. Since there are four beats in each measure, each measure gets a full pattern of the strum.

Remember, after you play the C note C♯ in some of the measures that have accidentals, don't forget to play the C note natural, when you see it again, in other measures.

FIGURE 20-3 *"Pretty Shacoon"*

FIGURE 20-3 *(cont.)*

PRETTY SHACOON

Adapted and arranged by R.T. Jacobs (Based on a Haitian folk song)

G
I once had pretty Shacoon
D7
I know I was a lucky man
She smiled at me all the time
G
I thought that she was all mine
She smiled at me all the time
A D7
I thought that she was all mine.

Chorus

G D7 G
Pretty girl please don't run away from me
D7 G
Pretty girl, you know how lonely I'll be
C G
What did I ever do to make you feel so blue
D7 G
I know I made you sad and now I feel so bad
C G
Oh please, don't go away, I'll be so good today
D7 G
If you just come back you'll see.

2 *I wish I could forget*
And then I would go away too
But I'm not lucky like you
So I sit with nothing to do
But I'm not lucky like you
So I sit with nothing to do.

Chorus

3 *Oh, since the day she left*
I'm trying so hard to forget
My poor heart feels the pain
My soul feels like it has chains
My poor heart feels the pain
My soul feels like it has chains.

Chorus

KEY SIGNATURE IN THE KEY OF A

Now we're going to learn a key signature with three sharps in it. The same general idea holds whether there are one, two, three, or more sharps in the key signature: if there is a sharp in the key signature, it indicates that a particular note must be played sharp throughout the piece of music.

The following song, "Tomorrow," has three sharps in its key signature, indicating that it's in the key of A. Play each F note, C note, and G note, sharp: F♯, C♯, and G♯. Accompany yourself with the Bnj B Strum and alternate the basses on each chord. Make sure you play the primary bass whenever you change to another chord, then alternate between the fourth, fifth, and sixth strings. I want you to do the full pattern of the Bnj B on each beat of the measure. That means you'll do four Bnj B patterns in each measure. Using B-du to line out the Bnj B pattern, this is how it would look:

FIGURE 20-4 *"Tomorrow"*

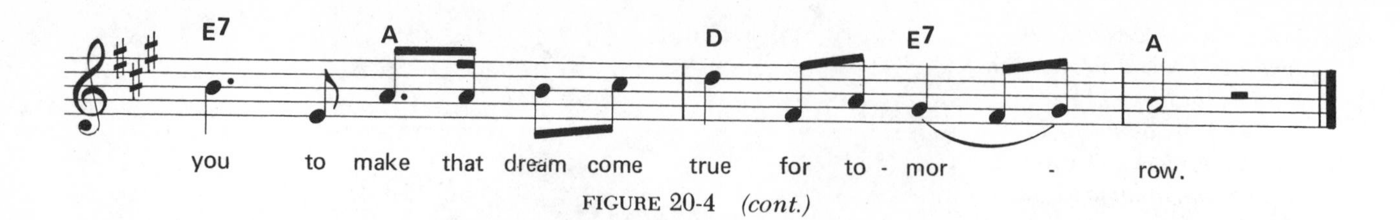

FIGURE 20-4 *(cont.)*

B-du B-du B-du B-du B-du B-du B-du B-du B-du
Last night I dreamt that the world was full of l o v e
B-du B-du B-du B- du B- du B-du B-du B-du B-du, etc.
but when I a - woke 'twas only a d r e a m Now dreams

TOMORROW

D E7 A D E7
Last night I dreamt that the world was full of love
A D E7
But when I awoke 'twas only a dream
D E7 A E7
Now dreams some times come true, but it's up to me and you
A D E7 A
To make that dream come true, for tomorrow.

2 *Sometimes I wonder if the world is out of tune*
But maybe it's just another dream
Well, yesterday is gone and now today is here
Let's tune up today for tomorrow.

3 *And now is the time for you and for me*
To sit by the fireside and sing
We'll sing of love and peace and dream of a beautiful world
That we could all live in for tomorrow.

4 *Well, it's now we're on the track and it's now we won't turn back*
And I believe the time is now, right now
For each and every one, to join in hand in hand
To build a better world for tomorrow.

5 *So come on young and old and gather all around*
And share in a melody with me
When we're in harmony, together we will sing
And make the bells ring out, for tomorrow.

On the next song, "This Time I'm On My Way," do the Bass-fingers-down-down-up-down-up strum. Alternate basses, playing two strum patterns for each measure. For example, using the B-fd-du-du to line out the pattern, this is how you'd do it:

B- fd- du-du B-fd- du- du B-fd-du-du B- fd- du-du
I'm on my way and I won't turn back I'm on my way

Although the strum pattern has four steps, this time, for the first time, you'll be doing *two* steps of the pattern for each beat in the measure. Try it *very slowly,* at first, until you get used to it.

FIGURE 20-5 *"This Time I'm On My Way"*

THIS TIME I'M ON MY WAY

Adapted and arranged with additional words by R.T. Jacobs (Based on a spiritual)

A E7
I'm on my way and I won't turn back
A
I'm on my way and I won't turn back
D
I'm on my way and I won't turn back
A E7 A
I'm on my way, this time, I'm on my way.

2 *It's a long hard road, but I won't turn back*
It's a long hard road, but I won't turn back
It's a long hard road, but I won't turn back
I'm on my way, this time, I'm on my way.

3 *There's many a one, who's gone before*
There's many a one, who's gone before
There's many a one, who's gone before
I'm on my way, this time, I'm on my way.

4 *Some have made it and some turned back*
Some have made it and some turned back
Some have made it and some turned back
I'm on my way, this time, I'm on my way.

5 *I asked my friends to join with me*
I asked my friends to join with me
I asked my friends to join with me
I'm on my way, this time, I'm on my way.

6 *If they say no, I'll go anyhow*
If they say no, I'll go anyhow
If they say no, I'll go anyhow
I'm on my way, this time, I'm on my way.

Repeat first verse

AROUND THE KEYS

First you had a key signature (the key of C) with no sharps or flats in it. Then you had a key signature (G) with one sharp in it, F♯. Next, you had a key signature (D) with two sharps in it, F♯ and C♯. And most recently, you learned a key signature (A) with three sharps in it, F♯, C♯, and G♯.

Have you noticed anything about each key that has one more sharp added to it? Think about this. How far is the key of G from the key of C in the musical alphabet? Counting C as one:

1 2 3 4 5
C D E F G

When you got to G, one sharp was added to the key signature. How far is the key of D, from the key of G in the musical alphabet, counting G as one? Right! It's five again, from G to D. In the key of D, you add another sharp to the key signature. You can figure out for yourself that the key of A is five away from the key of D. When you get to the key of A, another sharp is added. It goes around in fives, then, doesn't it?

There's an interesting consistency to all this. In the key of C, the I chord is the C; if you count up five in the musical alphabet, you'll get the V chord, the G. In the key of G, the I chord is the G; if you count up five, you'll get the V chord, the D. In the key of D, the I chord is D; if you count up five, you'll get the V chord, the A. You can see that each I chord is the V chord of the key before it.

Around We Go in a Circle of Fifths. In music, there is a system called a circle of fifths. Starting from the key of C and moving around the circle in a clockwise direction, each key is five away from the key preceding it, and adds one sharp to its key signature. Also, it's the fifth, or the V chord, of the key preceding it.

You already know the first five keys in the circle of fifths and their three main chords. You've sung and played songs in the keys of C, G, D, A, and E. I've only filled in half the circle for now. I don't want you to get dizzy from going around too fast. So, think about the circle of fifths for awhile and we'll get back to it a little later on.

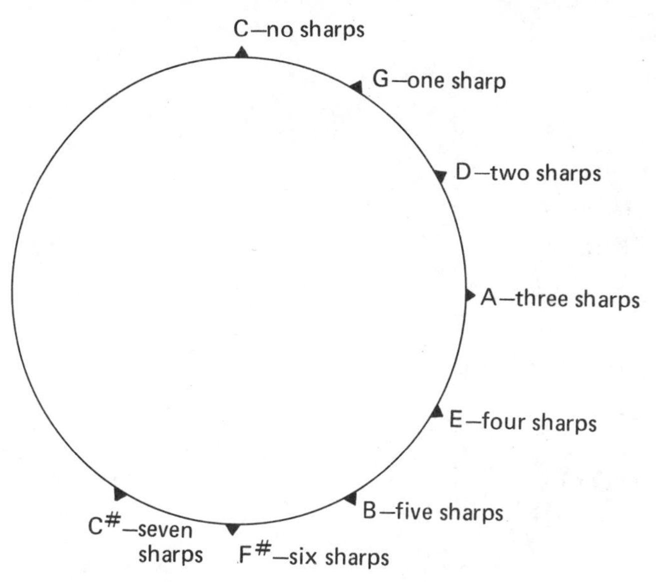

FIGURE 20-6 *Sharp side of the circle of fifths*

KEY SIGNATURE IN THE KEY OF F

I've purposely saved this key for last. You may wonder why. Because this key is a bit more difficult, I've provided chord-changing descriptions again. You may need to put a bit more effort into this key, but if you've gotten this far you know how nicely your efforts can pay off.

FIGURE 21-1 *Key signature of F*

Sometimes, you'll see a key signature like the one in Figure 21-1. This is the key signature for the key of F and it has one flat, the B flat (B♭). A flat lowers the note a half step. So, any B note that you see in a piece of music with that key signature has to be played B flat (B♭). Where you see a B in the following piece of music, instead of playing it on the fifth string, second fret, play it on the fifth string, first fret. Since the frets are a half step apart, that lowers the B one half step and it becomes a B♭.

FIGURE 21-2 *Flatting the B*

FIGURE 21-3 *"Hail, Hail, the Gang's All Here"*

Changing from F to C^7 to F

This change is exactly the same as the change from F to C to F, except that you add your fourth finger to the third string, third fret, for the C^7 chord. Do the Easy Strum when you sing "Hail, Hail the Gang's All Here."

In the next song, "The Peanut Song," a different situation arises when it comes time to play the B♭. It's easy enough to lower a note one fret, or flat it, as you did when you played Figure 21-2. But what do you do when the note to be flatted is one fret lower than the open string? How can you play a note lower than the lowest note on the string? Think about it. Where would you play the B♭ in Figure 21-4a? It's played on the third string, third fret, because as you learned at the beginning of the book, the frets on the guitar are like a keyboard on a piano: white key, black key, white key, black key, and so on. We know the musical alphabet is A, B, C, D, E, F, G. Since a sharp raises a note a half step (one fret up) and a flat lowers a note a half step (one fret down), if A on the third string is to be sharped, you raise it from the third string, second fret, to the third string, third fret. Calling on the musical alphabet, the next note (fret) would have to be a B. That would put B on the third string, fourth fret. Play that B, then play the B on the open second string. What do you hear? If your guitar is in tune, you should hear the same sound. That's because whether you play B natural (see Figure 21-4b) on the open second string or on the third string, fourth fret, it's the same B. (Isn't that something you do when you tune your guitar? When you press the fourth fret on the third string and tune the open second string to match, what are you doing? You're matching the sound of the open

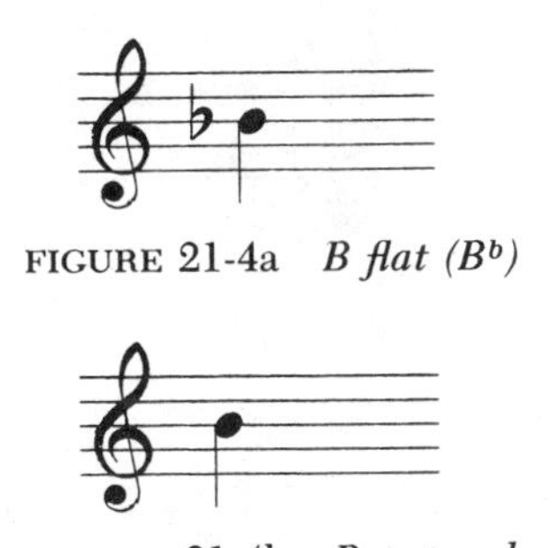

FIGURE 21-4a *B flat (B♭)*

FIGURE 21-4b *B natural*

B string to the sound of the B you're fingering on the third string, fourth fret.)

Since you can't play a note lower on a string than the open string itself, you have to play the flatted B in Figure 21-4a somewhere else. Conveniently, you could play it on the next lower string, the third string. Since a flat lowers a note one fret, if the third string, *fourth* fret, is a B, then B♭ is one fret lower on the third string, *third* fret.

Notice that A♯ and B♭ are in the same fret and that they sound exactly the same in pitch. Experiment and you will see that the same theory holds for other pairs of notes, like C♯ and D♭, D♯ and E♭, F♯ and G♭, and G♯ and A♭. That's because notes like C♯ and D♭ are really the same note. They're just spelled differently, musically speaking. Get used to recognizing the sharp (♯) sign and the flat (♭) sign.

FIGURE 21-5 *"The Peanut Song"*

This is the first time you've seen a $\frac{6}{8}$ time signature. When you sing the song accompany yourself with the Easy Strum. We'll play two strums to each measure. Since the time signature tells you there are six beats to a measure and each eighth note gets one beat, we're going to do one Easy Strum for the first eighth note and one Easy Strum for the fourth eighth note in each measure. So you're really dividing the measure in half and strumming for each half of the measure.

THE B FLAT (B^b) CHORD

Try out both versions of the B^b chord and choose the one you want to use. The first diagram is a better preparation for eventually playing barred chords. Notice that in the first diagram, it's really an A chord moved up one fret with a note added on the first string, first fret. You may find the second diagram easier because you're not fingering the fourth string in the third fret.

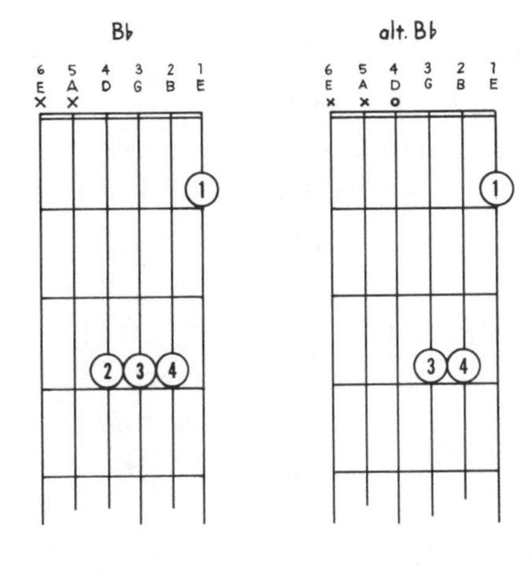

FIGURE 21-6a, b *Two versions of the B flat (B^b) chord*

Changing between F and B^b and C^7

The change between the F and the B^b chords is not too difficult, though the F chord, in itself, is not easy. How're you doing with that F chord?

If you're using the B^b chord that looks like the moveable A chord, this is what you do when changing from F to B^b: since your first finger is already covering the first two strings in the first fret on the F chord, adjust it to cover the first string only. Your second finger goes from the third string, second fret, to the fourth string, third fret, and your third and fourth fingers line up right behind your second finger on the third and second strings in the third fret.

If you're using the second diagram version of the B^b chord, when changing from the F to the B^b chord, adjust your first finger, in the first fret, and move your third finger from the fourth to the third string in the third fret. Put your fourth finger right behind it, on the second string.

When changing from the movable A version of the B♭ chord to the C^7, although it's a bit tricky, here's how you do it: your first finger goes from the first string to the second string, in the first fret; your second finger slides on the fourth string, from the third fret to the second fret; your third finger goes from the third string to the fifth string, in the third fret; and your fourth finger goes from the second string to the third string, in the third fret.

Changing to the C^7 chord from the second B♭ diagram is easier. Your first finger moves from the first to second string, first fret; your second finger presses the fourth string, second fret; your third finger goes from the third string to the fifth string, third fret; and your fourth finger moves from the second to the third string, third fret.

Because I've given you more than one choice for fingering the B♭ chord, the changes from the B♭ to other chords seem involved, but they're really not. Note that even the movable A version, using all four fingers of the left hand, is not the full B♭ chord. To do a full B♭ chord, you must barre all five strings in the first fret with your first finger. (The reason you barre just five strings is that the fifth string, first fret, is a B♭, and that's the bass for this chord. Barring chords is a more advanced method of playing chords; we're not going to take that up here.) Because you're not actually playing the full barred version of the B♭ chord, you don't have a primary bass string to strum from, so strum from the secondary bass string, the open fourth string, or from the fingered fourth string in the movable A version.

Changing from F to A^7 to F

When switching from the F to the A^7, your first finger goes to the fourth string, second fret, your second finger goes from the third string to the second string, second fret, and your third finger lifts off. When changing back to F, put your third finger down on the fourth string, third fret, switch your second finger from the second to the third string, second fret, and move your first finger from the fourth string, second fret, to barre the first two strings in the first fret.

Changing from A^7 to Dm to A^7

When going from A^7 to Dm, your first finger goes from the fourth string, second fret, to the first string, first fret; your second finger goes from the second to the third string in the second fret; and use either the third or fourth finger to play the second string, third fret. When changing back, your first finger goes from the first string, first fret to the fourth string, second fret, your second finger goes from the third to the second string, second fret, and your third or fourth finger lifts off.

Changing from F to G⁷

In this change, your third finger lifts from the fourth and transfers to the sixth string, third fret; your second finger goes from the third to the fifth string, second fret; and your first finger stands up to finger the first string in the first fret.

In the next song, "Aura Lee," we'll do the Bass-three-pull together-three strum. Remember, it's a four-step strum. Each one of the four steps of the strum gets one beat or count. Play a full strum pattern, B-3-(2)-3, for each measure of the music.

FIGURE 21-7 *"Aura Lee"*

AURA LEE

Arranged by R.T. Jacobs (Traditional)

F Bb
As the blackbird in the spring
C7 F
'Neath the willow tree
Bb
Sat and sang, I heard him say
C7 F
Lovely Aura Lee.

Chorus

F A7
Aura Lee, Aura Lee

D^m A^7
Lovely golden hair
F G^7
Sunshine came along with thee
C^7 F
And swallows in the air.

2 *Aura Lee, the bird may flee*
The willow's golden hair
Swing through winter shivering
On the stormy air.

Chorus

3 *Yet if those lovely eyes I see*
Gloom will soon depart
For to me, sweet Aura Lee
Is sunshine through the heart.

Chorus

4 *In that blush the rose was born*
Music when she spoke
Through those lovely eyes all things
Sparkling soon awoke.

Chorus

5 *When the mistletoe is green*
Take my golden ring
Love and light return with thee
And swallows with the spring.

Chorus

Changing from F to Dm to F

When changing from F to Dm, your first finger, which is barring the first two strings in the first fret, adjusts to finger only the first string. Your second finger doesn't move. Depending on which finger you use in the third fret on the Dm, either your third or fourth finger goes to the second string, third fret. Changing back to the F, your third finger goes to the fourth string, third fret. Your second finger doesn't move. Your first finger adjusts itself to barre the first two strings, in the first fret. Now you're back on the F chord.

Changing from C^7 to $B^\flat$

Review the change from $B^\flat$ to C^7 in "Aura Lee," depending on which $B^\flat$ you use, and then reverse the moves to change from C^7 back to $B^\flat$.

Changing from $B^\flat$ to Am

If you use the movable A version of the $B^\flat$, this change is very easy. Your first finger moves from the first to the second string, in the first fret, while your second and third fingers slide from the third fret to the second fret, on the fourth and third strings. Your fourth finger lifts up.

For the second B♭ diagram, with the third and fourth fingers in the third fret, it's an easy change also. Your first finger goes from the first to the second string, in the first fret, your second finger plays the fourth string, second fret, and your third finger slides from the third to the second fret on the third string. Your fourth finger lifts off.

Changing from Am to F

When going from Am to F, your first finger, which is on the second string for the Am chord, lays down to barre the first two strings in the first fret. Your second finger goes from the fourth to the third string, in the second fret. Your third finger leaves the third string, second fret, for the fourth string, third fret.

BASS–DOWN-UP–DOWN-UP STRUM

This is another variation of the basic waltz strum, the B-down-down. It's in three steps.

1. Brush the bass string and come to rest on the very next string.
2. With the flat side of your first fingernail, brush down, and immediately, brush up with the soft underside of the first finger.
3. Repeat the second step.

Each one of the steps is equal to one beat or count. Play one full pattern for each measure of the music.

Practice your chord changes with the Easy Strum and then with the Bass-down-up-down-up strum on the next song, "Spanish Is The Loving Tongue."

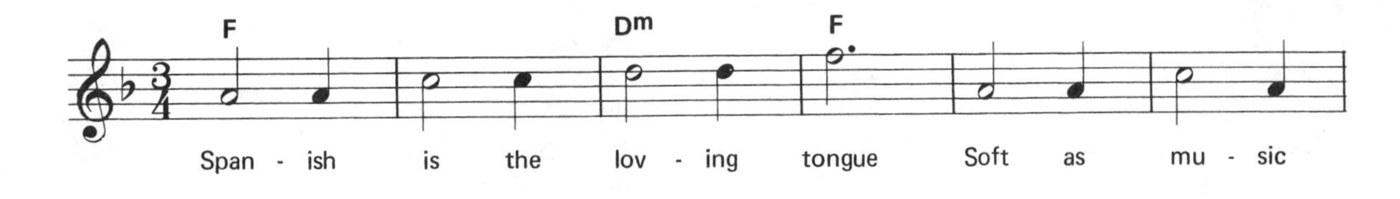

FIGURE 21-8 *"Spanish Is The Loving Tongue"*

FIGURE 21-8 *(cont.)*

SPANISH IS THE LOVING TONGUE

Adapted by R.T. Jacobs

F Dm F
Spanish is the loving tongue
C7
Soft as music, light as spray
F Dm F
'Twas a girl I learned it from
C7 F
Living down Sonora way
Dm C7 B♭ Am
I don't look much like a lover
F C7
Yet I say her love words over
F Dm
Often when I'm all alone
F C7 F
Mi amor, mi corazon.

2 *Nights when she knew that I'd ride*
She would listen for my spurs
Throw that big door open wide
Raise those laughing eyes of hers
How my heart would near stop beating
When I'd hear her tender greeting
Whispered soft for me alone
Mi amor, mi corazon.

3 *Moonlight on the patio*
Old señora nodding near
Me and Carla talking low
So the Madre couldn't hear

How those hours would go a-flying
And too soon I'd hear her sighing
In that soft and sorry tone
Mi amor, mi corazon.

4 *Never seen her since that night*
I can't cross the line you know
Wanted for a gambling fight
I suppose it's better so
Still I often sort of miss her
Since that last sad night I kissed her
Left her heart and lost my own
Adios, mi corazon.

KEY OF F FAMILY

Now you know the key signatures to five keys: C, G, D, A, and F. Also, you know that Am is the relative minor of C; they have the same key signature.

I'm sure you've noticed that the key of F isn't an easy key to play in. Perhaps you'd prefer to wait a little longer before attempting to play in this key; when you're ready to try it again, it'll be easier for you. Meanwhile, to get yourself ready sooner, keep going over the chord changes, especially those involving the F and B♭ chords.

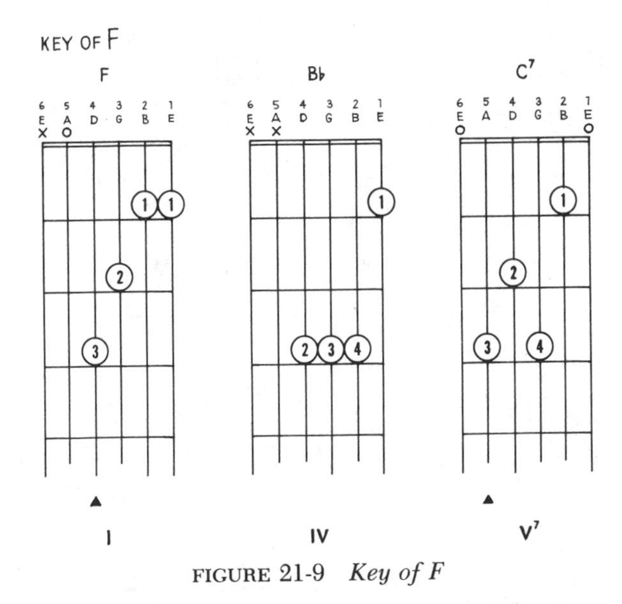

FIGURE 21-9 *Key of F*

Around the Circle of Fifths, Again

We left the circle of fifths in chapter 20 (see Figure 20-6). We filled in half the circle with the keys having sharps in their key signatures. There's also a circle of fifths for keys with flats. When you go around the circle for flat keys, you go around in a counterclockwise direction.

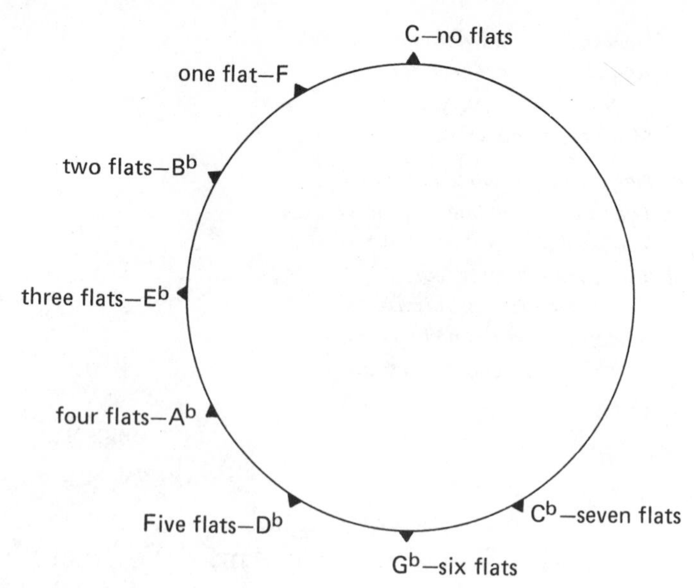

FIGURE 21-10 *Flat side of the circle of fifths*

You already know that the key of C has no flats in its key signature. The next key, the key of F, has one flat (B♭) in its key signature. As you travel around the circle, each flat key has one more flat in its key signature.

You'll most likely see those two incompletely filled circles of fifths nowhere else. You'll usually see the circle of fifths all filled in, with the sharp keys on one side of the circle and the flat keys on the other side.

Figure 21-11 illustrates the entire circle of fifths. This circle is not meant to confuse you or to lose you. It's around to help you understand some of the chord progressions you've

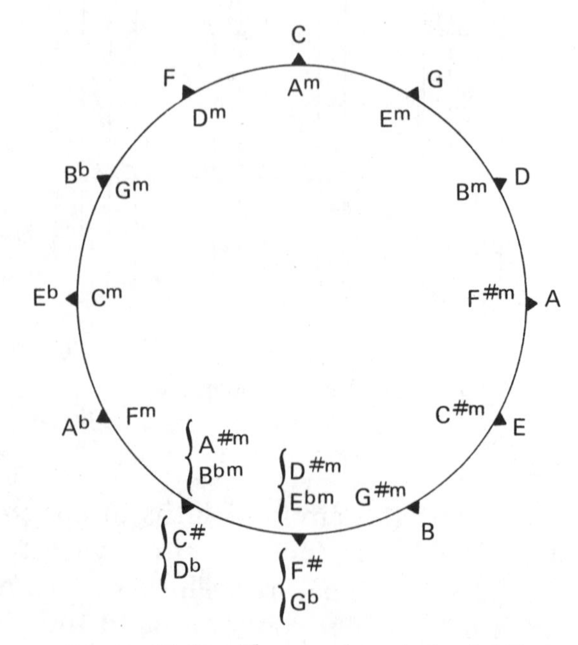

FIGURE 21-11 *The complete circle of fifths*

already learned in the songs you've been playing. It'll be useful, also, with the songs you intend to learn.

You should remember that the bracketed keys sound the same even though they have different names. For example the keys of C♯ and D♭ sound all the same notes even though they're spelled differently. In music, the letter name that's used for each note is called its musical spelling. To understand this better, finger the second fret on the second string. The note you hear is C♯, but it's also D♭: move one fret up from the C note on the second string, first fret, and you have C♯ in the second fret; move one fret down from the D note on the second string, third fret, and you have D♭, in the *same second fret.*

On the inside of the circle are minor chords. Each of the minor chords on the inside is the relative of the major chord on the outside of the circle. In fact, the relative minor has the same exact key signature as its relative major. So, the key of C major and the key of A minor have the same key signature: no sharps and no flats. The keys of G and Em have the same key signature, one sharp (F♯), and the keys of F and Dm have the same key signature, one flat (B♭). This association continues all the way around the circle.

The key of the relative minor begins on the sixth note of its relative major scale. Count and you'll see. Counting C as one, if you count up six, you'll get to A: Am is the relative minor of C major. See for yourself if counting up to the sixth note in every major key in the circle gives you the paired relative minor key on the inside of the circle.

What Does It All Mean? What does this circle of fifths mean to you? Well, for one thing, it's a good way to brush up on the I, IV, and V chords in any key. Notice that the two chords on either side of any key in the circle are IV and V chords of that key. For example, look at the C. On one side, you've got the F, or the IV chord, in the key of C. On the other side, you've got the G, or V chord, in the key of C. The G is also surrounded by the IV and V chords in its family. The same relationship holds for all the chords in the circle.

Now suppose you wanted to play in the key of F and counted, in the musical alphabet, to find the IV and V chords in the key of F family. You'd come up with C and B. If you played your song in the key of F with the C and B chords, it would sound awful. That's because if you look carefully at the circle of fifths, you'll see that the chord to the left of F is not B, but B♭.

So, should you be casually strumming your guitar one day

and someone says to you, "Can you play for me if I sing 'Jingle Bells' in B♭, here's what will happen. With a twinkle in your eye, you'll quickly reply, "Sure thing." That's because you know from your circle of fifths that the key of B♭ has E♭ and F for its IV and V chords. Or, you could change keys another way.

The Capo

You can always pick up a handy helper called a capo. (It's pronounced kay' poh.) It allows you to play in lots of different keys without having to know more than the chords in just a few keys.

The capo is a clamp made of metal or rubberized elastic that is used to barre all the strings at a paricular fret. You already know that each fret is a half step apart, musically. If you start counting from the first fret, and continue counting up to the fret the capo is on, you'll know how many half steps you've raised the pitch of each string by fretting it with the capo.

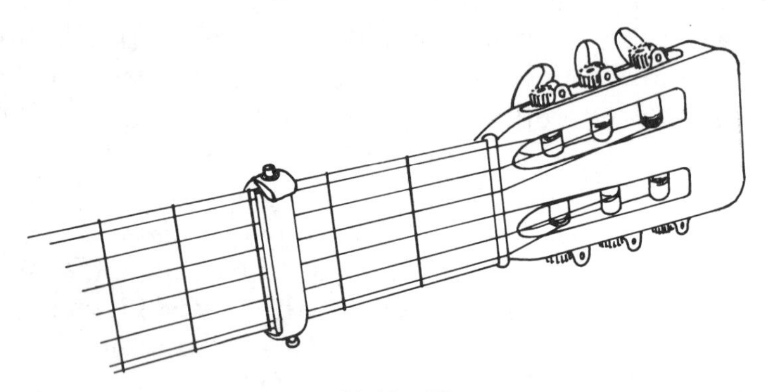

FIGURE 21-12 *The capo*

When you explored the sounds of your guitar you learned that fingering a string shortened it and raised the pitch. Whichever fret you put the capo on shortens the length of the strings by the amount of half steps (frets) you've counted, from the first fret up to the fret the capo is on. So, if you put your capo on the third fret and play a D chord, you would be sounding an F chord, not the D that you're fingering. That's because the capo in the third fret shortens and raises the strings (and thus the chord) three half steps: D♯, E, F.

Here's another way to look at it. Suppose you weren't too comfortable singing a particular song in the key of D. If you put the capo on the third fret and continue playing as if you're in the key of D, you'll be sounding the key of F. That's because it's three half steps from D to F in the musical alphabet, or three frets up, which is where your capo is. So, your D chord position with the capo in the third fret is sounding an F chord; your G chord position is sounding a B♭ chord; and your A7 chord position is sounding a C7 chord.

Getting back to "Jingle Bells" and the circle of fifths, if you put your capo on the first fret and played the chords for the key of A, you'd really be sounding the chords in the key of B♭. One fret up from A is A♯ *and* B♭. If your capo is in the first fret, you can play "Jingle Bells" for that person who wants to sing in the key of B♭ by playing the chords you know in the key of A. Even professional guitarists, who thoroughly know the chords in all keys, will use a capo to get certain qualities of sound that they prefer.

All the Way Up and All the Way Down. Now's a good time to take a look at the notation for every half step up to the fifth fret on the guitar fingerboard, for all six strings. Of course, you've been playing most of these notes right along.

In Figure 21-13, the scale first appears with sharps, going up the scale on the fingerboard notes. Musically speaking, this is called an ascending chromatic scale. (The word "chromatic" means by half steps.) Then, you'll see the fingerboard notes with flats, going down in a descending scale. You haven't played the Numbers Game for a while, but I purposely included it for the chromatic scales so you could see once more that some differently spelled groups of notes, such as C♯ and D♭, actually have the same sound.

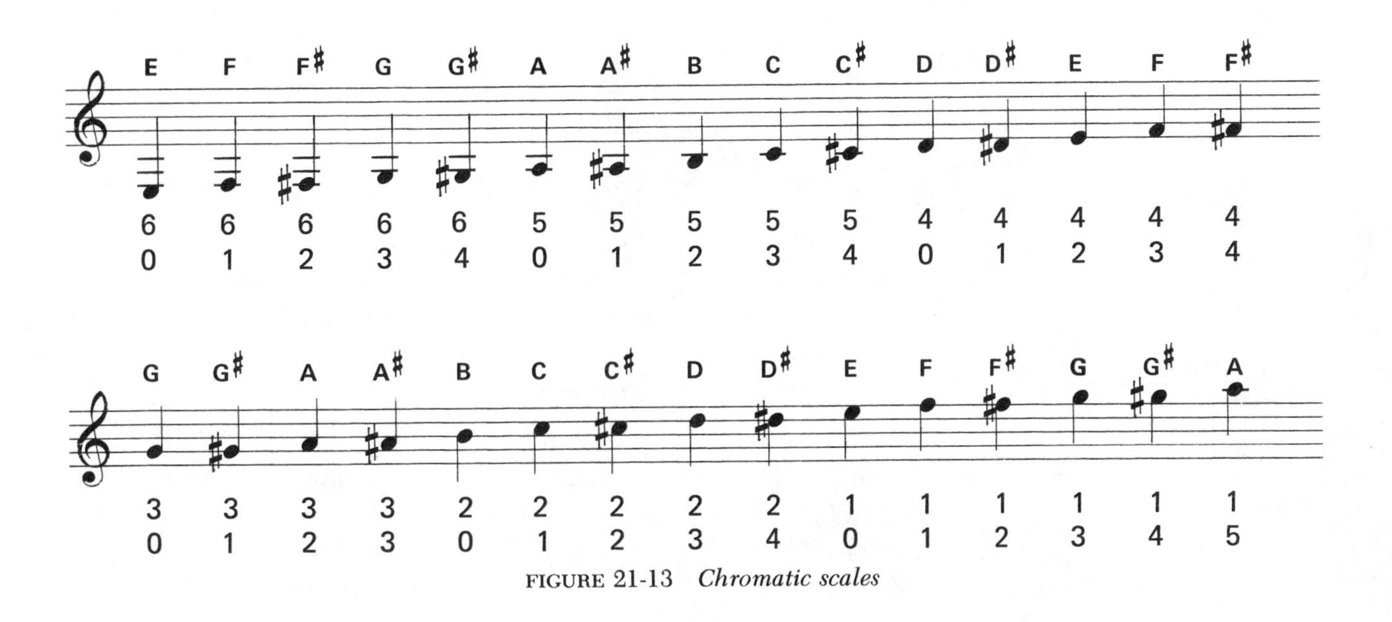

FIGURE 21-13 *Chromatic scales*

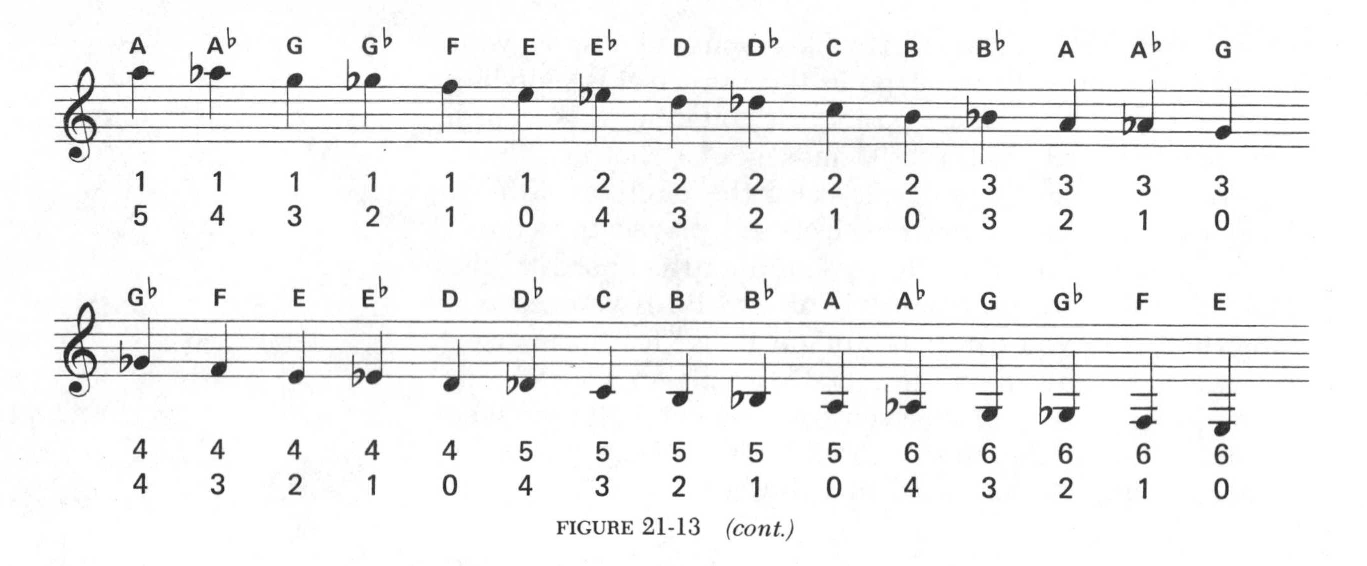

FIGURE 21-13 *(cont.)*

Finding Notes on the Fingerboard The following chart will help you to see where a lot of the notes you've been playing are on the guitar fingerboard. The fingerboard is shown up to the fifth fret only. Frets with more than one note encircled indicate where a single sound with two differently spelled notes occur.

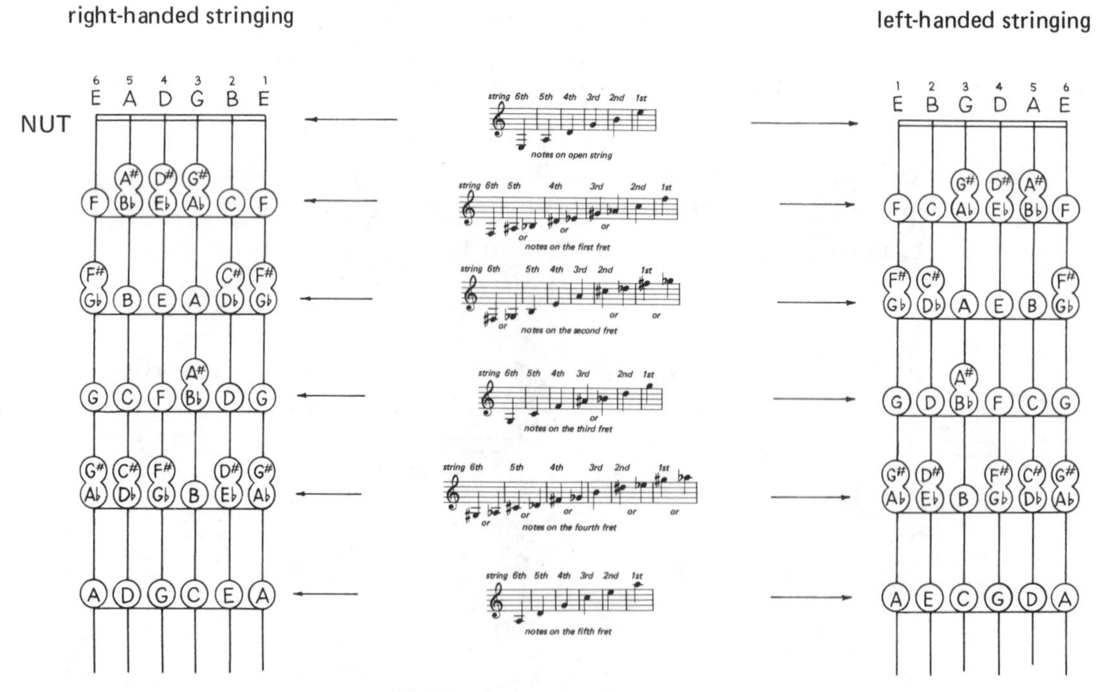

FIGURE 21-14 *Guitar fingerboard notes*

Transposing When you learned new songs and chords and numbers and notes, you learned them in certain keys. Sometimes, those keys may have been uncomfortable to sing in, too high or too low. *All of them can be played and sung in any key.* There's no rule that says you must play and sing a song in the key in which you first learned it. The key of any song can be transposed to a more comfortable key for your voice. The following table will show you the chords in the six major keys that you've learned. I've included the three main chords and the relative minors of those keys. I've also included the II and III chords of the keys because you already used them in the second section of this book. I've left out diminished chords, which are the VII chords of any keys, because we haven't learned about them.

Key					Relative minor
I	**II**	**III**	**IV**	**V**	**VI**
C	Dm	Em	F	G	Am
G	Am	Bm	C	D	Em
D	Em	F♯m	G	A	Bm
A	Bm	C♯m	D	E	F♯m
E	F♯m	G♯m	A	B	C♯m
F	Gm	Am	Bb	C	Dm

The Beginning. We're coming to the end of this book, but it's the beginning of many exciting, wonderful things to come for you. You've really worked hard if you've made it this far and you've surely done well. You haven't given up. Generally, you should feel stronger and better about yourself. Don't worry if you didn't completely grasp everything in this book. Certainly, you can't get all the answers from one place. It's like food. No one food does it all for you. You need lots of different foods to grow and stay healthy. If this book "fed" you in any way, that's great and I'm glad. Take what's enjoyable for you and be happy with it.

I feel as though I've known and been with you personally, throughout this book. We've become friends by making music together. Extend the good feeling by making more music and more friends with others.

When you learned new songs and chords and numbers and notes, you learned them in certain keys. Sometimes, those keys may have been uncomfortable to sing in, too high or too low. *All of them can be played and sung in any key.* There's no rule that says you must play and sing a song in

glossary

acoustic guitar non-electric guitar
action height of the strings above the frets
bar group of beats set off by bar lines; also the vertical line separating the groups of beats called a bar line
barre to cover more than one string with finger or other device
bass string lowest note of the chord and the string from which you begin the strum for the chord
bass strings fourth, fifth, and sixth strings on the guitar
chord diagram a miniature picture of guitar fingerboard, usually showing the first few frets
damping the strings stopping the vibrating sounds of the strings by covering them with your right hand
to finger, fret, or press a string to place your left hand finger down on a string in a particular fret
flat a note, lowered by one fret; one half step towards the guitar head
fret the metal strip or crossbar which divides the guitar fingerboard
key a group of notes belonging to a particular key family with a key family name
lining out fitting the strum pattern to the words of the song
measure a group of beats set off by bar lines
notation notes; written music
octave the space or distance between a note and the same note sounded eight tones higher or lower

pattern the design or form of a strum
picking or plucking pulling a string with your right-hand finger tip
pitch the high or low quality of a sound
pitch pipe a set of whistles or pipes for tuning the guitar that has the pitches of all six guitar strings
primary bass string the string, open or fingered, that represents the lowest note of a chord
rhythm everything that has to do with the long or short quality of a musical sound
rubato no strict timing; play it as you feel it
sharp a note raised by one fret; one half step toward the guitar body
slur the curved line that joins two or more notes sung to one syllable of a word
staff the framework of lines and spaces that music is written on
tie the curved line that joins two notes of the same pitch; the second note *isn't* sounded, but the first note *is* sounded and held for the time value of both notes.
timbre the difference in quality of sound when different voices or instruments sing or play the same pitch
transposing changing to another key
treble strings first, second, and third strings on the guitar
tuning fork a tuning device made of steel with two prongs that is struck against an object and then placed lightly on a surface; it vibrates to a specific note, usually A-440
waltz time three beats to a measure

x on a chord diagram, 'x' above a string means, don't strum that string.
o on a chord diagram, 'o' above a string means, although it's an unfingered(open) string, it can be strummed.
▲ this mark under a chord diagram, shows the primary bass string of the chord, and the string to strum from.

index

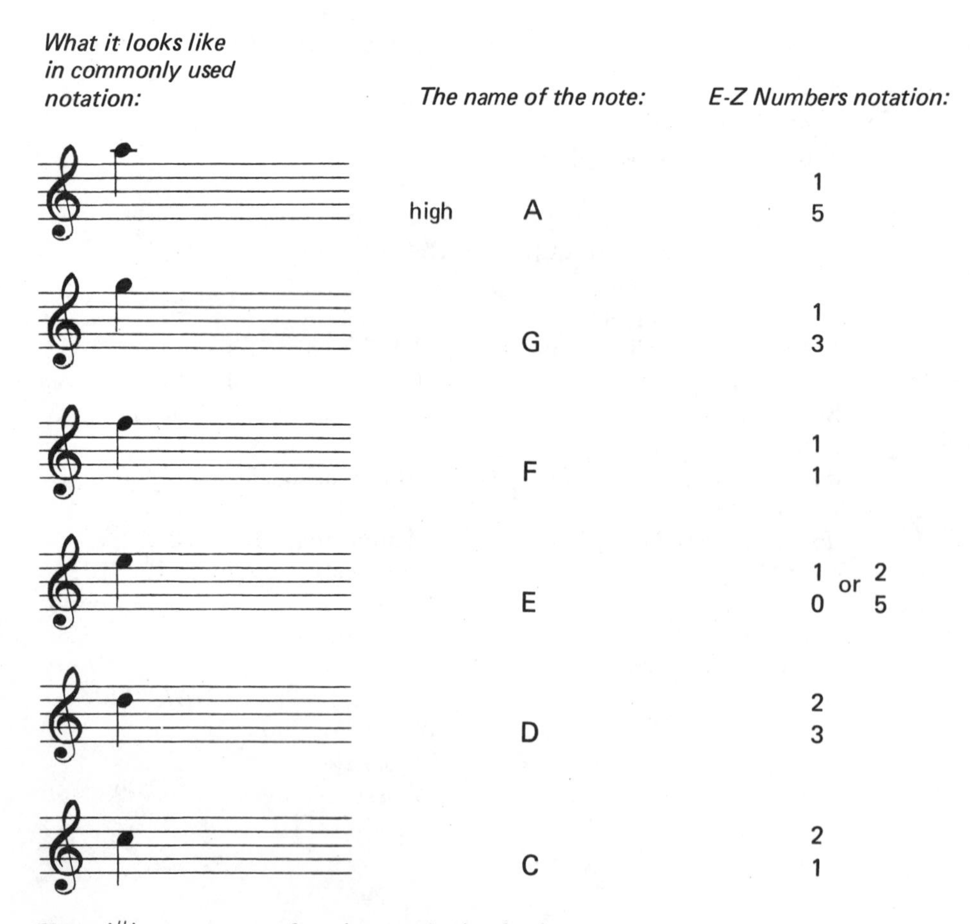

What it looks like in commonly used notation:		The name of the note:	E-Z Numbers notation:
	high	A	1 5
		G	1 3
		F	1 1
		E	1 0 or 2 5
		D	2 3
		C	2 1

Sharp (#) notes are one fret closer to body of guitar.
Flat (b) notes are one fret closer to head of guitar.

What it looks like in commonly used notation:	*The name of the note:*	*E-Z Numbers notation:*
	B	*string* 2 or 3 *fret* 0 or 4
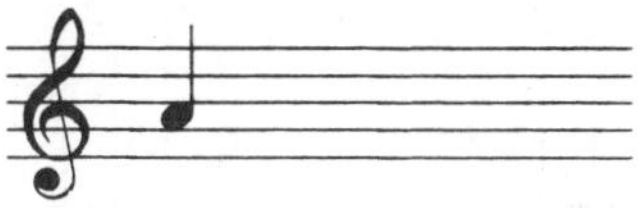	A	3 2
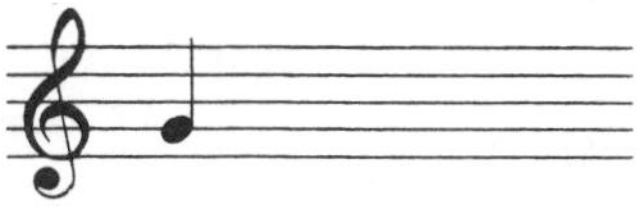	G	3 or 4 0 or 5
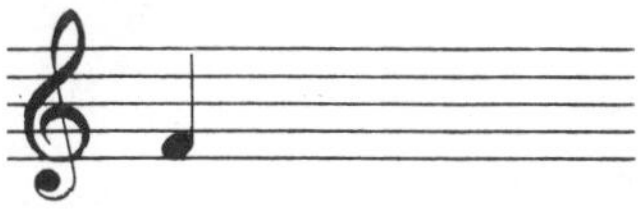	F	4 3
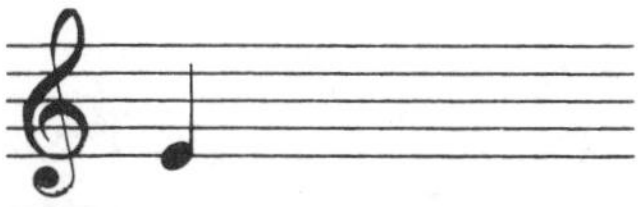	E	4 2
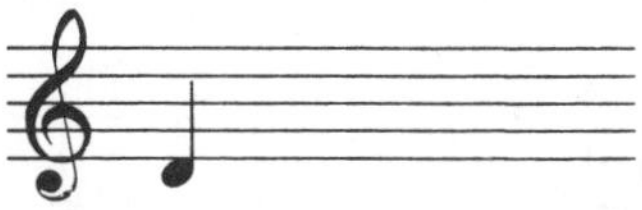	D	4 or 5 0 or 5
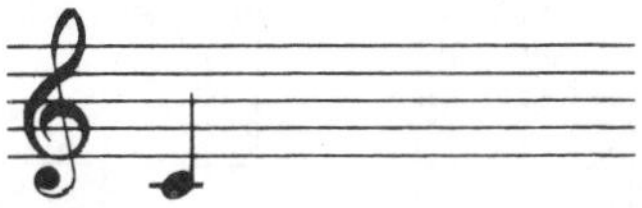	middle C	*string* 5 *fret* 3
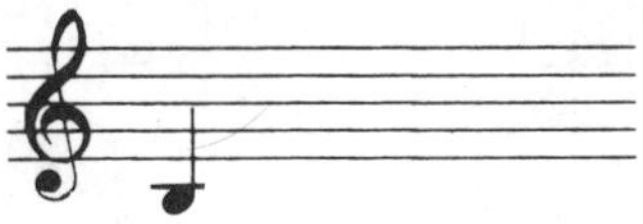	B	5 2
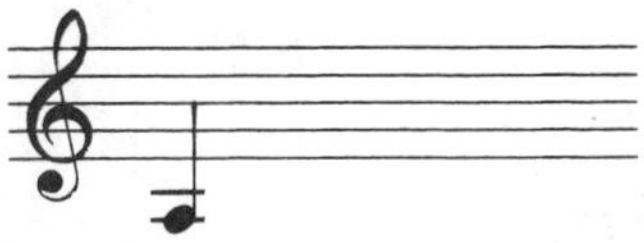	A	5 0
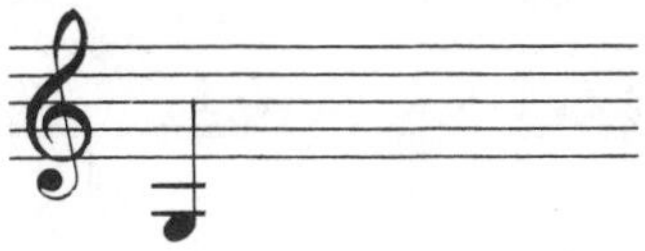	G	6 3
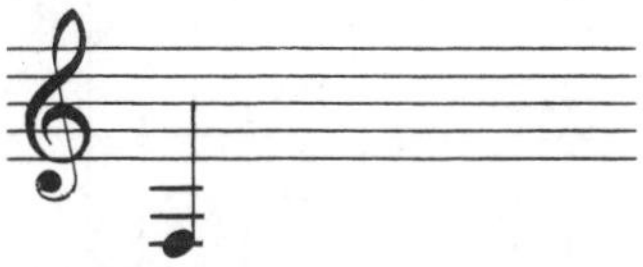	F	6 1
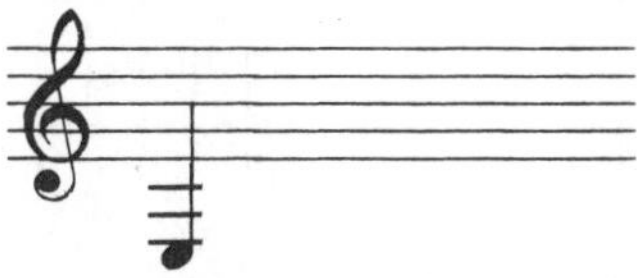	E	6 0

Sharp (#) notes are one fret closer to body of guitar.
Flat (b) notes are one fret closer to head of guitar.

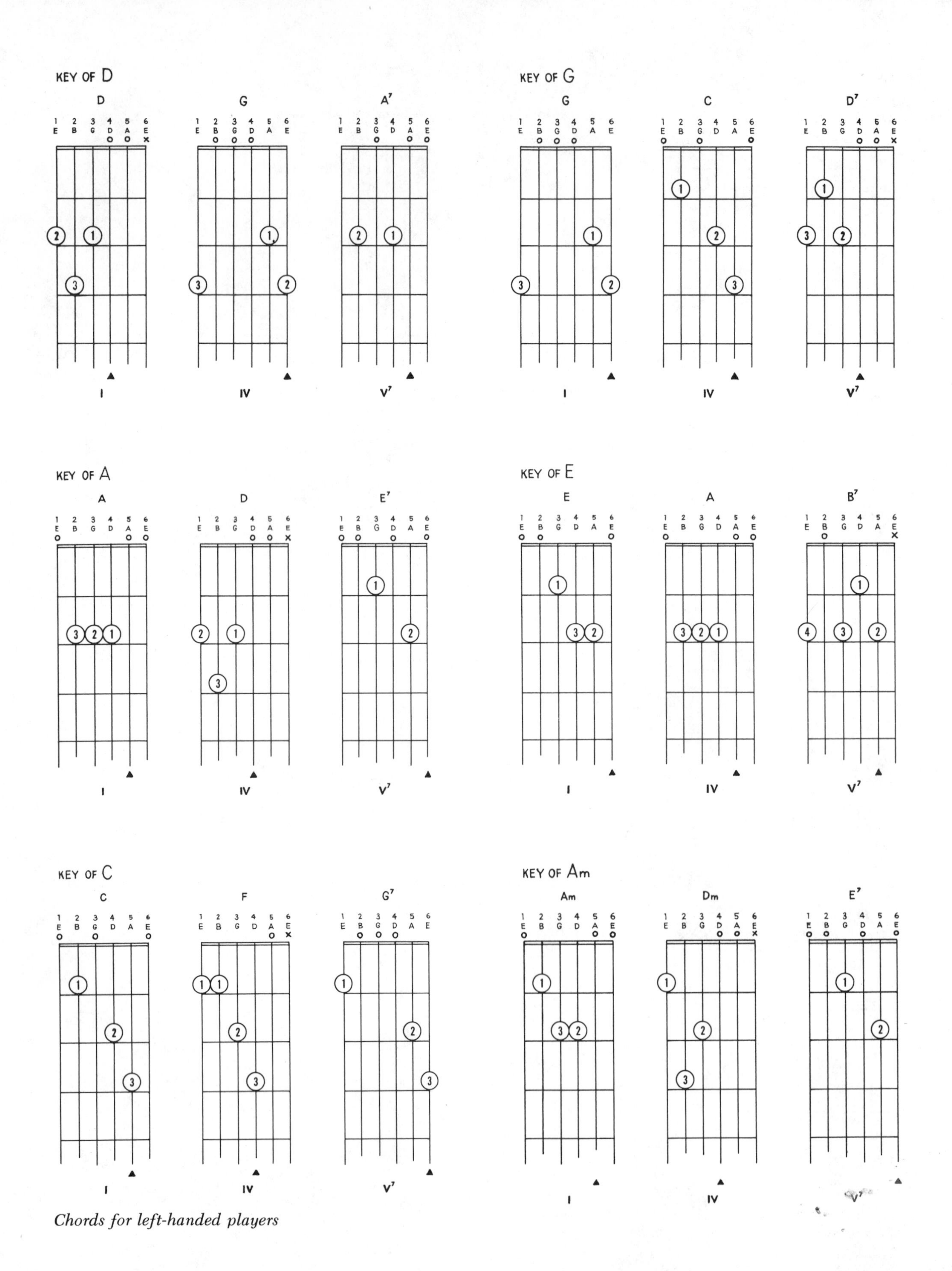

Chords for left-handed players

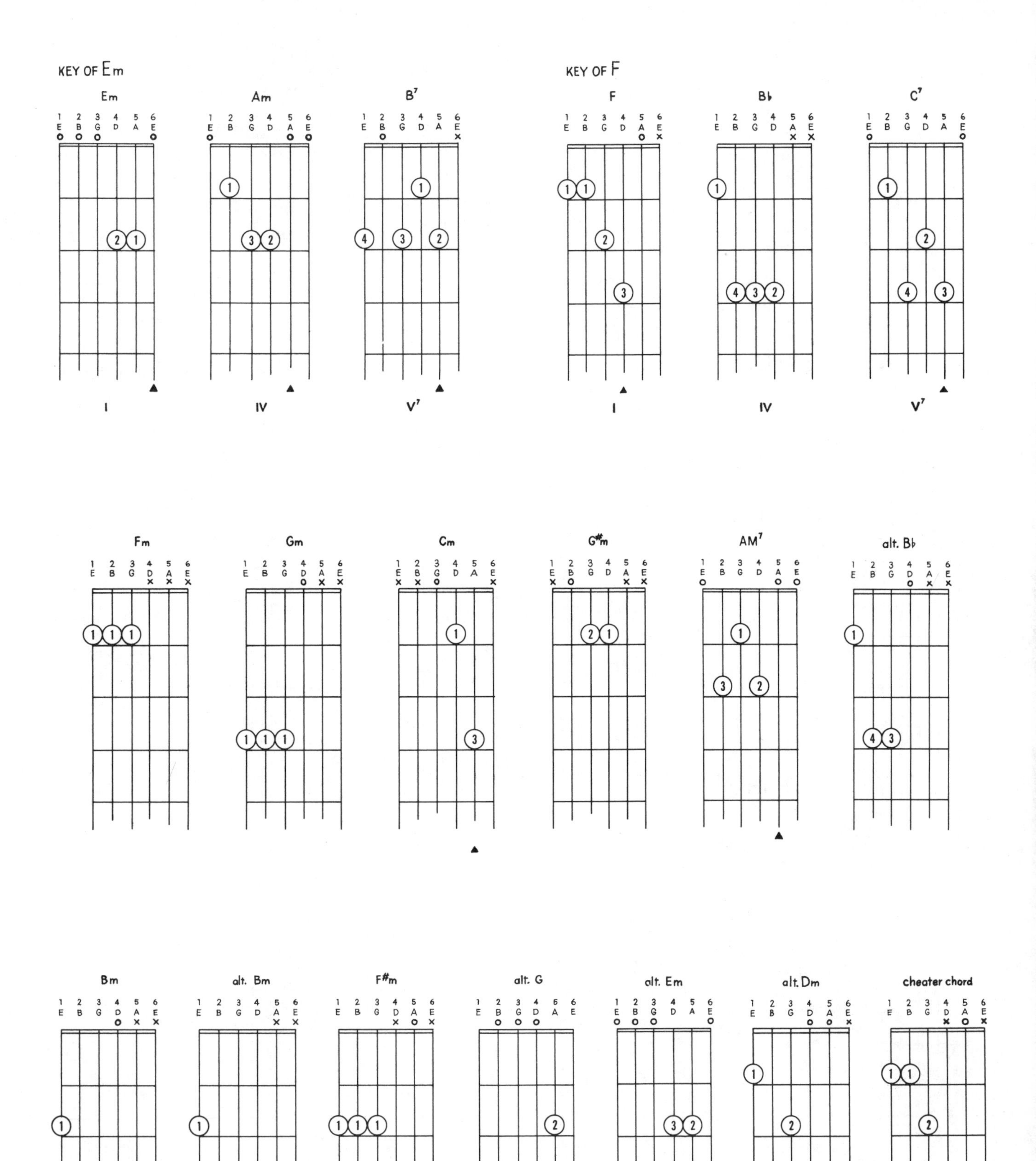

Bm
alt. Bm
F#m
alt. G
alt. Em
alt. Dm
cheater chord

Chords for left-handed players (cont.)

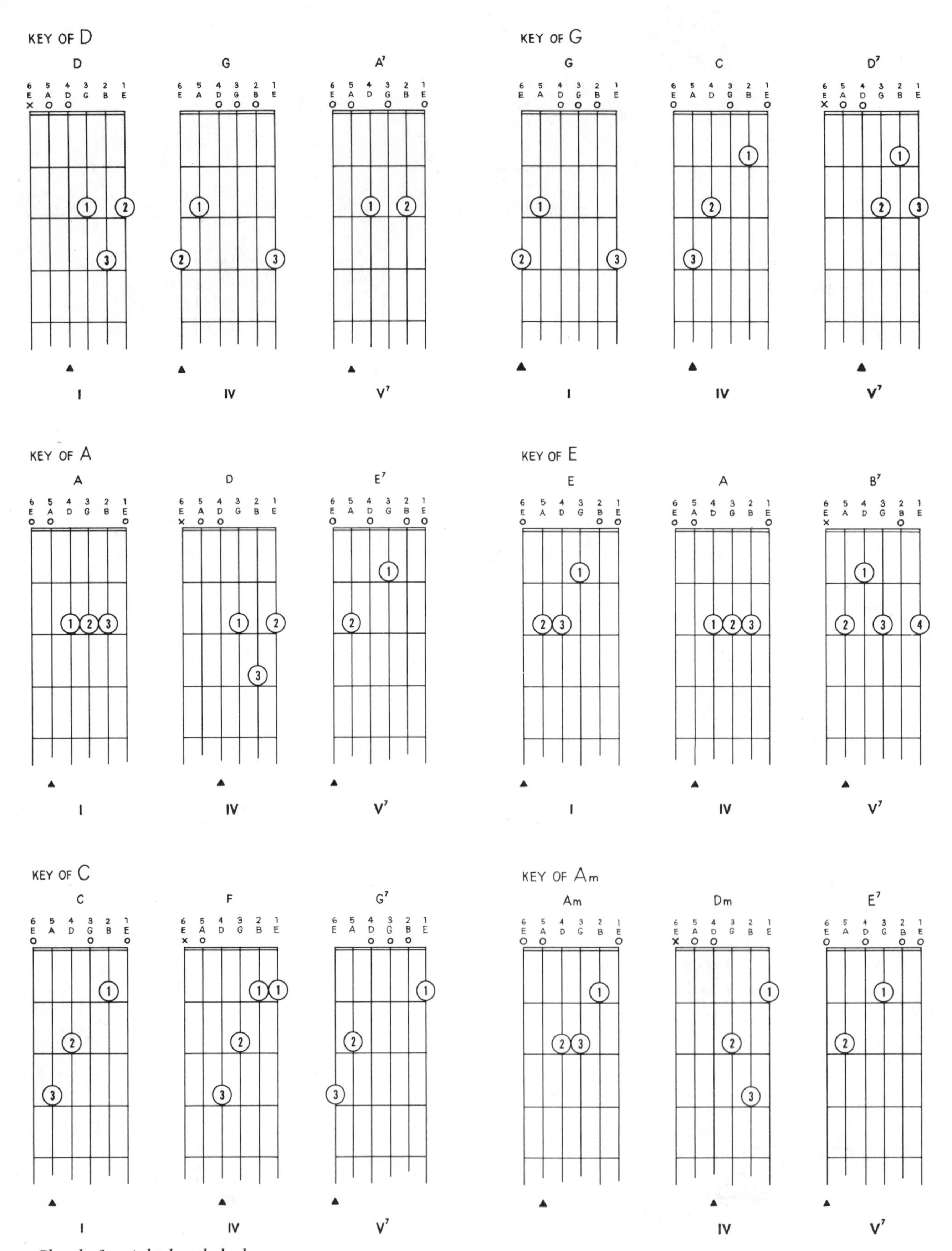

Chords for right-handed players

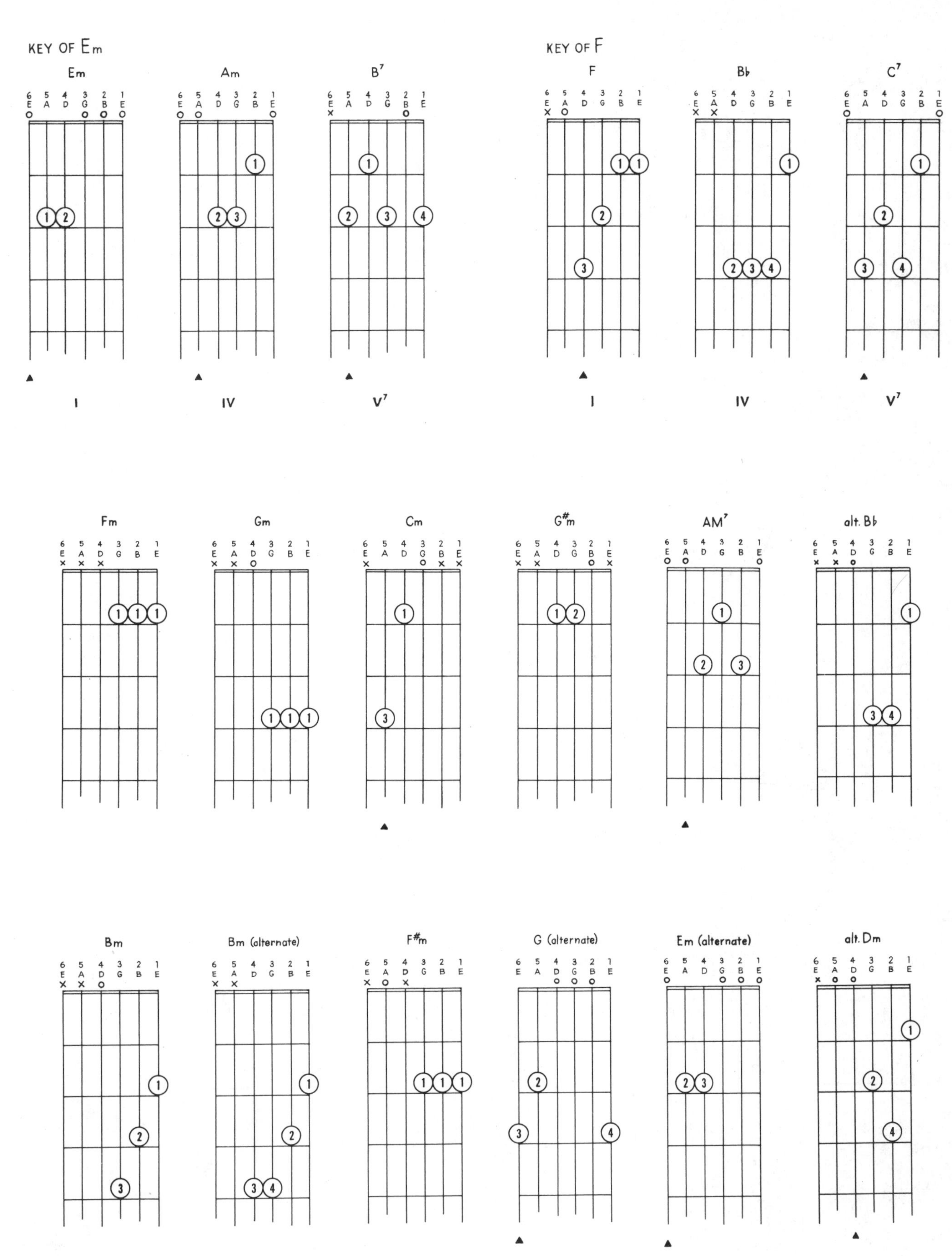

Chords for right-handed players (cont.)